INDIA

Text by
MAURIZIO TADDEI

Foreword by
CLEMENT GREENBERG

MONUMENTS OF CIVILIZATION
INDIA

CASSELL
LONDON

Frontispiece:
Khajuraho: A detail of the sculptured exterior
of the Temple of Kandariya Mahadeo. It dates from
the second quarter of the eleventh century A.D.

For permission to quote English translations of ancient texts, we gratefully acknowledge the following:

From *Anabasis Alexandri* by Arrian, trans. by E. Iliff Robson. Vol. II, page 209 (1958 edition). The Loeb Classical Library and Harvard University Press.

From "Atharva Veda" XIX:15 in *Hymns from the Vedas*, trans. by Abinash Chandra Bose. Published by Asia Publishing House, Bombay, India. Copyright 1966 by Abinash Chandra Bose.

From *Kautilya's Arthasastra*, trans. by Dr. R. Shamasastry. Fourth edition printed in 1951. Published by Sri Raghuveen Printing Press, Mysore, India. Courtesy of M. S. Srinivas.

CASSELL & COMPANY LIMITED
35 Red Lion Square, London WC1R 4SG
and at Sydney, Auckland, Toronto, Johannesburg,
an affiliate of
Macmillan Publishing Co., Inc.,
New York

English translation copyright © 1977 by Mondadori, Milano-Kodansha, Tokyo; originally published in Italian under the title *Le Grandi Civiltà: INDIA ANTICA*. Copyright © 1972 by Mondadori-Kodansha, Tokyo. Copyright © 1972 by Kodansha Ltd., Tokyo, for the illustrations. Copyright © 1972 by Mondadori, Milano-Kodansha, Tokyo, for the text.

First published in Great Britain 1977
ISBN 0 304 29495 0
Printed and bound in Italy by Mondadori, Verona

Editorial Director
GIULIANA NANNICINI
American Supervisor
JOHN BOWMAN
Graphics Editor
MAURIZIO TURAZZI

CONTENTS

FOREWORD

Two months in India made me an addict of her ancient sculpture. That includes her temples, which are sculpturally shaped in their construction as well as in their adornment. The ancient Indians were particularly, *especially* sculptors; they were obsessed by volume-enclosing surfaces.

An addiction does not necessarily mean a preference. Preferences in art depend, or should depend, on pure aesthetic judgment. My addiction to Indian sculpture does depend partly on that, but it also depends on a certain suspension or adulteration of aesthetic judgment. I am fascinated by the very unevenness of Indian sculpture, by its failures as well as successes — or rather by the spectacle these make, the spectacle of this unevenness in all its profusion. It speaks for a unique vitality. No other tradition of sculpture can show its like. No other tradition shows an equal longevity, not even the ancient Egyptian or the Chinese: there, the lapses of quality amount to actual interruptions of quality. In India the lapses get swallowed up in a sustaining unevenness, as it were, in a self-renewing unevenness; when they finally amount to an interruption, it is at the end only.

The constant self-renewal of Indian sculpture over the course of two millenniums sets at naught such orderly notions of rise and decline as the history of artistic quality seems to impose elsewhere. In India different schools or regional tendencies came and went, crossed and entwined, with one now rising while another was declining, and so on. What in any other artistic tradition might look like decadence could in India body forth a culmination or climax. Who would believe, before seeing, that such flamboyant detail and elaboration as are found in Hoysala sculpture of the twelfth century could make for such contained perfection? Or that such perfection could come so late in a millennial tradition? Conversely, some of the far earlier Buddhist sculpture in northern India manages to look decadent in all its vigorous clumsiness. It is as though the complicatedness of the history of quality of India echoed the complicatedness of detail in so many Indian works of art themselves. (Do I have to say that complicatedness is not the same thing as confusion?)

Under all this there must be, among other things, the centrifugal drive of the Indians, their urge to differentiation. It manifests itself in religion, politics, language, social distinctions, dress, diet, physical size, skin color — in almost everything except hair and eye pigmentation. But there is also an opposing tendency to blend or gradate differences, and this makes for still more complicatedness.

From the first, Indian art focused on the nude or nearly nude human figure. It was perhaps confirmed in this respect by the influence of Hellenistic art, which came relatively early during the Buddhist phase. But whereas the Greeks emphasized the masculine, Indian art feminizes. Often, especially in Hindu art, you have to look twice at a partially clothed figure to recognize it as male. Yet there is no suggestion of the homosexually tinged feminization of the male form that is seen so often in late Greek and in Roman sculpture. With the Indians it is more a question of reconciliation, of the softening of differences, than of femininity as such, even granted that their art paid more attention to the female nude than has any other art, not excluding Western European. It could be said even that the Indian "will to art" is actually a very masculine one, and that it drives toward the feminine precisely because it is so masculine. (Just as it is my paradoxical impression that the Indians could so abundantly depict or describe sexual activity because sex was not really that much on their *minds,* in their *heads.*)

Indian temple architecture, in its urge to reconcile differences, wrestles with rectilinearity and rectangularity on behalf of the curved and rounded. But it never entirely suppresses either of the former, not even in the Buddhist stupa. Some of the extraordinary beauty of the "medieval" Hindu temple arises from the way in which it resolves or contains this struggle: as in the swelling, tapering towers at Khajuraho, to name one example out of many. The Hindu temple can be stupendous, but it seldom inflates itself into the merely colossal; somehow it remains in human scale, or commensurable with human scale — which is not to say that the profusion of chiseled detail and the multiplicity of projecting and reentering angles, lateral and vertical, don't bewilder the eye on closer approach.

Here the obsession with three-dimensionality, with sculptured form, is partly responsible. Whatever else he did not suppress or exclude, the Indian architect and artist did suppress flat surfaces or planes. And it seems to follow from this obsession with three-dimensionality that the Indian painting that got started in the Buddhist period should be the only kind outside Greco-Roman and Western European to shade or model representations of the human form in a consistent way in order to achieve an illusion of relief and volume. The Greek influence cannot account for this altogether. Other peoples, exposed to that influence at much closer quarters, did not accept it; the Indians did, and the explanation lies with them, not with the Greeks or the Romans. Moreover, Buddhist painting came to full fruition in Ajanta, centuries after the influence or presence of Hellenistic art was first felt in the subcontinent, which would indicate that it proceeded to that climax on its own momentum.

In Ajanta, too, there is the effort to blend differences. Relief (incorporating highlights as well as shadings) and flatness are reconciled with a kind of explicitness whose like cannot be found in Western pictorial art. As Maurizio Taddei points out in his text, painting at Ajanta does not concern itself with an illusion of space in which volumes are contained. Rather it creates an illusion of volumes from within which space presses outward. Space, volume, mass are as though summoned from some inner center or source.

At this point I cannot refrain from drawing one of those tenuous-seeming analogies that I usually hurry to disallow when drawn by other people. As given as they were to sculpture and the sculptural, the art in which the Indians have, as I think, excelled most signally (as Christian Europe has excelled in music) is that of the dance. They are the incomparable masters of human physical movement as a means to artistic creation. The movements of dance start from within the body. Well, I sense a kind of analogous movement not only in the painting of ancient India, but also in her sculpture and architecture, Buddhist, Hindu, and Jain. Surfaces, shapes, masses, spaces do not so much gather around a center as issue from it: swelling, thrusting, bristling. The stupa is, of course, an arch-example of this centrifugal pressure. So, in a different way, are the cliffside reliefs at Mamallapuram. But something similar is exemplified, even if much less obviously, in the sculpture of a cave-shrine like the one at Elephanta.

This movement outward from an inner center — once again it is the Indian centrifugal urge. Or has the analogizing become too facile and overdone by now? Is this the sort of thing the understanding grasps at in order to explain to itself what is beyond conceptual understanding? As all art, good and bad, Indian and other, is. Quite likely. But at any rate, my addiction to Indian sculpture does not derive from any intellectual construct or analogizing interpretation; it derives from direct experience, plain experience.

Clement Greenberg

INTRODUCTION

Before immersing ourselves in ancient India, we might consider how such a study can also serve as a valid instrument for a deeper understanding of the present. But let us rid ourselves at once of the deceptive but widely held opinion that history as a succession of political and military events in the past can be a "key" to the present. What allows us to comprehend the phenomena of the present is an understanding of the historic roots of such phenomena, not the establishment of an illusory parallelism between the past and present. The Roman and British empires, for instance, essentially had little in common, once we exclude certain recurrent forms of ideology, mystifications promulgated for political ends; these empires had nothing substantial in common because the social and economic conditions that determined their existence were different. Thus the opposition between the centers of power (Rome or England) and their subject nations (such as Egypt or India), although similar from a political point of view, concealed a deeper and more articulated reality in which the social classes of the dominating and dominated nations and their relationships were fundamentally different. The point of all this for our study of India is that we must be prepared to consider the complexity of its full history on its own terms.

Another misconception about history in general should also be dispelled. History is not — and cannot be — the impartial study of the epochs that have preceded ours. The historian is committed (even if he does not want to be) to a work that requires continuous choice, which in turn will obviously reflect his own ideological premises. Ultimately there is the choice of the very facts to be considered; avoiding such a choice means writing a sterile chronicle. Moreover, even this line of action would finally not succeed, since the sources for such a chronicle would hardly be characterized by complete impartiality. All of which is to say that we are not claiming that this is somehow to be an impartial reading of India's history.

To begin with, we are to approach India from a very special angle: through a consideration of its ancient "great monuments." These will principally be temples, monasteries, sanctuaries cut out of rock, stupas, sculptures and relief carvings — mostly with religious associations and, as a group, comprising the major remains of artistic interest that ancient India offers to archaeology. But we shall not be limited in our examples, any more than we shall be confined by the political boundaries of contemporary India.

This would also seem to be the point to remind ourselves of certain basic premises of such an exposition. First of all, we shall not consider these monuments as the expression of some abstract "India"; on the contrary, we will place the works geographically as well as chronologically. (The essential facts of the geography will be provided in the course of this introduction.) In the second place, we must ask for whom each single work was made, whether it is sculpture or architecture, specifying the person or persons who commissioned the work, not as individuals but as representatives of a class or social group. This means both placing the work in its proper context and utilizing it for the reconstruction of that very context. And thirdly, it needs to be repeated that, for the purposes of historical reconstruction, it is not the unique masterpiece that counts but rather the current, "fashionable," even "mass-produced" work. The less exceptional an object, the more significant its recovery by modern archaeology; the more a work can be associated with a type or a model, the more certain we may be that it was accepted by the society in which it was produced.

Among the various goals of this study of the ancient monuments of India will be the search for the historic roots of what at times appear to be the "constants" of Indian thought. The historical explanation of their genesis will allow us to see to what extent these supposed "constants" adhere to reality — that is, the social reality of the country. Meanwhile, we shall be seeing to what extent they are merely artificial survivals that, without being ignored, should be taken for what they are: vestiges, remnants, things that, once relevant, have now lost their reason for existing. This is the case, for example, with *ahimsa*, the theory of non-violence espoused by Gandhi: if valid in ancient India, as a policy in today's world it cannot stand up to reality. Given the massive external aggression that Asia has been subject to in our time, the non-violent response today seems rather pathetic.

Just as with such intellectual constructs, the first thing we must effect when faced with a work of art is an act of demystification, clarification, the stripping away of that supposed universal value with which it is so easily veiled, in order to single out its function in the society that produced it. It should thus be quite clear that, just as history cannot be impartial, so archaeology and art history cannot be impartial: they can only be critical. Eventually we shall see how the history of ancient India has been used for more or less declared purposes of political propaganda. Here we limit ourselves to the statement that in today's India even a quite obvious assertion — for example, that the Taj Mahal of Agra is a product of the Islamic culture of India — has a political implication. In fact, it means spurning the theory of the Jana Sangh, the political organization of the extreme right-wing Hindu nationalists, who claim that the Taj Mahal (and the Quwwat-ul-Islam mosque at Delhi, another typically Moslem work) is a Hindu monument taken over and used by the Moslems. This is obviously an extreme but by no means isolated case, and the task of the serious scholar is to show everyone what a work like the Taj Mahal (and for that matter, every Indian monument) represents in reality, so that Moslems and Hindus alike can laugh when the Jana Sangh asks the Indian government to order the removal of the tomb of Shah Jahan "to a more appropriate place" and preserve the Taj Mahal as a Hindu memorial.

We shall try to apply all these principles — expressed perhaps in such a simple manner as to appear ingenuous — in the pages that follow. But before moving on, let us establish some geographic context for ancient India, so necessary, as we have said, for a precise delineation of its history and monuments. And when we refer to "ancient India" we mean the territory that includes other states outside today's Republic of India: part of Afghanistan, all of Pakistan, Bangladesh, Sri Lanka (formerly Ceylon), part of Burma, and Nepal. History — or, more exactly, politics — has determined the borders (occasionally absurd) within this region; but the extreme limits of India have been set by nature. For the geologist, India is divided into three basic areas: the peninsular plateau south of the Vindhya mountains — that is, the Deccan; the extrapeninsular mountainous region of the Himalayas, which marks the limits of the land from the northwest across to the northeast, and includes parts of Afghanistan, Baluchistan, and areas of Burma; and the Indus-Ganges plain, which extends from the Indus valley in Sind to the Brahmaputra valley in Assam and which includes the two vital areas of the Punjab and Bengal and part of the new state of Bangladesh.

Viewed this way, India seems relatively well defined, but from a climatic viewpoint India is somewhat more variegated. There is the Himalayan area with its consistently cold climate and heavy rainfall on the eastern and central slopes; a desert area with hot, dry summers and cold and dry winters, which includes a good part of Afghanistan, Baluchistan, and Sind (present-day Pakistan) and part of Rajasthan; a region composed of part of the Punjab, Uttar Pradesh, and Rajasthan — with Delhi as the center — characterized by cool winters and very hot and dry summers; a vast region with much precipitation and high temperatures, on the eastern side, extending from Orissa to Bengal, Assam, and the hilly area of Burma, and also penetrating Magadha and the heart of Madhya Pradesh. Finally, peninsular India can be divided into a relatively thin area along the western coast, from Bombay to Cape Comorin, hot and extremely rainy; another area, with very hot summers and mild winters with moderate rainfall, which extends from Kathiawar into the interior of the Deccan and includes most of Maharashtra, the state of Mysore, and Andhra Pradesh; and another area with hot summers and cool, humid winters with moderate winter rainfall, this area including a broad strip of the Cape Comorin coast up to the northern end of Andhra Pradesh and taking in the entire state of Madras.

India remains what it has always been, a fundamentally rural country with its population most unevenly distributed. The physical and climatic aspects are, naturally, the causes of these phenomena. The peninsular area is relatively poorer in the center (the Deccan), where large areas of laterite (the reddish residue of rock decay) render cultivation difficult; the western coast (Malabar) is richer, as it has an equatorial-type climate (like that in Sri Lanka); while the eastern coast (Coromandel), almost devoid of monsoons, depends on the large rivers in the Deccan. Of these many rivers, only two — the most northerly ones, the Narmada and the Tapti — flow into the Arabian Sea; the Narmada skirts the southern slopes of the Vindhya mountains. The other large rivers in the peninsular region flow eastward into the Bay of Bengal: they are, from north to south, the Mahanadi, which flows into Cuttack in Orissa; the Godavari, which comes from the western Ghat mountains north of Bombay and, crossing the Deccan, flows into Andhra Pradesh with a large delta contiguous with the Kistna River, whose sources are in Maharashtra, south of Puna; and finally the Pennar flows into the area north of Madras, while the Kaveri crosses the Tamil region.

The basin of the Ganges and the Yamuna, rich in waters, is formed at the mouth of these rivers in the delta shared by the Brahmaputra River, and is suitable for the cultivation of rice (in the lower basin) and wheat (in the upper basin); in Bengal and Magadha there are three good annual crops. The Indus, in Pakistan, has a more irregular flow than the Ganges, one that necessitates a more complex irrigation system. For long stretches, this large river does not offer any apparent benefit to vegetation; the middle and lower basins of the Indus are joined to Baluchistan, with its steppes and cases, and to the arid regions of Rajasthan, without any appreciable differences.

Farther north, the Punjab — "Land of the Five Rivers," divided between modern India and Pakistan — stands up well to the reduced violence of the monsoons and is today one of the most productive areas in the subcontinent, thanks also to a well-developed irrigation system. The Punjab is literally formed by five large rivers, the Indus and four of its affluents on its left: the Jhelum, the Chenab, the Ravi, and the Sutlej. Still farther north, the affluents of the Indus come in from the right side: the Kabul is the river that takes in the waters coming from Afghanistan and from the northern regions of Pakistan brought by the Panjshir, the Kunar, and the Swat rivers. Here in the north, a double crop is not exceptional in the mountainous strip with its large and varied forest areas and numerous fertile valleys.

From time to time, various regions have functioned as the political and cultural center of India. Leaving aside the proto-historic period — with the development of the urban Harappa culture between about 2500 to 1500 B.C — it is the agricultural area of Magadha (the southern part of modern Bihar) where the first unified state in India, the Maurya empire, sprang up; with it, Indian art of the historical period effectively began (about the third century B.C.). Later, other centers would contend for the position of political preeminence held by Magadha, but it will be this rich region that once again gives birth to the next great empire, that of the Guptas (starting in the fourth century A.D.), in which there grew up an art that is traditionally known as the "classical" art of India (although the major centers of production were outside Magadha). But before considering these great monuments, we must go back quite a few centuries to look at the society that provided the roots for all subsequent manifestations of Indian civilization.

ANCIENT INDIA

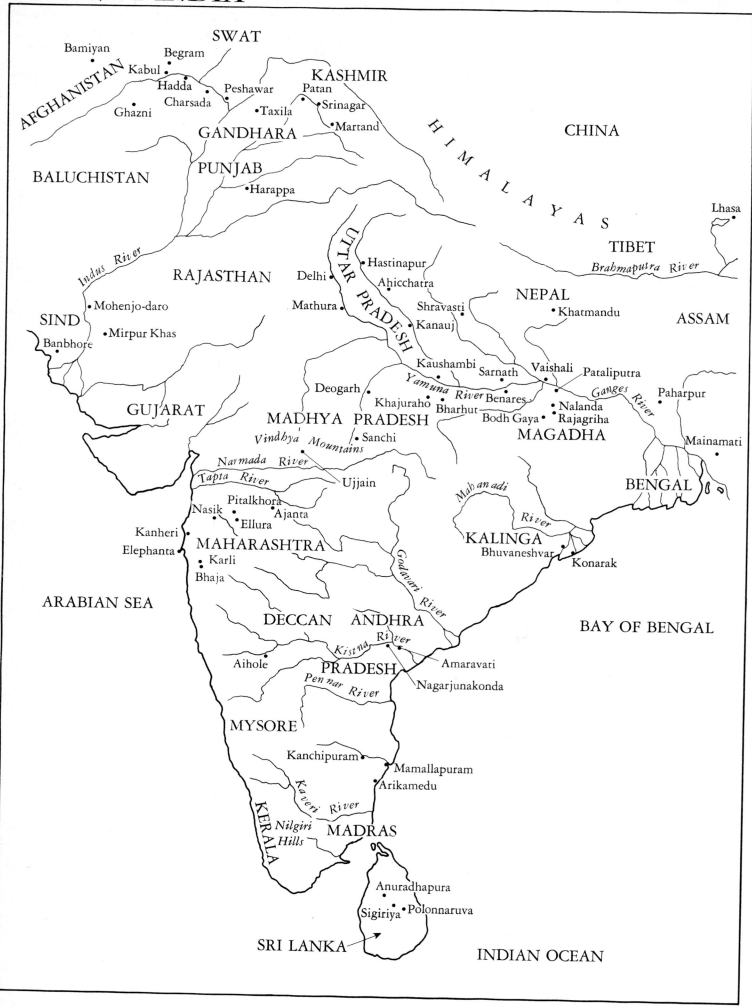

SWAT

Bamiyan

Begram

AFGHANISTAN

Kabul

Hadda

Peshawar

Charsada

Ghazni

Taxila

GANDHARA

KASHMIR

Patan

Srinagar

Martand

CHINA

H I M A L A Y A S

Lhasa

TIBET

Brahmaputra River

BALUCHISTAN

PUNJAB

Harappa

RAJASTHAN

Delhi

Hastinapur

Ahicchatra

UTTAR PRADESH

Mathura

Shravasti

Kanauj

NEPAL

Khatmandu

ASSAM

Indus River

SIND

Mohenjo-daro

Mirpur Khas

Banbhore

Kaushambi

Sarnath

Vaishali

Pataliputra

GUJARAT

Deogarh

Khajuraho

Yamuna River

Benares

Bharhut

Bodh Gaya

Nalanda

Rajagriha

Paharpur

MADHYA PRADESH

Sanchi

MAGADHA

Mainamati

Vindhya Mountains

Narmada River

Tapta River

Ujjain

Mahanadi River

BENGAL

Nasik

Pitalkhora

Ajanta

Ellura

KALINGA

Kanheri

Elephanta

MAHARASHTRA

Karli

Bhaja

Bhuvaneshvar

Konarak

Godavari River

ARABIAN SEA

DECCAN

ANDHRA

Kistna River

BAY OF BENGAL

Aihole

PRADESH

Amaravati

Pennar River

Nagarjunakonda

MYSORE

Kanchipuram

Mamallapuram

Arikamedu

Kaveri River

KERALA

Nilgiri Hills

MADRAS

Anuradhapura

Sigiriya

Polonnaruva

SRI LANKA

INDIAN OCEAN

EARLY INDIA: BUDDHISM
CHALLENGES TRADITIONALISM

/

The Transformation of Indian Tribal Society

1.   Mohenjo-daro: Bust of a man, most probably a priest; he wears some obviously special garment, decorated with the trefoils, each of which was originally filled with a red paste. Much has been written about this whitish limestone statue and about similar ones found at sites of the Harappa Culture phase of the Indus Valley Civilization; in particular there have been attempts to relate the statues to Sumerian-Mesopotamian works. But too much remains unknown to allow any definitive explanations. (New Delhi: Central Asian Antiquities Museum)

Historical India, whatever other differences may have divided it, has long been united in recognizing an ideal proto-history. It is the period that gave rise to the most ancient works of Indian literature: the *Vedas* — including the collections of hymns *(Rig-Veda)*, chants *(Sama-Veda)*, prayers *(Yajur-Veda)*, and magic formulas *(Athar-Veda);* the rituals and theological manuals for the Brahmanic schools (the *Brahmanas*); the traditional stories *(Puranas);* the esoteric philosophical texts (the *Upanishads*); and the two great epic poems, the *Ramayana* and the *Mahabharata*. These works were actually written down over a long period of time: the earliest Vedas were composed before 1000 B.C., while some of the other works did not get written down for another 1,500 years. But they express the essence of the early age much as Homer's epics speak of an earlier period; the Indian works have long been accepted as enlightening us about the so-called Vedic period.

Ironically, this idealized proto-history has turned out to be quite recent compared to India's actual first proto-historic phase, the Indus Valley Civilization, which archaeology has revealed only within the last half century. Beginning before 3000 B.C., this civilization climaxed about 2200 B.C. in what has now become known as the Harappa Culture phase, named after one of the two known principal centers, the other being Mohenjo-daro. At these and other centers along the Indus Valley, an urban way of life developed, quite different from the India portrayed in the ancient literary texts, a way of life characterized by a well-developed civil organization, a high level of artistic ability (Illustration 1), and intensive trade activities with not only their adjacent hinterlands but even overseas and far overland (the Persian Gulf and Mesopotamia).

What especially distinguishes the Harappa Culture, though — both in relation to our own views of ancient civilizations and in relation to the traditional Vedic texts — is the style of urban life apparently maintained in the cities. These were built according to grid plans, and contained efficient drainage systems; public edifices, such as baths and granaries, that required considerable building technique; and living quarters that suggest strongly structured social groups. Put in the most general terms, this was a society divided into classes, among which, it is obvious to assume, particular importance was assumed by the mercantile class that made its profits from the excess production of the land (excess, that is, with respect to the basic subsistence of the agricultural community). Significant portions of the crops were amassed in immense granaries and then redistributed, partially for the basic needs of the local population and partially for trade purposes. All this helped to confirm the city as the center of power.

But we cannot become more deeply involved in the Indus Valley Civilization, since we have enough to do with understanding the works of later periods. However, we might mention that the study of this civilization still offers many challenges, not the least of which is the writing. Its decipherment and interpretation are being worked on by many scholars, and it is still possible that a more "literate" knowledge of this ancient period will allow us to connect it more directly with the traditional Indian civilization of the Vedic and later periods. Already we may accept the presence of certain persistent cultural elements, such as the fertility cult, in Indian religion as going back at least to the Indus Valley Civilization. But the significant fact for us at this point is that India seems to have lost every conscious link with her first urban civilization: the proto-history relevant to India and to us is that of the tribal society.

At one time it was glibly assumed that the end of the Indus Valley Civilization was to be explained by the arrival in India of certain particular nomadic, cattle-rearing, warrior-exalting tribes from the north. But now it is generally accepted that even if the final destruction of the cities was relatively sudden, their decadence had begun long before. One theory is that the partial cause for the destruction was the deterioration of the surroundings due to tectonic movements that caused the amassing of such quantities of alluvium (from the periodic flood waters) as to overwhelm the settlements. Yet too little is known about this ancient civilization — not to mention what it is that causes the "end" of any civilization — to say what brought about the end of this Indus Valley Civilization.

As for the tribes that penetrated the subcontinent from the northwest about 1500 B.C., bringing a new type of culture and social organization, they have traditionally been called "Aryans." Although science has for some time demonstrated the complexity of the concept of race when the attempt is made to attribute biological purity, the utilization of this pseudo-concept persists into our own times, often with disastrous consequences (and perhaps at their worst with the use of the very term "Aryan" by the Nazis). "Aryan," flatly stated, is not an ethnic or biological term; the element that objectively unifies these people is the fact that they spoke languages belonging to the same group, variously defined as Indo-European, Indo-Germanic, or Aryan-European. (We might recall the celebrated retort that "the Aryan race" is no more valid than the concept, for example, of a "brachycephalic language.") Yet once this is understood, we may return to employing the term "Aryan" to describe this historical-cultural group, with the awareness that this is merely a convenience.

When the Aryans reached India, they were divided into three groups: the warriors, the priests, and the "common" people. These groups are often called "social classes" in the literature on this period, but the term seems decidedly improper. The concept of a social class implies not only a division of labor among different groups but also a different arrangement of these groups with regard to the basic means of production. In the patriarchal organization of tribal society there is no surplus of production that a group can appropriate, beyond mere matters of prestige. Yet there do exist differences in the accumulation of goods on the part of individuals, and there is a more or less rigid specialization in labor. Once settled in a sedentary life, the Aryans had to create an organization suitable for this new way of life. The figure of the tribal chief could have undergone a substantial evolution in these new conditions, either by disappearing or by changing into a king. It is probable that the first forms of monarchy in India grew out of the election of a leader from among the tribal chiefs. However, even when a sovereign was elected, his power was limited by the existence of assemblies, and republican tendencies persisted for a long time in India.

But the principal characteristic of Aryan-Vedic and post-Vedic India is the transition from the Aryan invaders' classless tribal organization to a division into "castes." It seems that castes developed both from inside and outside the primitive tribe, and it is possible that they reproduced in part a social division among the pre-Aryan populations of India, those dark-skinned *dasa* regarded as the prime enemy by the Aryans. Later the term *dasa* came to mean an individual of inferior caste, a servant, or even a slave. But originally it was the name of a subject population — namely, the indigenous population of India — and hence placed at the bottom of the social ladder. So we may at least feel sure that the division into castes

Sarnath: Reconstruction of the Lion Capital, showing the Buddhist symbol, the "wheel of the law," that originally rested on the lions' backs.

2.   Sarnath: The Lion Capital of Asoka, some 6 feet 10 inches high, and dating from the third century B.C. This has become the most famous Indian sculpture because it has been adopted as the symbol of the Republic of India and is used on money, stamps, state seals, etc. But such diffusion is deserved by this loveliest example of a group of similar monuments erected by Asoka — pillars crowned by sculptured capitals that merged the traditional *axis mundi* with astral symbolism that in turn merged Asoka's Buddhist and political aspirations. The Sarnath capital, found in 1904, is made of sandstone that was given a high polish. Four lions, erect on their forelegs, sit on a round plinth decorated with four wheels that alternate with a lion, an elephant, a bull, and a horse; below this is a bell-shaped capital in the Persian tradition. But if elements of this work invite direct comparison with sculpture and architecture at the Achaemenid palace of Persepolis, other elements (such as the four animals on the plinth) have more in common with the Hellenistic tradition. (Sarnath: Archaeological Museum)

Free us Indra, from the fear of all that we
 are afraid of.
May thou, with thy saving power,
 turn away the hater and the enemy.

We call on Indra, bounteous Giver,
 we will be prosperous in men and cattle.
Let not the demon hosts approach us;
 turn the hostiles away on all sides.

Adorable Indra, our Savior,
 Virtra-slayer and Furtherer of our highest
 aims,
May he be our protector from the end,
 from the middle, from behind and from in
 front.

Lead us to a free world, wise One,
 where lie divine luster, sunlight and
 security.
Valiant are the arms of thee, the powerful;
 we will take to their vast shelter.

May the mid-region free us from all fear,
 and both Heaven and Earth make us
 secure;
let there be for us no fear from behind,
 no fear from in front, no fear from the
 north or the south.

Let there be no fear from friend, no fear
 from foe,
 no fear from the known, no fear from
 what lies before us unknown,
let there be no fear for us from night, no
 fear from day; let all the quarters be my
 friends.

Atharva Veda XIX:15

THE BRAHMANIC LAW

There are three branches of the law. Sacrifice,
study, and charity are the first.
 Austerity alone is the second. And to dwell
as a chaste student in the house of a teacher is
the third. All these attain the worlds of the
blessed. But only he who is firmly grounded in
Brahman obtains immortality.

Chandogya-upanishad II, xxiii: 1–2

3. **Northwest India: This terra-cotta
figurine (7 inches high), dating from the third
or second century B.C., is one of numerous
such figures found in the northwestern region
of India. Their elaborate headdresses and
jewelry have gained them the name of "the
Baroque Ladies," but they were almost certainly variations of the mother goddess, or
fertility-cult figures. (Paris: Guimet Museum)**

did not precede the Aryans' change to a sedentary existence, but was rather a result of this.

But it is difficult to explain the origin of the castes historically. The fact is that in Sanskrit (the classical literary language of India, and as such a direct link back to the language of the early Aryans) the term for "caste" is *varna* — "color." This indicates that originally the differentiation did have racial roots and was based, at least ideologically, on skin color. However, we cannot assume that this explains the origins of the four principal castes that came to play such a role in Indian life. The first three, in fact, seem to represent an evolution from the division of the early Aryan tribes as canonized by the priests themselves: these were the warriors, or *kshatriyas,* the military aristocracy who ended by wielding secular powers; the priests, or *brahmans,* who dominated in the spiritual and intellectual realms; and the cultivators, the *vaishyas,* the masses who worked the land. The fourth caste, the *shudras,* originally included the pre-Aryan inhabitants, *dasas* and all those of mixed origins; eventually they were taken into the Hindu community in a subordinate position and took on the role of farmers, while the *vaishyas,* formerly the Aryan cul-tivators, moved up the scale and became landowners and merchants.

The *Manavadharmasastra* — the "Law Code of Manu," a work com-posed in the first two centuries of our era — explains the origins of the four castes, giving legal justification to the Vedic cosmogony: "The Lord, Svayambhu, he who exists for and by himself, in his desire for the prosperity of the world, gave birth to the Brahmans, the Kshatriyas, the Vaishyas, and the Shudras, from his mouth, from his arms, from his thighs, and from his feet. . . . And in order to protect the universe He, the most resplendent one, assigned separate duties and occupations to those who had sprung from out of his mouth, his arms, his thighs, and his feet. . . . All those races of this world that are excluded from the commu-nity of those born from the mouth, the arms, the thighs, and the feet of Brahman are called Dasas, both those who speak the language of the Mlechchhas [barbarians] and those who speak that of the Aryans."

The transformation of the castes into inflexible and virtually non-communicating groups is a phenomenon of a later, historical India. In antiquity, the castes were much more open, and the passage of groups from one caste to another, in either direction, caused no astonishment. It is understandable that this would take place in a society that had to adapt a legal-religious scheme to an extremely mutable reality. The *Man-avadharmasastra* itself gives a list of tribes that fell down the social ladder: "As a result of their omitting the sacred rites and of their not having consulted the Brahmans, the following tribes of Kshatriyas have gradu-ally sunk in this world to the condition of the Shudras: the Paundrakas, the Codas, the Dravidas, the Kambojas, the Yavanas [Greeks], the Shakas [Scythians], the Paradas, the Pahlavas [Parthians], the Cinas, the Kiratas, and the Daradas." This passage has little historical significance, since some of the tribes are clearly foreign, and it is difficult to imagine they ever had status as *kshatriyas:* clearly the Brahmans are attempting to keep their people "in line" by this kind of revisionism. But what matters to us is that this traditional text recognizes that entire groups could pass from one caste to another. And in case it has not been understood, individuals could also pass from caste to caste, for any number of reasons.

Such a division of society can evidently be maintained only if the society itself is able to produce the legal and ideological means to punish infrac-tions. In India, the basic instrument for the conservation of this structure became the principle of the impurity of the lowest castes and the outcasts. Although it was only in a later epoch that this principle took hold in the extreme forms that everyone has heard about, there is no denying that the *Manavadharmasastra* clearly provides the intellectual foundations for the practice. Perhaps a comparable mode in the Western tradition was the effect that excommunication from the Catholic Church once played in history. Even in our own time we see survivals of this: thus, when the dictator of Argentina, Juan Peron, went too far in obliterating the tradi-tional social lines in his country, it was the Papal excommunication that freed many people to turn against him.

But this kind of analogy raises a question of primary importance. To what extent may we see the phenomena of ancient India in Western terms — specifically at this point, can we consider castes as classes as we understand the latter within the frame of Western sociology? The fact that the caste system was so rigidly established by a priori intellectual traditions — that it was independent, in other words, from the organic relationship with the means of production — excludes a definition of the castes as purely economic classes. But then economic classes do not necessarily coincide with social classes. To focus on our particular concern, however, we may say that the division into castes tended to preserve the ancient and authoritative tribal divisions as well as to assert the new privileges the Aryans came to enjoy over the indigenous, dark-skinned inhabitants of India; these latter then became, for all practical purposes, an economic and social class.

The Indian caste system was obviously a hybrid system. The fundamental division into classes was that which set on one side the *dvijas* ("born twice," first by biological birth, and secondly through initiation), which included the brahmans, kshatriyas, and vaishyas; while on the other side were the shudras, the "servants" of society. (They were never reduced to quite the state of slavery as has existed in other societies, because — as we shall see — the ruling class had other means of appropriating their production.) This is, of course, an oversimplification of the problem; for one thing, the full explanation would have to be articulated in a chronological account of Indian society. But the opposition between the ruling class and the servants — for the most part the farmers — seems valid. The further division of the ruling class into three parts then may be seen as having undoubted social importance. But it allowed for such otherwise apparent contradictions of pure social classes as the fact that brahmans could lead totally different kinds of lives, from influential politicians to hermit plant-gatherers. Perhaps we might best conclude by accepting the definition Max Weber, the great sociologist, gave to caste: *Stand,* a German word that is best rendered as "status group." Many of the great monuments we are about to explore will be understood if we keep in mind the concept of "status."

But if Indian monuments are to be viewed to some extent as based on such subtle constructs as status, it is also true they rested on very tangible economic foundations. And so we should mention, if but briefly, the question of the relationships of the principal classes of ancient India with the means of production. The idea of the "Asiatic mode of production," which has been taken up today by many persons and with diverse connotations, was set forth by Karl Marx in various writings. (The one that most clearly expressed his intuition, "Pre-Capitalist Forms of Production," remained unpublished for a long time and was never given definitive form by Marx.) By "mode of production" is meant a particular form of exploitation of nature and man, with its concomitant social organization. As Chesneaux has put it: "The Asiatic mode of production is characterized by the combination of the productive activities of the village communities with the economic intervention of a state authority that exploits them and at the same time directs them." This latter aspect must be emphasized: that is, the function of the state as controller and general entrepreneur. In the last analysis, the state is the sole proprietor. We should keep this in mind when we approach some of the ambitious architectural monuments.

Marx emphasized the fundamental fact that in ancient India private property — ownership of the land as such — did not exist; even in the most extreme instances, it was more a form of concession that allowed individuals to participate in the income of the state, not really to own property. The sole proprietor was the state, which appropriated the production surplus and redistributed it, particularly in the great hydraulic works that supported the fields and communities. The state thus represented the superior unit that identified itself with the interests of the community. Here, then, lies the origin of those forms of idealization of state authority that we shall be seeing in so much of the architecture and figurative arts. And if such groups as the aristocracy, the priests, and the

ADULTERY AS A DISRUPTIVE FORCE

Men who commit adultery with the wives of others, the king shall cause to be marked by punishments that cause terror, and afterwards he shall banish them.

For by adultery is caused a mixture of the castes among men; hence follows sin, which cuts up even the roots and causes the destruction of everything.

Manavadharmasastra VIII: 352–353

THE THREE BIRTHS

According to the injunction of the revealed texts the first birth of an Aryan is from his natural mother; the second happens on the tying of the girdle of *munga* grass; and the third on the initiation to the performance of a sacrifice.

Among those three, the birth symbolized by the investiture with the girdle of *munga* grass, is his birth for the sake of the Veda; they declare that in that birth the *Savitri* [verse] is his mother and the teacher his father.

They call the teacher the pupil's father because he gives the Veda; for nobody can perform a sacred rite before the investiture with the girdle of *munga* grass.

He who has not been initiated should not pronounce any Vedic text except those required for the performance of funeral rites, since he is on a level with a *sudra* before his birth from the Veda.

Manavadharmasastra II:169–172

4. **Northern Pakistan:** A selection of terra-cotta figurines, more of the "Baroque Ladies," or mother goddesses, dating from the third or second centuries B.C. (Rome: private collection)

5. **Sari Dheri:** A fragment of a terra-cotta figurine, some 2½ inches high, and dated to the third or second century B.C. (Rome: National Museum of Oriental Art, gift of D. H. Gordon)

The naive-primitive execution of these "Baroque Ladies" and certain similarities with some terra-cotta figurines found at Harappa and Mohenjo-daro at first caused scholars to date them to a much earlier age than they are dated today; the revision has been due to findings at other excavation sites.

6.   Sanchi: This is a view of the hill of Sanchi, situated about 5 miles southwest of present-day Vidisha, in Madhya Pradesh. The first Buddhist monuments on this hill probably date from Asoka's time, when the great emperor had a stupa and a pillar built here. The subsequent development of this complex was due to the continuous support of a monastic community offered by rich merchants of the region. The hill rises about 300 feet above the plain. In this photograph, the three main stupas can be seen: on the upper terrace, at the far left edge, is Stupa 3; Stupa 1 the prominent one to the left; and Stupa 2 the dark structure (far right) on the lower slope.

Following pages:
7.   Sanchi: A detail of the sculptured railing of Stupa 2, dated to the beginning of the first century B.C. The relief decoration of Stupa 2 is concentrated on this railing, which has four "elbow-bend" entrances rather than the ornate portals typical of Stupas 1 and 3. Although the stupa was the work of Buddhists, it is interesting to note that the railing's carvings include only a few Buddhist motifs. The stupa itself was opened and half destroyed early in the 19th century, and was then damaged again by Alexander Cunningham, who at least discovered the relics chamber almost at the center. The reliquary, made of white sandstone, had the following inscription: "The relics of all the masters, including *Arhat* Kasapa-gota and *Arhat* Vachi-Suvijayata, the master." Within were four small steatite reliquaries, bearing the names of the Buddhist "saints" whose relics they contained; evidently they had been preserved in different places until they were brought together in the one larger reliquary of this stupa. (All the reliquaries are now in the British Museum in London.)

bureaucracy all benefited from their support of this supreme authority, it is also true that they could not privately monopolize the means of production. Thus priests, like their temples and other religious structures, may be seen as serving as agents of this supreme power.

The Roots of Religion in Early India

We are not going to be able to go back and search for the roots of even the most important phenomena of Indian religion in the deepest past. It would be no easy task, in any case, because Indian religion has never been a closed theological system, but a complex of often contrasting experiences that has never hesitated to make use of disparate religious elements of various origins, merging them in an adventure of thought that has never been afraid of the most daring leaps. It is as difficult today as it was in the past to establish, for example, what orthodox Hinduism is; it is somewhat less difficult perhaps to single out an orthodox Hindu since devoting oneself to certain practices — the observance of certain rites and the respect for certain taboos — has always been much more essential than the adherence to a particular philosophic concept. Indian thought is not autonomous but finds its liberation only in religion: India has no "lay" philosophy, any more than its traditional political philosophy could be separated from its religious life.

What does concern us here is the Vedic religion, expressed in the four collections of the *Vedas*, previously mentioned as being among those traditional "sources" of India's ideal history. The *Vedas* were written down over a period of some centuries, with a definitive version dating from about 800 B.C. (approximately the same time that Hesiod and Homer were being written down in the Greek world), and they do not present a homogeneous picture. "In fact it is possible," Tucci has written, "to distinguish in the *Vedas* a stratification that, if one follows it in detail, almost marks the stages of the contrasting form of religious thought, documents the fortune of the various gods, shows how this god takes the place of another one, and how all, little by little, lose their primitive characters and assume others until they are finally transmuted into manifestations of supreme entities, still vague and undetermined but whose appearance marks the dawn of Indian speculation." Of course we must realize that what is here being described was the religious experience of the ruling class as elaborated by the brahmans, not the popular religion (although some reflection of the latter may perhaps be found in the *Atharva-Veda*).

But this then raises the question of what popular religion in Aryan-Vedic India means? Certainly we must think of various levels of popular religiosity, which reflect if anything the two different roots of Indian society: the tribal-nomadic root and the agricultural pre-Aryan one. Of the divine figures who appear in the *Vedas*, two take on ever-growing importance: Vishnu, originally a sun god, and Rudra, the god of tempests and epidemics. Rudra almost prefigures Shiva, in whom were eventually merged the pre-Aryan elements, especially those connected with fertility. (A seal from Mohenjo-daro, for instance, one of the centers of the Indus Valley Civilization, shows a horned and ithyphallic being, probably one of the various pre-Aryan antecedents of Shiva.) Next to these two was Indra, the hero-god, the deification of the tribal warrior-chieftain.

But the gods are not the chief protagonists of the Vedic religious life: the *Vedas* attach the greatest importance to sacrifices as an elaboration of the priestly caste. The world itself, mankind, the castes — all derive from the sacrifice of Purusha, the cosmic man. The sacrifice, regulated by a rigorous ritual, whether domestic or public, was the religious foundation of the social system in India, the instrument through which the priest, the protagonist in the public sacrifice, made himself the guardian of the preservation of that system.

THE UNDYING SELF AND CASTE DUTY

The god Krishna said to Arjuna: You have grieved for those who deserve no grief, and you talk words of wisdom. Learned men grieve not for the living nor the dead. Never did I not exist, nor you, nor these rulers of men; nor will any one of us ever hereafter cease to be. As in this body, infancy and youth and old age come to the embodied self, so does the acquisition of another body; a sensible man is not deceived about that. The contacts of the senses, O son of Kunti! which produce cold and heat, pleasure and pain, are not permanent, they are ever coming and going. Bear them, O descendant of Bharata! For, O chief of men! that sensible man whom they pain and pleasure being alike to him afflict not, he merits immortality. There is no existence for that which is unreal; there is no non-existence for that which is real. And the correct conclusion about both is perceived by those who perceive the truth. Know that to be indestructible which pervades all this; the destruction of that inexhaustible principle none can bring about. These bodies appertaining to the embodied self which is eternal, indestructible, and indefinable, are said to be perishable; therefore do engage in battle, O descendant of Bharata! He who thinks it to be the killer and he who thinks it to be killed, both know nothing. It kills not, is not killed. It is not born, nor does it ever die, nor, having existed, does it exist no more. Unborn, everlasting, unchangeable, and primeval, it is not killed when the body is killed. O son of Pritha! how can that man who knows it thus to be indestructible, everlasting, unborn, and inexhaustible, how and whom can he kill, whom can he cause to be killed? As a man, casting off old clothes, puts on others and new ones, so the embodied self casting off old bodies, goes to others and new ones. Weapons do not divide it into pieces; fire does not burn it; waters do not moisten it; the wind does not dry it up. It is not divisible; it is not combustible; it is not to be moistened; it is not to be dried up. It is everlasting, all-pervading, stable, firm, and eternal. It is said to be unperceived, to be unthinkable, to be unchangeable. Therefore knowing it to be such, you ought not to grieve. But even if you think that it is constantly born, and constantly dies, still, O you of mighty arms! you ought not to grieve thus. For to one that is born, death is certain; and to one that dies, birth is certain. Therefore about this unavoidable thing, you ought not to grieve. The source of things, O descendant of Bharata! is unperceived; their middle state is perceived; and their end again is unperceived. What occasion is there for any lamentation regarding them? One looks upon it as a wonder; another similarly speaks of it as a wonder; another too hears of it as a wonder; and even after having heard of it, no one does really know it. This embodied self, O descendant of Bharata! within every one's body is ever indestructible. Therefore you ought not to grieve for any being. Having regard to your own duty also, you ought not to falter, for there is nothing better for a Kshatriya than a righteous battle. Happy those Kshatriyas, O son of Pritha! who can find such a battle to fight — come of itself — an open door to heaven! But if you will not fight this righteous battle, then you will have abandoned your own duty and your fame, and you will incur sin. All beings, too, will tell of your everlasting infamy; and to one who has been honored, infamy is a greater evil than death. Warriors who are masters of great cars will think that you abstained from the battle through fear, and having been highly thought of by them, you will fall down to littleness. Your enemies, too, decrying your power, will speak much about you that should not be spoken. And what, indeed, more lamentable than that? Killed, you will obtain heaven; victorious, you will enjoy the earth.

Therefore arise, O son of Kunti! resolved to engage in battle. Looking alike on pleasure and pain, on gain and loss, on victory and defeat, then prepare for battle, and thus you will not incur sin.

Bhagavadgita II:11–37

INDRA

He who just born chief god of lofty spirit by power and might became the gods' protector,
Before whose strength in majesty of valor the two worlds trembled, He, O men, is Indra.
He who fixed fast and firm the earth that staggered, and set at rest the agitated mountains,
Who measured out the air's wide middle region and gave the heaven support, He, men, is Indra.
Who slew the dragon, freed the seven rivers, and drove the kine forth from the cave of Vala,
Begat the fire between two stones, the spoiler in warriors' battle, He, O men, is Indra.
He who created all these things that perish, who chased away the humbled race of Dasas,
Who like a hunter conquering takes as booty the foeman's treasure. He, O men, is Indra.

Rigveda II:12

THE PRIMEVAL SACRIFICE

When the gods performed the sacrifice with Purusa — the primeval eternal Man, the Supreme Being — as the oblation, then the spring was its clarified butter, the summer the sacrificial fuel, and the autumn the oblation.

The sacrificial victim, namely, Purusa, born at the very beginning, they sprinkled with sacred water upon the sacrificial grass. With him as oblation the gods performed the sacrifice, and also the Sadhyas [a class of semidivine beings] and the risis [ancient seers].

From that wholly offered sacrificial oblation were born the verses and the sacred chants; from it were born the meters; the sacrificial formula was born from it.

From it horses were born and also those animals who have double rows of teeth; cows were born from it, from it were born goats and sheep.

When they divided Purusa, in how many different portions did they arrange him? What became of his mouth, what of his two arms? What were his two thighs and his two feet called?

His mouth became the brahman; his two arms were made into the *rajanya;* his two thighs the *vaisyas;* from his two feet the *sudra* was born.

The moon was born from the mind, from the eye the sun was born; from the mouth Indra and Agni, from the breath the wind was born.

From the navel was the atmosphere created, from the head the heaven issued forth; from the two feet was born the earth and the quarters, or the cardinal directions, from the ear. Thus did they fashion the worlds.

Rigveda X:90

What type of edifices would then be erected by such a society, one that, if slowly, was opening itself to exchanges with the surrounding world? In particular, India was interacting with Iran, from which region the Indians probably adopted the use of iron. (The appearance of iron in India is still of an uncertain date, but recent excavations indicate that 800 B.C. is a likely date.) Vedic India — which we may think of as generally lasting from about 1500 to 500 B.C. — has not left us any temples, since its rituals had no need of enclosed structures just as it had no need of idols; the Vedic priests required simply consecrated space. As for the excavations of this period, the excavation of Hastinapur (in Uttar Pradesh, the north-central region) is one of the most extensive, yet even here there are few remains of the early centuries. In the second period (about 1100–800 B.C.) no town-planning can be recognized in the dwellings, but simply remains of walls of mud or sun-dried bricks and walls of reed with mud plaster. The main ceramic production is represented by the so-called Painted Gray Ware, also common to many other localities in northern India, some of which are mentioned in the *Mahabharata* (such as Mathura, Ahicchatra, Kurukshetra, etc.). About 800 B.C. Hastinapur was abandoned, and archaeology confirms what was stated in the *Mahabharata:* Hastinapur was swept away by a Ganges flood, and the capital of the region was moved to Kaushambi. And if the impression of architectural activity in Vedic India is disappointing, the field of figurative arts is no better. The sole remains known at this time are fragments of terracotta figurines of animals, among which a hump-backed ox is recognizable.

Much time was to pass before the Indian city ceased to be a mere "enlargement" of the village, both as regards form and type of habitation. This was a process whose initial phase can be said to end with the city-capital of the Maurya epoch, which began in the fourth century B.C. And this lag is especially notable because the sixth century B.C. marked a period of great social and religious renovation in India. By then the country found itself in a position to push aside what remained of the old tribal organization, specifically the division into castes. Such a social arrangement, which had met the needs of a simple agricultural society, now had to take into account the emergence of new groups devoted to new activities, especially commerce. Thus, coins appeared for the first time in India; although these were but small pieces of silver or copper that bore impressions of punches, they signify a major turning point in any society: wealth was no longer measured only by the number of cattle owned.

The great majority of merchants belonged to the *vaishya* caste, but the *Manavadharmasastra* allowed *brahmans* and *kshatriyas* to indulge in commerce, even if only under conditions of particular necessity. Among the businessmen there quickly emerged a group of bankers and financiers *(sreshthin)* who were particularly respected by the sovereigns themselves. It is clear that the merchant, in order to engage in his activity, needed a complex of guarantees of order: political stability, safety along the trade routes, peace with neighboring countries. And his new social status, based on his acquired wealth, in order to be recognized and accepted, required some adaptation of the traditional principles of caste. Two kinds of instruments were needed to accommodate these new social demands: political and ideological. Simultaneously, the figure of the absolute sovereign was taking shape, the ancestor of the "despot" of India's medieval period. Meanwhile, by means of wars and confederations, India was going through a process of territorial unification. The final result was to be the empire of the Maurya, but as early as the sixth century B.C. the king seems to have taken on those characteristics that we tend to associate with the great Mauryan king, Asoka. The merchants were supporting these kings with their wealth; the kings reciprocated with their benevolence and with guarantees of security.

Among the various "heresies" that arose as pressures against the Brahmanic ordering of society in this period of India's history, two registered almost immediate impact. These were Jainism — with its emphasis on the doctrine of non-violence *(ahimsa)* — and the doctrine of determinism preached by the Ajivikas. But it was still another "heresy," Buddhism, which turned out to be the most extraordinarily efficient ideological instrument for adapting Indian society, and we shall go deeply only into this religion because it was Buddhism that influenced India in such a profound way and for such a long period. Although Jainist groups are still active in India today, and have a certain social importance, Jainism has never taken on that character of a universal religion as has Buddhism. Buddhism set against the ritualism of the Brahmans its moral law, which makes the individual responsible for his actions and free from the prison of castes, no longer dependent on the Brahman in his inner life and his behavior, engaged in a struggle to acquire merits that represent a true *brahman* existence, not in the narrow sense of belonging to a caste but in the sense of "noble" and "just."

Thus a surprisingly explicit passage from the *Dhammapada*, an ancient Buddhist text, states: "Not by matted hair, not by lineage, not by caste does one become a Brahman. He is a Brahman in whom there are truth and righteousness. He is blessed. What is the use of matted hair, O fool, what of the raiment of goatskins? Thine inward nature is full of wickedness; the outside thou makest pure." Self-control, then, is the Buddhist ideal. The *Dhammapada* says that "if a man were to conquer in battle a thousand times a thousand men, and another conquer one, himself, the latter is indeed the greatest of conquerors." The Buddhist has to travel down a long moral road: the word of the Enlightened One shows him the way, but he will be able to follow it only by himself and not through the virtue of others. All this, no matter how it may sound to modern ears, was novel and threatening to the society that had developed through some one thousand years of Vedic India, and it was the teaching of one who had every reason to want to preserve that traditional society.

Siddhartha, the historical Buddha — also known as Gautama, his surname, and Shakyamuni, "the sage of the Shakyas" — was born about 563 B.C. at Lumbani, near Kapilavastu, a town near the border of Nepal. (The exact date of birth is uncertain, as tradition proposes another quite different chronology.) He belonged to one of the old Aryan-Vedic tribes the Shakyas, in which his father belonged to the royalty; as a youth, Siddhartha was destined to follow the career of such a leader by means of perfect training under the Kshatriya traditions. But things developed differently, and after certain mystical insights he abandoned his family and home and went off to devote himself to various traditional Vedic-mystical practices. But as he came to feel the uselessness of this ascetic life, he directed his mind toward the mystery of death and rebirths. Finally, in 531 B.C., he attained Enlightenment by meditating under the Bodhi Tree at Gaya; there he achieved the recollection of his past lives, the consciousness of life and death, the knowledge of having destroyed desire, and awareness of successive rebirths in oneself. From Gaya, Siddhartha, now the Buddha ("Enlightened One"), went to Sarnath, near Benares, and there, in Deer Park, preached the Law for the first time. Buddha then spent his long life traveling throughout India, preaching and working miracles and making converts. His death (the achievement of *nirvana*, a total extinction that freed him from any further rebirths) occurred in 483 B.C.

One of the important things to realize is that Buddha was not a god; he was merely the one who clarified things. Primitive Buddhism, which is known through the *Pali Canon* (the oldest collection of Buddhist texts, in Pali, a dialect of the Vedic-Aryan language), had nothing to do with salvation or devotion; rather, the means of liberation was innate in man, who only through his own efforts could reach it by avoiding the endless cycle of deaths and rebirths. Buddha had merely shown the way. Therefore, primitive Buddhism rejected any form of image worship; there was not even any reason to reproduce Buddha's person (although in a later period the Buddhists elaborated some legends about how the first image of Buddha was taken from his very shadow).

Respect for a particular ritual was not required for a Buddhist, either; instead, the Buddhist was expected to follow an ethical norm that left little room for mere forms. Sacrifice, the undisputed foundation of Vedic society, was rejected with scorn. The story of King Okkako, induced by the Brahmans into sacrificing a large number of cows, is narrated in the

THE TRUE BRAHMAN

For whoever amongst men lives by cow-keeping — know this, O Vasettha — he is a husband-man, not a Brahmana.

And whoever amongst men lives by different mechanical arts — know this, O Vasettha — he is an artisan, not a Brahmana.

And whoever amongst men lives by trade — know this, O Vasettha — he is a merchant, not a Brahmana. . . .

And I do not call one a Brahmana on account of his birth or of his origin from a particular mother; he may be called bhovadi, and he may be wealthy, but the one who is possessed of nothing and seizes upon nothing, him I call a Brahmana.

Whosoever, after cutting all bonds, does not tremble, has shaken off all ties and is liberated, him I call a Brahmana. . . .

The man who does not mix with householders nor with the houseless, who wanders about without a house, and who has few wants, him I call a Brahmana.

Whosoever, after refraining from hurting living creatures, both those that tremble and those that are strong, does not kill or cause to be killed, him I call a Brahmana.

The man who is not hostile amongst the hostile, who is peaceful amongst the violent, not seizing upon anything amongst those that seize upon everything, him I call a Brahmana. . . .

For what has been designated as "name" and "family" in the world is only a term, what has been designated here and there is understood by common consent.

Adhered to for a long time are the views of the ignorant, the ignorant tell us, one is a Brahmana by birth.

Not by birth is one a Brahmana, nor is one by birth no Brahmana; by work one is a Brahmana, by work one is no Brahmana.

By work one is a husbandman, by work one is an artisan, by work one is a merchant, by work one is a servant.

By work one is a thief, by work one is a soldier, by work one is a sacrificer, by work one is a king.

So the wise, who see the cause of things and understand the result of work, know this work as it really is.

By work the world exists, by work mankind exists, beings are bound by work as the linch-pin of the rolling cart keeps the wheel on.

By penance, by a religious life, by self-restraint, and by temperance, by this one is a Brahmana, such a one they call the best Brahmana.

He who is endowed with the threefold knowledge, is calm, and has destroyed regeneration, — know this, O Vasettha, — he is to the wise Brahman and Sakka.

Sutta-Nipata 612–656

COME THOU NOT BACK TO BIRTH!

Hast thou not seen sorrow and ill in all the springs of life? Come thou not back to birth! Cast out the passionate desire again to Be. So shalt thou go thy ways calm and serene.

Therigatha I:14

8. **Pitalkhora: A relief depicting the "Great Departure" of Buddha, found in Cave 4 and dated to the second to first century B.C. The relief shows the moment when Siddhartha — who, as was traditional, was not actually represented — left his hometown, Kapilavastu, on horseback. But what is of particular interest at this point is that the city gate bears a likeness to the *toranas* of the Bharhut and Sanchi stupas. (New Delhi: National Museum)**

Suttanipata (one of the early sacred texts of Buddhism) in order to explain the many diseases that struck man as a result of that crime. "This iniquity of violence is of ancient origin," says the Sublime Buddha to the Brahmans who had questioned him. "Innocent creatures are sacrificed by priests who assault them with weapons in their fists. This ancient, ignoble custom is condemned by the sages; the people who see such things censure the priest who sacrifices." Freed from such ritualistic forms that the Brahmans had required, the king had new obligations imposed on him by a new moral code. This code, moreover, was functional within the new society in which the merchants had come to represent the most innovational group. Naturally the development of commerce not only involved the interests of those who devoted themselves to a specifically commercial activity, but also — in certain respects, more importantly — the interests of those who have surplus products. It is thus easy to see how only those groups of Brahmans who were deprived of their privileges connected with rites and sacrifices would become a conservative force, resistant to the appeal of this new teaching. Probably, too, these traditionalist Brahmans kept on their side the poorest rural classes, among whom the spread of Buddhism was never comparable to that which took place in

the urban environment. Buddhism in early India, then, was — if not a cause — definitely related to the shiftings of power within society, shiftings that saw the emergence of new forms of political, economic, and social forces that were putting pressure on the traditional Vedic way.

"The new philosophy gave man control over himself," has written the distinguished Indian scholar, D. D. Kosambi, and one must agree with him in judging the political vision of early Buddhism as "an intellectual achievement of the highest order [in] a society that had just begun to conquer the primeval jungle." Yet the man who would acquire control over himself is not any and every man, although the Buddhist texts cite examples of men of low birth who attained nirvana after an existence of prestige among the highest castes. But in general the "new man" would be only the one who had the intellectual, hence cultural, and thus probably economic, means to take the difficult path that leads to the suppression of desire. Buddha replaced an aristocracy of lineage with one of intellect; it is understandable that this should be so, and it would be ingenuous to reproach Buddhism for this limitation. However, it is necessary to point this out in order to understand the function of Buddhism itself in the development of Indian society and in order to understand the modifications (sometimes profound) that Buddhism had to undergo simultaneously with the evolution of that society.

In any case, it would seem that, under the influence of Buddhism, the individual would become enormously important in the new Indian society. Yet Buddhism never accepted that the individual existed; rather, what we think of as "an individual" was but an agglomerate of components that disintegrates at the moment of death. Buddhism was not afraid of this contradiction between the theory of *anatta* (that is, non-*atman*, the existence of an individual soul) and the theory of rebirth. Actually the contradiction arises only in our Western logic, which considers good and evil from the point of view of the individual. Not so for Buddhism, which in the succession of deaths and rebirths sees principally

9.   Pitalkhora: Left: A *yaksha* from Cave 3, standing some 42 inches high, and dated to the second to first century B.C. This is an extremely rare piece, in part because it is one of the few such figures to have been executed in the round, but especially because of an inscription it bears: "Made by Kanhadasa, goldsmith." Although epigraphical evidence dates this inscription to the second century B.C., stylistically the work has much in common with the sculptures of the Great Stupa at Sanchi. (New Delhi: National Museum)

10.   Pitalkhora: Right: A *yaksha* from Cave 3, dated to the second or first century B.C. and probably one of the oldest pieces of sculpture from Pitalkhora and from western India in general; certainly it is one of the finest "archaic" works of Indian art. Standing some 66 inches high, it was used as a guardian of the gate on the left side of the entrance to Cave 3. There are still traces of the original yellow paint on the face and the red of the lips. (Bombay: Prince of Wales Museum of Western India)

THE BIRTH OF THE BODHISATTVA

It is in accordance with the normal order of things that in the moment in which the bodhisattva, the venerable one, leaves his mother's womb, the mother, woman of heroic lineage, is neither sitting nor lying down; by merely standing she gives birth to a warrior. And it is the norm that, as soon as he is born, the bodhisattva takes seven steps unassisted and, turning his glance toward the four cardinal points, exclaims: "This is the Orient and I orient myself toward Nirvana; this is the South and I will bring good to all creatures; this is the West and this is my last birth; this is the North and I shall go beyond the flux of existence." And it is the norm that as soon as the bodhisattva is born, the gods hold upon his head golden umbrellas and fans with gem-studded handles. And it is the norm that, as the bodhisattva is born, there appear in the sky two waterfalls, one hot and the other cold, which, falling on the head of the Buddha, sprinkle him. And it is the norm that there arises before the mother and genetrice of the bodhisattva, the venerable, a pond from which water runs, in order that his mother do with that water that which one does with water.

And it is the norm that as soon as the bodhisattva is born the gods of the atmosphere shower on him lotus flowers.

Vinaya of the Mulasarvastivadin

THIS IS NOT THE WAY

The thought came to me, monks, "I shall live with both body and mind withdrawn from sensual pleasures, and with my thoughts of them, my fondness for them, my feverish longing for them and my attachment to them subdued. Although I undergo unpleasant, bitter, cruel and severe feelings which torment my soul and my body, I shall be capable of the state of 'further man,' of knowledge, insight and enlightenment. . . ."

So, monks, I restrained and curbed body and mind with thought. And as I thus restrained and curbed body and mind with thought, perspiration poured out of my armpits and fell hot and steaming to the ground. From my face and my brow the perspiration poured out and fell hot and steaming to the ground. . . .

Then, monks, I said to myself, "There are people here who, prescribing what is pure, make their meals of jujube fruit and of jujube bark. . . . of sesamum. . . . of rice. . . . complete abstinence from food. Let me now, then, practice complete abstinence from food. And then, monks, as I practiced complete abstinence from food this body of mine became exceedingly lean . . .

I would try, monks, to grasp the front of my body, but it would be my backbone that I held in my grasp. I would try, monks, to stand erect, and immediately I would tumble forward in a heap. Then, monks, having after vain endeavor stood up well and properly, I would chafe my riblike limbs with my hands. But then the hairs on my body, rotten at the roots, fell off. . . .

Then, monks, I said to myself, "Those worthy recluses and brahmans who undergo . . . have in the past undergone unpleasant, bitter, cruel, and severe feelings which assail their souls and their bodies do so to gain perfection, but in no wise do they attain it . . . . have they attained it. . . . This is not the way to enlightenment. . . .

Mahavastu 123–130

---

the perpetuation and, finally, the extinction of *karma* (action, in the moral sense, and its consequence), independently from the individuals who are its bearers. So while we may speak of Buddhism as a new and renovative force within ancient Indian society, we should not make the mistake of ascribing to it various characteristics we associate with Western tradition.

Eventually we shall be reading of the edicts of Asoka, the emperor who openly identified himself with Buddhism, and we shall understand the coldly propagandistic element present in the message of non-violence, peace, and concern for the good of all living beings. But we need not for this reason refuse to regard the contents of those texts as one of the high achievements of human civilization. Outside of India, no country in the third century B.C. was promulgating political propaganda in these terms: this at least is to the credit of Buddhism, even if the results in practice proved to be less than lasting peace.

Ceramics and Cities of Early India

For the moment we shall turn away from the impact of early Buddhism on some of the aspects of religious, intellectual, social, and political life in India, and try to see what was taking place in the more tangible productions of the period. If we were to resume an examination of the stratigraphy of Hastinapur, for instance — mentioned on page 27 — we would notice a series of basic innovations in the third period (beginning of the sixth century to the beginning of the third century B.C.). Painted Gray Ware disappears, giving way to the new "luxury" ware, Northern Black Polished Ware, made of well-baked and purified clay, with a smooth and exceptionally lustrous surface that is usually black or metallic steel-blue. (There are also examples of coarser red and gray pottery.) With some exceptions, the forms of this Northern Black Polished Ware were also new compared to those of the preceding period. The new black ceramics provide a most useful element for the archaeologist in dating his work, because of its vast distribution; it is found from Amaravati (on the Kistna River) to Bengal, and over into the northwest, although sporadically, at Taxila, Charsada, and Udegram (Swat). By this time, too, iron was being used for tools; people had houses built with mud bricks or bricks baked in furnaces; there were drainage pits made of terra-cotta vessels or rings (in this latter case these were sometimes water wells); and there were drainage canals with brick facing. The first coins are also beginning to circulate, both punch-marked coins and also copper coins with no inscriptions. This growth of coin minting, together with the widespread distribution of Northern Black Polished Ware, is a clear sign of the new economic conditions, particularly of large-scale commercial activity.

The course of Indian history as revealed at Hastinapur is further confirmed by excavations at Ahicchatra, Kaushambi (near the confluence of the Ganges and the Yamuna), at Vaishali (Magadha), and at Benares (the site of Rajghat). At many of these sites, however, the Northern Black Polished Ware was clearly imported. It now seems certain that the distribution center of this pottery was the central basin of the Ganges, as the excavations at Kaushambi in particular demonstrate, although elsewhere there are indications of local production. The production of terra-cotta figurines also went through considerable qualitative development at Hastinapur. The elephant was a particular favorite; the terra-cottas representing elephants have stamped impressions in the form of a wheel *(cakra)*, leaves, and circles. Human figures also appear, among which the females with rich headdresses, large earrings, and elaborate dresses are particularly characteristic. Some human figures were executed from casts, unlike the animal figures, which continued to be modeled by hand.

Kaushambi presents problems of particular historical significance. Excavations have brought to light many elements, among which are the grandiose fortifications; their first phase precedes the appearance of Painted Gray Ware, which is accompanied by red, and red and black pottery and which does not disappear when the Northern Black Polished Ware enters the scene. Vaishali was the capital of the Licchavi dynasty and preserves the stupa where a part of Buddha's relics were said to have been deposited. Still another structure dating from this period was Ghoshitarama, the famous monastery of Kaushambi; its first phase at least goes back to the fifth century B.C.

The cities of this period, from what is known of them, were constructed according to a rough town-planning system, certainly nothing comparable to the one used at the centers of the Harappa Culture. Panini, a famous Indian grammarian who lived between the second and first centuries B.C., suggested this when he spoke of the various parts of the typical city of the time: the residential structures, the shops gathered together in a bazaar, the royal storehouses, the Council chambers, the sites for dramatic performances. On the whole, though, the remains of Indian cities before the Maurya epoch do not confirm the impression of grandeur that the Buddhist texts of the time would have us imagine.

One site that is fairly important for its civil architecture is Takshashila in the western Punjab — a city that has passed into history under its Greek name, Taxila. The site has been the object of several major excavations, particularly those of Sir John Marshall (1913–34) and of A. Ghosh (1944–45); results of the latest excavations have largely remained unpublished, while the most ancient part of Taxila, set on the Bhir Mound, has yet to be fully explored. One of the city's richest quarters, however, has been brought to light; this has a stratigraphic succession that goes from the fifth to the second centuries B.C. The domestic habitations were rather poor: houses built with limestone and a calcareous stone (kanjur) in a rather coarse manner — especially in the oldest level — and covered by a thick plaster of mud mixed with straw. The houses, usually two or more stories, consisted of an inside court with rooms that opened on to its sides; there was no town-planning system for their construction, so that the plan of the Bhir Mound seems highly chaotic. However, there was a drainage system and a sewage disposal system (with cesspools). The sole edifice of a religious character is perhaps the apsidal structure discovered in 1944. And, as mentioned, Northern Black Polished Ware also appears at Taxila.

Taxila's importance, even in this early period, must have been considerable, thanks to its fine position on the road that linked India to Afghanistan; its importance was naturally to increase with the territorial unification effected by the Maurya rulers. In this regard, the discovery of two hoards (in 1924 and in 1945) containing jewels and bent-bar coins is of particular interest. The hoard found in 1924 is dated to about 317 B.C., because of the presence of a coin of Philip III Aridaeus (a half-brother of Alexander the Great); the hoard found in 1945 is from approximately the same period. Both the works of gem-engraving and the jewelry indicate some "Occidentalization" of the Taxila culture: Greek-Asian works are accompanied by Achaemenid work, perhaps of local production but certainly of "classical" inspiration. Taxila probably preserved a kind of semi-independence within the sphere of the Persian-Achaemenid Empire, of which Gandhara was a satrapy at least from the time of Darius I (who ruled from about 520 B.C.). And Achaemenid domination left its mark, particularly on the economic and political structure of the region, as testified by such elements as the satrapy organization, the official use of the Aramaic language (Kharoshthi, the characteristic writing of the northwestern region of ancient India, developed from the Aramaic alphabet), and the use of Achaemenid units in coinage. However, it is quite probable that the splendid specimens of Achaemenid gem-engraving and jewelry work found in the excavations of Bhir Mound had been imported to Taxila during Alexander the Great's campaign, or shortly thereafter.

On the same road leading to Afghanistan there lay Charsada (Pushkalavati), near the confluence of the Swat and Kabul rivers, and a short distance from Peshawar. Charsada displayed certain parallels with the development of Taxila, even if it differed in certain aspects, among

LET AN ANIMAL NOT RECEIVE THE ORDINATION

At that time there was a serpent who was aggrieved at, ashamed of, and conceived aversion for his having been born as a serpent. Now this serpent thought: "What am I to do in order to become released from being a serpent, and quickly to obtain human nature?" Then this serpent gave himself the following answer: "This Sakyaputtiya Samanas lead indeed a virtuous, tranquil, holy life; they speak the truth; they keep the precepts of morality, and are endowed with all virtues. If I could obtain pabbajja with the Sakyaputtiya Samanas, I should be released from being a serpent and quickly obtain human nature."

Then that serpent, in the shape of a youth, went to the Bhikkhus, and asked them for the pabbajja ordination; the Bhikkhus conferred on him the pabbajja and upasampada ordinations. At that time that serpent dwelt together with a certain Bhikkhu in the last Vihara. Now that Bhikkhu having arisen in the night, at dawn was walking up and down in the open air. When that Bhikkhu had left the Vihara, that serpent, who thought himself safe from discovery, fell asleep in his natural shape. The whole Vihara was filled with the snake's body; his windings jutted out of the window.

Then that Bhikkhu thought: "I will go back to the Vihara," opened the door, and saw the whole Vihara filled with the snake's body, the windings jutting out of the window. Seeing that, he was terrified and cried out. The Bhikkhus ran up, and said to that Bhikkhu: "Why did you cry out, friend?" "This whole Vihara, friends, is filled with a snake's body; the windings jut out of the window." Then that serpent awoke from that noise and sat down on his seat. The Bhikkhus said to him: "Who are you, friend?" "I am a serpent, reverend Sirs." "And why have you done such a thing, friend?" Then that Naga told the whole matter to the Bhikkhus; the Bhikkhus told it to the Blessed One.

In consequence of that and on this occasion the Blessed One, having ordered the fraternity of Bhikkhus to assemble, said to that serpent: "You serpents are not capable of spiritual growth in this doctrine and discipline. However, serpent, go and observe fast on the fourteenth, fifteenth, and eighth day of each half month; thus will you be released from being a serpent and quickly obtain human nature."

Then that serpent, who thought, "I am not capable of spiritual growth in this doctrine and discipline," became sad and sorrowful, shed tears, made an outcry, and went away.

Then the Blessed One said to the Bhikkhus: "There are two occasions, O Bhikkhus, on which a serpent who has assumed human shape manifests his true nature: when he has sexual intercourse with a female of his species, and if he thinks himself safe from discovery and falls asleep. These, O Bhikkhus, are the two occasions on which a serpent manifests his true nature.

"Let an animal, O Bhikkhus, that has not received the upasampada ordination, not receive it; if it has received it, let it be expelled from the fraternity."

Mahavagga I:63

So it was evident that Alexander was not in-capable of higher thought, but he was, in fact, grievously under the sway of ambition. For once when he came to Taxila and saw those of the Indian wise men who go naked, he desired very much that one of these men should join him, since he so much admired their endur-ance. On this the oldest among these wise men, whose pupils the others were, called Dan-damis, said that he would not join Alexander, and would not permit any of his school to do so. For he is said to have replied that he was just as much a son of Zeus himself as Alexan-der was, and that he had no need of anything from Alexander, since he was contented with what he had; he perceived, moreover, that those who were wandering about with Alexan-der over all those countries and seas were none the better for it, and that there was no end to their many wanderings. He did not then desire anything that Alexander could give him, nor did he fear being kept out of anything of which Alexander might be possessed. While he lived, the land of India was all he needed, giving to him its fruits in their season; and when he died, he would merely be released from an un-comfortable companion, his body. Alexander then hearing this reply had no mind to compel him, realizing that the man was indeed free.

ARRIAN: *Anabasis* VII 2:2–4

which not the least is the rarity of Northern Black Polished Ware. One of the most interesting results of the 1958 excavation, carried out by Sir Mortimer Wheeler, was the discovery of a moat protected by a rampart covered by sun-dried bricks: it was from these very fortifications that the inhabitants of Charsada opposed the Macedonian invader in 327 B.C. Much further south, in Madhya Pradesh, is the site of Ujjain, which provides a more varied picture of life during this "transitional" period in India. There is, for instance, an octagonal structure of square bricks that, if it is in fact pre-Mauryan, demonstrates that an evolved technique of stone construction was known at this time. At Ujjain, too, the whole of the ceramic production is interesting. It seems, for example, that Northern Black Polished Ware was produced here, as is shown by the large number of fragments of poor quality, some of which are unvarnished on the inside: as slight as such a defect might seem to the untutored observer, it suggests strongly to the specialist that such ceramics were probably not imported from the centers of that ceramic ware. This, in turn, suggests a diffusion of a general culture, albeit at a provincial level in many places.

But finally, in the total picture that the excavations provide of India from about 600 B.C. to the coming of Alexander's expedition in 327 B.C., what most surprises us is the extreme poverty of artistic production, architectural or figurative. It is a failing that can be explained only par-tially by the fact that such production must have been made of wood or other perishable materials. The only building works of any ambition seem to have been the fortifications. To those already mentioned, we might add the outside wall of Rajagirha, the capital of Magadha until the middle of the fifth century B.C., when it was succeeded by Pataliputra. This wall, which extends for about 25 to 30 miles, was considered the sole remains of a pre-Mauryan structure until the discovery of the Indus Valley Civilization. Now, of course, far more of the period has been uncovered, and although nothing yet is known to equal the great intellec-tual achievements of Buddhism and Jainism, there is increasing evidence from more and more sites and sources of, if by no means monumental artistic activity, at least a more dynamic society than once assumed.

The Mauryan Epoch: India's First Centralized Empire

We have seen how in Buddha's time India was freeing herself from the ancient tribal structure and organizing herself into states, whether king-doms or republics. The sovereign had already taken on, or was in the process of taking on, a divine character, while the Brahmans, for all practical purposes, had become the intermediaries between the king and the people, thus changing their function in the social organization with-out losing any of their privileges. The elaborate structure of Indian soci-ety was still reproduced and consolidated in traditional forms, as in the horse sacrifice *(ashvamedha)*, during which the king invested himself with dominion over the lands that a predestined victim-horse was allowed to wander over. Here is how the ritual was carried out in its original Vedic form. First the horse was given an ablution in a pool, in which a dog was then sacrificed. Then the horse, watched over by four hundred nobles, was let free to wander where it pleased for an entire year, setting off to the northeast. When the year was over, after another bath and still more complicated rites, the horse was tied to a pole and suffocated to death with a cloth. The king's wife then had to sleep next to the dead horse, covered with the same veil, while around them young people and women shouted jokes and scurrilous words. The horse was then cut into pieces, which were roasted and offered to Prajapati, the Cosmic Man. It was typical of India that such a primitive rite would be maintained even as the social realities became more sophisticated.

And we have also seen how Buddhism integrated itself into the new social realities, contributing to their renewal. The influence of Buddhism had become particularly strong in Magadha (present-day southern Bihar), where a state with a relatively efficient political and administrative organization was formed. The most important of the ancient kings of Magadha was Bimbisara, who ascended the throne some time in the second half of the sixth century B.C. The history of the dynasty of Bimbisara — who was assassinated by his son and successor Ajatashatru about 493 B.C. — is the history of the unification of the eastern region of the Ganges basin, realized through wars and alliances. When the last of Bimbisara's descendants was deposed and replaced by his viceroy, Shishunaga, in 413 B.C., the kingdom of Magadha continued to retain all its power, although traditional accounts speak in harsh terms about the character and capabilities of these sovereigns.

The Shishunaga dynasty lasted only about a half century, when a usurper, Mahapadma Nanda, took over the throne of Magadha, initiating the first non-*kshatriya* dynasty in India. Some sources claim that Mahapadma had been born to a mother belonging to the *shudra* caste, others that he was the son of a barber and a courtesan. It is difficult to know how much truth is in such assertions; but what does seem to be true is that for the first time a king comes from a lower caste; perhaps he was a *vaishya* (as was evidently the person who usurped the throne from the Nanda dynasty, Chandragupta Maurya). In any case, this entire period — from about 550 to 321 B.C. — despite its tormented succession of dynasties, usurpations, and assassinations (tradition has it that the five successors of Ajatashatru were all parricides), experienced a consistent development of the state's military, political, and economic strength. The merchants, who in Bimbisara's time had already carried decisive political weight, took direct control of some of the real levers of power; the class structure remained the same, in other words, but power groups were shifting within it. There was no basic change with the means of production, so that most farmers never felt the effects of any new situation; meanwhile the *brahmans* and *kshatriyas* did not see their economic privileges threatened.

Then, with the usurpation of the throne from the Nanda dynasty by the young Chandragupta Maurya, India's political history took a major turn. Chandragupta filled in the political vacuum left by the invasion of Alexander the Great in the northeast; Alexander essentially went through like a whirlwind, and since he died within a few years, it was left to one of his several successors, Seleucus Nikator, to cope with India. In 303 B.C. a solution of equilibrium was established between the two powers, through the transfer of a good part of present-day Afghanistan and Pakistan (Arachosia, Gedrosia, Paropamisadae) to the Mauryan sovereign; there was also an exchange of gifts and ambassadors, and possibly even a celebration of marriage between members of the ruling families. Political considerations as well as military defeats must have played a role in the Greeks' decision to co-exist with Mauryan India at this time.

As for the character of Chandragupta's somewhat sudden and new "empire," we must realize that he did not rest content with mere territorial expansion but he also allowed for strong internal economic differentiations within the new state. Magadha, with its capital Pataliputra, was essentially an agricultural region, and it now found itself at the head of an empire that included vast areas, like the northwest, in which animal husbandry was the principal form of natural exploitation. It is easy to see how all this would lead to a series of expanded possibilities for trade, with an enlarged domestic market as well as a greater variety of potential goods available for export.

We cannot assume, however, that the increased trade led to a productive reinvestment of profits. In fact, businessmen's profits were strictly limited by law. The *Arthasastra* was a study of government and economics attributed to Kautilya, the Brahman who, according to tradition, was Chandragupta Maurya's chief mentor and counsel. This valuable text states that a license was needed in order to buy grain from the farmers for commercial purposes, that the price was fixed by the authorities, and that the percentage of profit was also established at a fixed level, even if this sometimes differed according to the nature of the product involved.

THE SUPERINTENDENT OF COMMERCE

The superintendent of commerce should ascertain demand or absence of demand for, and rise or fall in the price of various kinds of merchandise which may be the products either of land or of water, and which may have been brought in either by land or by water path. He shall also ascertain the time suitable for their distribution, centralization, purchase, and sale.

That merchandise which is widely distributed shall be centralized and its price enhanced. . . .

That merchandise of the king which is of local manufacture shall be centralized; imported merchandise shall be distributed in several markets for sale. Both kinds of merchandise shall be favorably sold to the people.

He shall avoid such large profits as will harm the people.

There shall be no restriction to the time of sale of those commodities for which there is frequent demand; nor shall they be subject to the evils of centralization.

Or pedlars may sell the merchandise of the king at a fixed price in many markets and pay necessary compensation proportional to the loss entailed upon it.

The amount of vyaji due on commodities sold by cubical measure is one-sixteenth of the quantity; that on commodities sold by weighing balance is one-twentieth of the quantity; and that on commodities sold in numbers is one-eleventh of the whole.

The superintendent shall show favor to those who import foreign merchandise; mariners and merchants who import foreign merchandise shall be favored with remission of the trade-taxes, so that they may derive some profit. . . .

Arthasastra II:16

As Marx put it: "From the time that the circulation of goods develops, there also develop the need and desire to fix and preserve the result of the first metamorphosis, the goods transformed into the chrysalis of gold or silver. . . . It is especially in the first periods of circulation that . . . gold and silver become *per se* social expressions of over-abundance — that is, wealth." This form of hoarding, which Marx singled out in modern India, was probably present as a phenomenon in Mauryan India as well. In fact, the large donations of money frequently mentioned in Buddhist texts seem to indicate the need for such displays of personal wealth: piety and prestige were simultaneously proven. And among the beneficiaries of such donations, the various monastic communities were soon to assume first place.

We shall soon have occasion to observe the tangible results of such donations. For the present, we might observe that, in some cases at least, the merchant seems to have been an agent of the state authority. But what is not clear is how the surplus production taken by the state was transformed into goods — that is, commercialized. To begin with, what actual domestic goods were involved? Archaeological finds do not indicate that the cities were carrying out any crucial economic function, but doubtless the developing bureaucracy helped to open up markets; territorial unification was certainly a factor. We may thus imagine that the surplus from the countryside, drawn upon by agents of the state, was sold in the cities and in the army, and that part of the proceeds flowed back into the country in the form of major irrigation works, the digging of wells and cisterns, the transplanting of trees. Another part was used for the maintenance of the army and other large public works — roads, warehouses, religious edifices. And still another part was hoarded or used for the acquisition of luxury items by those at the center of power. The Greek writer Strabo described the extravagant clothes worn by the richest Indians, while the *Arthasastra* confirms Strabo's observation about the gems that flowed into the royal treasury. Out of all this emerges an image of the cities of Mauryan India as essentially parasitical: they were basically made up of the royal palace and the habitations of the king's functionaries and bureaucrats. Even if India never supported a mere "show town" built for prestige purposes only — as, for example, Persepolis in the Achaemenid Empire — the Indian city served no essential economic purpose.

The characteristic of the Indian economy during the Mauryan epoch — which lasted from 321 to 185 B.C. — may be summed up by essentially two elements: state control of agriculture, industry, and commerce; taxation of various kinds for the population. Such a system was necessary to support the Indian state that had developed, the prime need being its military obligations. It seems clear that a system like the one in force in the Mauryan empire could enjoy the maximum efficiency when non-productive expenses did not place the state in the position of having an urgent need for money, thus preventing it from undertaking works for the improvement of its main support, agriculture. The village community, even if self-sufficient, could not engage in major works, since it was stripped at the same time of production surplus and initiative. And yet, expenses such as those for military needs, which had quite an effect on the budget, could not be eliminated even during peacetime because the army (consisting mostly of *kshatriyas*) was so intimately connected — through caste interests — with political power. Any major military obligation, for example, such as those that Chandragupta imposed on the state funds, must have left little margin for other expenses.

Undoubtedly this was one of the reasons why Chandragupta never initiated, so far as we know, any great building enterprises. Besides, labor was never in particular abundance, any excess being absorbed by the lower ranks of the army. Thus the two conditions necessary for prestige building activity — financial resources and surplus labor — were still lacking in India. But we cannot be sure of the details of the state's finances. Probably the state raised the price of products in moments of particular need, in order to increase the yield of taxes and to recoup the money paid out to the troops. But if it comes to that, taxation was probably not the principal source of the state's income, even though it was the one that affected the masses of people most directly. The suggestion has been made that the basis of royal power was the extraction of minerals and metallurgy. Certainly the *Arthasastra* describes the positions of mines superintendent, iron-works superintendent, and such. The monopoly of the mines and the mineral trade, says the scholar R. S. Sharma, "was not only the source of large intake, but also of power for the central authority, because only the state could furnish the army with metal weapons, and agriculture and industry with the necessary tools."

All these characteristics we have been viewing as elements of Chandragupta Maurya's reign may also be traced in similar forms through the rest of the Maurya period. As for the castes, the situation must not have differed much from the one described for the preceding epoch. We may suppose there was some improvement in the condition of the *shudras* when the need for labor was at a peak; yet even then, as we shall see, this need was sometimes satisfied by the forced transferral of great masses of farmers. A passage from the *Indica* of Megasthenes, Seleucus' ambassador at the Mauryan court of Pataliputra, is most significant in this regard. He speaks of a society divided into seven castes: philosophers, farmers, soldiers, breeders (i.e., those who practiced animal husbandry), artisans, magistrates, and counselors. It has been observed that Megas-

BUILDING OF A FORTIFIED TOWN

Demarcation of the ground inside the fort shall be made first by opening three royal roads from west to east and three from south to north. . . .

In the midst of the houses of the people of all the four castes and to the north from the center of the ground inside the fort, the king's palace, facing either the north or the east shall, be constructed, occupying one-ninth of the whole site inside the fort.

Royal teachers, priests, sacrificial place, water reservoir, and ministers shall occupy sites east by north to the palace.

Royal kitchen, elephant stables, and the store-house shall be situated on the sites east by south.

On the eastern side, merchants trading in scents, garlands, grains, and liquids, together with expert artisans and the people of Ksatriya shall have there their habitations.

The treasury, the accountants office, and various manufactories shall be situated on sites south by east. . . .

To the south, the superintendents of the city, of commerce, of manufactories, and of the army as well as those who trade in cooked rice, liquor, and flesh, besides prostitutes, musicians, and the people of Vaisya caste shall live. . . .

To the west, artisans manufacturing worsted threads, cotton threads, bamboo-mats, skins, armors, weapons, and gloves, as well as the people of Sudra caste, shall have their dwellings. . . .

To the north, the royal tutelary deity of the city, ironsmiths, artisans working on precious stones, as well as Brahmans shall reside. . . .

In the center of the city, the apartments of gods, shall be situated.

In the corners, the guardian deities of the ground shall be appropriately set up. . . .

Either to the north or the east, burial or cremation grounds shall be situated; but that of the people of the highest caste shall be to the south of the city. . . .

Heretics and outcasts shall live beyond the burial grounds.

Arthasastra II:4

ON TRADE ROUTES

My teacher says that of the two trade routes, one by water and another by land, the former is better, inasmuch as it is less expensive but productive of large profit.

Not so, says Kautilya, for a water route is liable to obstruction, not permanent, a source of imminent dangers, and incapable of defense, whereas a land route is of reverse nature.

Of water routes, one along the shore and another in midocean, the route along and close to the shore is better, as it touches at many trading port towns; likewise river navigation is better, as it is uninterrupted and is of avoidable or endurable dangers.

My teacher says that of land routes, that which leads to the Himalayas is better than that which leads to the south.

Not so, says Kautilya, for with the exception of blankets, skins, and horses, other articles of merchandise, such as conch shells, diamonds, precious stones, pearls and gold are available in plenty in the south.

Of routes leading to the south, either that trade route which traverses a large number of mines, which is frequented by people, and which is less expensive or troublesome, or that route by taking which plenty of merchandise of various kinds can be obtained is better.

Arthasastra VII:12

thenes confused caste with occupation, and yet it is interesting to note that in the category of "philosophers" both Brahmans and Buddhist monks as well as religious men of other faiths were included, and all were exempt from taxation. Even if technically inexact, Megasthenes' passage offers a view that adheres to the social reality of India at that time perhaps more than do contemporary Indian texts.

Another important component of the Mauryan social structure were the artisans and merchants' guilds *(shreni)*. These ended by controlling the entire field of handmade goods and finally by carrying considerable economic and political weight. Their original function was to protect the individual members, sometimes from superior castes, rather than to organize commercial competition. The favor these guilds showed to the heterodox religions is well documented, because it was in their interest to limit the privileges of the *brahmans* and the *kshatriyas*. Yet the *vaishyas*, as we have said, had limits imposed on their economic activities, especially that of price control by the state authority. This explains why the merchants in the Mauryan period never enjoyed the power that their fortunes would have granted them, and why their position always remained complementary to that of the *brahmans* and the *kshatriyas*. And although there were certainly periods of great social tensions, which saw the *brahmans* and the *kshatriyas* opposing the *vaishyas*, the system was generally to the advantage of all three *dvija* ("twice-born") castes, because it allowed them to exploit the other groups. Priests, administrators, soldiers, merchants — they finally knew they were all necessary to one another. If anything, it is understandable that there would be greater dissatisfaction among the artisans who, as producers of goods, might well see the fruit of their work put in danger by unfavorable decrees concerning the prices. Viewed in this light, the rebellious stance occasionally assumed by the guilds becomes understandable.

Asoka's India: The State as a Personal Projection

Chandragupta Maurya — who according to the Jains was converted to Jainism in the last years of his life — was succeeded in 297 B.C. by his son Bindusara. (The ancient Greeks referred to him as "Amitrochates," perhaps derived from the Sanskrit *Amitraghata*, "destroyer of enemies.") Bindusara led an expedition into the Deccan and was successful enough there and in his other operations so that, on his death in 272 B.C., almost the entire subcontinent was part of the Mauryan empire. But it was Bindusara's son and successor, Asoka Piyadassi (286–232 B.C.), who developed into the most imposing of India's early rulers. Like all leaders of the time, he began with a series of military campaigns. Thus, Asoka saw to the conquest of Kalinga (Orissa), the only region in India that had offered strong resistance to the Mauryas; Kalinga also threatened the safe passage of goods along the southern route. The expedition against Kalinga in 260 B.C. was a total military success and led to the mass deportation of much of the population. Evidently there was an urgent need for labor elsewhere in the empire, and although technically speaking slaves did not exist in India, we need not imagine that many workers were any the less oppressed. Besides, we may also assume that the labor used in non-agricultural works (mines, state industries, etc.) was kept in a condition not unlike slavery. So to this extent the mass deportation was simply part of the general pattern of the status of the mass of people.

Yet it was after his campaign in Kalinga that Asoka had carved in a rock one of his most famous edicts (No. XIII): "The country of the Kalingas was conquered by King Piyadassi, Beloved of the Gods, eight years after his coronation. In this war in Kalinga, men and animals numbering one hundred and fifty thousand were carried away captive from that country, as many as one hundred thousand were killed there in action, and many times that number perished." We may allow for the

exaggerations of all figures at this time, but even so, the tradition was that all those people killed and deported so upset Asoka that he was filled with remorse and turned to Buddhism. "All men are my sons," says another of the edicts. Asoka's conversion to Buddhism was more than a religious conversion; it was presented as a crisis of conscience. The message that the sovereign had inscribed on rocks and pillars all over the empire (the westernmost inscriptions being the two at Qandahar, Afghanistan) do not contain specifically confessional connotations, but speak of peace, respect

12. Sanchi: Stupa 1, viewed from the north. The existent stupa — some 120 feet in diameter and 54 feet high — is a work of the Shunga — or possibly Andhra — period. The railing is a later addition. The fragment of a column and the bell-shaped capital (seen to right of the *torana*) belong to a pillar from the

Gupta age; the tiny stupas set along the modern access path date from a much more recent time. This stupa was badly damaged by archaeologists in the nineteenth century, and the surrounding area was greatly changed due to the demolition of various remains.

for individuals, justice, non-violence. War is rejected as a means of conquest; true victory is not that won with weapons but that of *Dhamma:* this was the Prakrit form of the Sanskrit word *Dharma,* "Law," a concept that is perhaps best approximated in Western terms as "natural law." It has rightly been observed that *Dhamma* does not really refer to "Buddhist law"; yet the reference appears clear when one considers the text of the edicts in which Asoka spoke to the monastic communities. In these he presented himself as a zealous neophyte worried about the unity of the

13. Sanchi: Stupa 1, seen from the south. The staircase of Temple 40 can be seen in the foreground, columns from Temple 18 (a seventh-century aspidal edifice) to the left, and Stupa 3 is at the right, rear. Stupa 1 was probably founded by Asoka, although its present appearance is due to the complete reconstruction of the Shunga or post-Shunga period. In the interior, however, are remains of an older stupa, perhaps the original one, with a diameter half that of the present one. The masonry of the larger stupa consists of sandstone blocks covered by a thick, robust stucco (visible in Illustration 12); that of the earlier, interior stupa is large, baked bricks, held together by mud. The dimensions of these bricks (61″ × 10″ × 3″) are about the same as those found in certain edifices dated to the Maurya period, and so seem to confirm the site's connections with Asoka.

Buddhist "church" and as one who threatened sanctions against those who would upset such unity.

The two-sided aspect of Asoka's propaganda thus appears evident: on the one hand, he supported Buddhism; on the other, he recognized all faiths and respected the traditional social hierarchies. There emerged from this union a political ideology that had its roots and stalk in the Buddhist religion but could spread its cover over any circumstances. Just as Buddha revealed the Law to men after meditating on the pain of humans, so Asoka, upset by the suffering of the victims of the Kalinga expedition, proclaimed to his subjects his personal conception of *Dharma:* the moral law accompanied by civil law. And just as Buddha at the time of his first sermon made the Wheel of the Law (the *dharmacakra*) turn, so the king is the *cakravartin,* "he who makes the wheel turn." By this time, too, the process of the sovereign's deification was certainly well advanced, even though Asoka took care to speak as a man, as Buddha spoke as a man. But the king was becoming idealized in that he was the state, he guaranteed justice, peace, prosperity, pity, and non-violence; in the same way, Buddha was not to be venerated, but the Law was to be followed. It must be admitted, though, that if Asoka expected political support from the monastic community (the *samgha*), he could not rely solely on the Buddhists. Thus the ideology he elaborated, despite its overt appeals to Buddhism, had to carefully maintain an equilibrium among all the religious groups in his India.

We have no images of Buddha from this period, nor are there any images of Asoka (or of the other Maurya kings). This is no accident. Indeed, the use of symbols that are religious and political at the same time was much more appropriate to Asoka's attitude, because the symbol allows for a more immediate identification of the sovereign with the "divine." This process of identification was expressed by Marx (in his previously cited essay, "Pre-Communist Forms of Production"): "A part of the surplus labor [of the self-sufficient agricultural community] belongs to the superior community, which in the end exists as a *person;* this surplus labor is manifested both in the form of tribute, etc., and in the form of collective work, in part to glorify the unity — that is to say, the royal despot — and in part the idealized system — that is, the god." This formulation corresponds exactly with the idea we have formed of Indian society in the Mauryan epoch, and is applicable not only to the execution of major public works but also to the erection of official monuments.

And it is with the official monuments of Asoka's reign that we finally arrive at our first tangible remains since those of the Indus Valley Civilization. If, at times, it has seemed that India has gone almost 2000 years with no art to speak of and nothing but economic, social, political, and religious "conditions," this is to a great extent due to the fact that these

THE EDICT OF QANDAHAR

After ten years of reign, King Piyadassi made
known to men the doctrine of piety, and from
this moment he has made men more pious and
all things prosperous throughout the whole
earth; and the king refrains from killing living
creatures; and other men, including all hun-
ters and fishermen of the king, have desisted
from hunting; and if some were intemperant
they have curbed their intemperance in so far
as they are able; obedient to father and mother
and elders, they will thus live more pleasantly
and better in the future than before.

Greek Text of the Bilingual Inscription of Qandahar

PROVISION OF COMFORTS FOR MEN AND ANIMALS

Everywhere in the dominions of King
Priyadarshin, the beloved of the gods, as well
as among his neighbors, the Cholas, the Pan-
dyas, the Satiyaputra, the Keralaputra, as far
as the Tamraparni River [Sri Lanka], and in
the territories of Antiochos the Greek king and
the kings the neighbors of that Antiochos —
everywhere have been made the healing arrangements of His Sacred and Gracious
Majesty the King in two kinds, healing arrangements for men and healing arrangements for beasts. Also, medicinal herbs for
men and for beasts, wheresoever lacking, have
been everywhere both imported and planted.
Roots also and fruits, wheresoever lacking,
have been everywhere imported and planted.
Along the roads, wells have been dug and trees
planted for the enjoyment of man and beast.

Edict of Asoka (Rock II,) Text from Girnar
(Kathiawar)

AGAINST VIOLENCE IN SEXUAL INTERCOURSE

He who defiles a maiden of equal caste before
she has reached her maturity shall have his
hand cut off or pay a fine of 400 panas; if the
maiden dies in consequence, the offender shall
be put to death.
He who defiles a maiden who has attained
maturity shall have his middle finger cut off or
pay a fine of 200 panas, besides giving an
adequate compensation to her father.
No man shall have sexual intercourse with
any woman against her will.
He who defiles a willing maiden shall pay a
fine of 54 panas, while the maiden herself pay
a fine of half the amount.

Arthasastra IV:12

SOME MISCELLANEOUS OFFENCES

When a person misappropriates the revenue
he collects as the agent of a household, violates
by force the chastity of a widow of independent living, when an outcaste [Candala] person
touches an Arya woman, when a person does
not run to render help to another in danger,
and when a person entertains, in dinner dedicated to gods or ancestors, Buddhists,
Ajivakas, Sudras and exiled persons, a fine of
100 panas shall be imposed.

Arthasastra III:20

very "conditions" did not allow for the creation of works of art. But it is
also true that the deep foundation of "conditions" that was being laid
down in India over these many centuries was now strong enough to
support the great monuments that were to arise over the coming centuries. There were the stupas, for instance, the moundlike structures
built to contain the relics of Buddha or of others revered by the Buddhists. Tradition attributes to Asoka the construction of a great number of
stupas, all supposed to bear the name of *Dharmarajika;* there is a *Dharmarajika* stupa at Taxila and another at Butkara (Swat), but these
monuments were completely redone in later epochs.

What does remain of Asoka's building activity are the monumental
pillars, reproductions of the traditional-mythical *axis mundi,* set up to
mark places in some way considered sacred from far back in time. Some
doubts have been raised about the theory that connects the pillars of
Asoka with important spots along roads; it is suggested that they probably had more to do with sacred Buddhist edifices erected by Asoka
himself. However, at least in some instances the two functions could have
overlapped; moreover, in a later era an isolated pillar would have
functioned as a reference point for wayfarers.

A legitimate suspicion has also arisen that some of the pillars are older
than Asoka, since the king himself tells us (for instance, in the edict
inscribed on his pillar VII) that he had ordered his words inscribed on
stone pillars wherever they existed. But he might be referring to pillars
already erected by himself. In fact, in this same edict he states that he has
set up pillars bearing inscriptions about the *Dharma;* it is not evident that
this was any innovation on his part. What is interesting, in fact, is that in
these symbolic monuments Asoka goes back to precedents from imperial
Persia, but with essential variations. Some of the formal parts of his
inscriptions may recall the inscriptions of the Achaemenid emperors (the
dynasty that reigned in Persia between the sixth and fourth centuries
B.C.), but the contents and "tone" are entirely different. And if certain
stylistic, typological, and technical details (such as the high polish of the
sculptured surfaces) look to Achaemenid precedents and make us think
that Iranian stonecutters, or at least those working in the Persian tradition, were used in Mauryan India, we must not lose sight of the fact that
the symbolic lexicon has been "Indianized." The king is not the powerful
lord of good who sets himself up against the powers of evil, as in
Achaemenid representations; he is, rather, the highest functionary in the
perfect state, he who benignly indicates to his children-subjects the way
that leads to the realization of a harmonious social system, the guarantor
of social balance, the counterpart of Buddha in the political sphere.

Consider the pillar of Lauriya Nandagarh, near Nepal. The shaft is an
absolutely smooth and tapered monolith, surmounted by a bell capital in
the form of a lotus (with the petals turned downward) on which is seated,
his front legs erect, a roaring lion. The bell-shaped capital is certainly of
Iranian inspiration, although it reminds us more of some Achaemenid
bases rather than their corresponding capitals. The lion also derives from
similar images on the Achaemenid palaces; the same can be said of the
four lions that decorate the capital of Sarnath (Illustration 2), still one of
the most extraordinary remains of India's past. But a close look reveals
the plinth that separates the bell-shaped capital from the four lions,
backed against one another; this plinth bears a relief decoration that is
stylistically different, more Hellenistic than Achaemenid in its naturalistic
representation of the four animals (a lion, elephant, bull, and horse) that
alternate with the four small wheels. Surmounting the entire capital was a
large wheel, resting on the backs of the four large lions. This expressed a
complex symbolism, with religious references that were both astronomi-
cal as well as Buddhist. Thus, the lion, a very old solar symbol, was also a
reference to Buddha, in that the lion belonged to the Shakya tribe, and
Siddhartha also bore the name of Shakyasimha, "the lion of the Shakyas."
The wheel, meanwhile, could be both the wheel of the king, the *cakravartin,* and a specific allusion to the Buddhist *dharmacakra.* None of these
were equivocations but were intended ambivalences, in which the very
essence of Asoka's propaganda is recognizable.

The Function of Art and Architecture in Asoka's India

It remains to be explained how this complex symbolism, whose roots seem to be partly foreign, was received by Indian culture. The problem can be posed also from a stylistic point of view, since we find no precedent in India for artistic works of such a high degree of sophistication. Iranian elements were to remain for a long time in Indian art, and the northwestern border region will later produce a rich harvest of art, the art of Gandhara, of a Graeco-Roman derivation: but in both cases, these phenomena were restricted to the elite of society. At the basis of official Mauryan art, however, there was something even more forced, something absolutely foreign to India at that time: more than just the ideology of the ruling class, the pillars of Asoka reflect, however genial or ephemeral, the political vision of a despot. This helps to explain how it is that the foreign elements seem to come out of nowhere to be imposed instantly on the Indian culture. In the end, of course, Asoka and the Maurya dynasty passed away, and only a few of Asoka's pillars remained in their original locations; others have long since been moved elsewhere. Among these latter, one of the most interesting "moves" was that of the pillar from Topra (a locality not definitely placed, but in the Ganges-Jumna region); despite being damaged, it stood over thirty-six feet high and had a diameter of over nine feet at the base; it was taken to Delhi by Firuz Shah Tughlaq in the last half of the fourteenth century A.D., where he had it placed on the roof of his fortress-palace — suggesting how much admiration even this Moslem sovereign had for a relic of Asoka's India.

We have concentrated on the "official" monuments of Asoka because they are exceptionally meaningful for an examination of that emperor's political attitude. We may now try to gain a slightly broader perspective on the artistic and architectural achievements of the late Mauryan age. Megasthenes, the ambassador of Seleucus, spoke with admiration of Pataliputra, the capital (near present-day Patna) where Chandragupta, the first of the Mauryas, had settled. His enthusiastic description conjures up the image of some palace of delights outdoing — the comparison is his — the cities of Achaemenid Persia in beauty. The excavations (carried out in 1896, 1912, and then again in 1955–56) have not been able to furnish precise confirmation of this image. Yet even the little we know leads to some consideration. The 1912 excavation, for instance, partially brought to light a hall with eighty, perhaps more, columns, some ten feet high; their arrangement reminds us of the similar "audience halls" (apadana) in the palace at Persepolis. And this is not just some impressionistic comparison. In the matter of technique, for instance, we note that, just as at Persepolis, the stone is flanked by timber, particularly the horizontal elements such as architraves. The columns of the Pataliputra structure were polished, this characteristic of Mauryan work also being derived — as we have seen with Asoka's capital at Sarnath — from a technique probably imported by Achaemenid artisans. Fragments found in 1955–56 suggest that there had once been a monolithic pillar at Pataliputra, perhaps isolated like those of Asoka. And the earliest excavation yielded a Persian-style capital decorated with volutes, palmettes, and other motifs, slightly incoherent in their composition, but all sharing the feature of having been imported.

In addition to the remains of the palace at Pataliputra, there are remains of the fortifications; some scholars believe these were pre-Mauryan. In any case, the wooden devices are particularly significant. The foundations consisted of cross-pieces some thirteen feet long, set horizontally, on which some wooden posts were placed vertically, these being at the time of the 1912 excavations still nine feet high. There was also a large wooden tunnel, the function of which has not been discovered, there being two opposing yet equally valid hypotheses: it could

14.   Sanchi: A detail of the western *torana*, a work of the beginning of the first century A.D. The pot-bellied *yakshas*, used as atlantes, are comparable to the *yaksha* of Kanhadasa (in Illustration 9), certainly an older work. Of the relief scenes depicting episodes from the life of Buddha (*jatakas*), we can recognize several. On the pillar in the foreground, top-left side, is the *Mahakapi-jataka*, showing the flight of the monkeys over the bridge formed by the body of Buddha, who had been incarnated as a monkey and who sacrificed himself in this way in order to save his companions. Below this is a panel showing the *adhyesana*, the traditional scene of the gods' invoking Buddha to preach the Law. On the pillar in the background, in the top facing panel, is the *Sama-jataka*, which shows the episode of the Young Sama, who was accidentally killed by the king of Varanasi; below that is the episode of Mucilinda, a mythical serpent-deity (*naga*) who protects Buddha from rain. Note that in both stories from the life of Buddha, the Enlightened One is represented by symbols and not in human form.

A SEVENTH-CENTURY A.D. CHINESE TRAVELER REPORTS ON INDIA

At Benares there is a stone *stupa* built by Asoka-raja. Although the foundations have given way, there are still 100 feet or more of the wall remaining. In front of the building is a stone pillar about 70 feet high. The stone is altogether as bright as jade. It is glistening, and sparkles like light. Those who pray fervently before it see from time to time, according to their petitions, figures with good or bad signs. It was here that Tathagata [the Buddha], having arrived at enlightenment, began to turn the wheel of the law [i.e., to preach].

HSUAN-TSANG: *Si-yu-ki* VII

have been a passageway inside an earthen fortification, or it could have been a structure filled in with earth to provide extra strength.

Still other features of Mauryan wooden architecture may be reconstructed through an examination of the four caves cut out of the rock of the Barabar Hills, near Gaya. They are generally attributed to Asoka (or to his grandson, Dasaratha, by some scholars). Here, too, we see the polished surfaces typical of Mauryan art, an element we have noted already, of Persian derivation; this fits in well with the fact that the very idea of rock-cut structures may also date from the Achaemenid or pre-Achaemenid tradition of rock tombs and reliefs. Of the caves at Barabar, the one of Lomas Rishi merits particular attention. It is a rectangular chamber with a barrel vault, and a cella with a lateral facade, all cut out of the natural rock; the relief sculpture on the facade is notable for reproducing a wooden structure that is considered to date from a much earlier period. Another cave at this site, known as Sudama, has a circular cella and an inscription of Asoka's: "This Nyagrodha cave is dedicated to the Ajivikas by King Piyadassi twelve years after his coronation." In still another cave an inscription specifies that the king intended it to be used as a refuge for ascetics during the rainy season, so that they might protect themselves from floods.

It should not come as any surprise that the Buddhist Asoka made donations to the Ajivikas, the heterodox group that had sprung up about the same time as Buddha: as we have noted, Asoka worked hard to maintain good relations with all the religious groups of his society. The entire Barabar complex was originally an Ajivika foundation, furthermore, even though the caves were later occupied by Buddhists and Hindus. There is some doubt about the chronological attribution of the Lomas Rishi cave facade, however, with its decoration of elephants and a stupa, which seems to exclude any reference to Asoka. We cannot neglect the fact, either, that elephants and stupas have no particular connection with the Ajivika doctrine, while they are not at all out of place in a Buddhist context.

Alongside such works commissioned by the king, non-official India does not offer anything that appeals on an aesthetic level. However, we must assume that in this period some effort was being made to "dress up" those modest sanctuaries that developed around sacred trees, known to us from later representations. Like the trees, too, water and rocks were considered sacred habitations of the *yakshas* (masculine) and *yakshis* (feminine), the genii or nature spirits that were survivors of the pre-Aryan religion of India. Some statues of *yakshas* and *yakshis* have been attributed to the Mauryan, and even the pre-Mauryan age, but we shall go into detail about these works in a later section. And behind the conception of the pillar as an *axis mundi*, and thus as an official-political symbol, there was the much older idea of the pillar as a substitute for the sacred tree.

The religiosity reflected in these primitive sanctuaries and images may also be associated with certain works in clay characteristic of the northwestern region: the so-called Baroque Ladies (Illustrations 3–5). These are terra-cotta female figurines that resemble in some ways the protohistoric figures from the Indus Valley Civilization. Archaeologists have given them the name "Baroque" because of their extremely elaborate hair styles and decorations. But their steatopygous ("fat-buttocked") shape and the emphasis on female sexual characteristics lead us inevitably to believe that they were goddesses of fecundity, mother-goddesses, whether or not they were connected with the Persian or Scythian goddess, Anaitis or Anahita, as has been suggested. The problem of assigning an age to these humble images has given rise to a long argument among scholars. At first placed by some in the second, or even third, millennium B.C., the Baroque Ladies have been dated (by D. H. Gordon, using brilliant intuition as much as specific evidence) to a period between 100 B.C. to A.D. 100. Not until the excavations at Charsada (by Sir Mortimer Wheeler, in 1958) was it possible to base a date on concrete facts: *e.g.*, the association of the Baroque Ladies with ceramic material such as Northern Black Polished Ware and the so-called Lotus Bowls,

15. Sanchi: The southern *torana* of Stupa 1. Dated to the beginning of the first century A.D., this is considered to be the oldest of the four portals; but not that much time passed between the creation of the first and last: thus, the right pillar of the western portal was donated by the same man who had also donated the median architrave of this southern portal. Of the four portals, this one is also the most badly damaged; the smooth parts are substitutions for the lost original sections (although part of the right pillar is kept in the local museum). The surviving relief panels on the left pillar (the top one clearly depicting the Wheel of the Law on a pillar) are the work of the ivory-carvers of Vidisha, a valuable inscription notes. Visible behind the *torana* is the railing to the gallery around the drum of the stupa, with the stairway leading to it.

datable with fair precision. The date proposed by Wheeler, circa 250–100 B.C., seems acceptable. Still, aside from certain "baroque" elements, there is basically no new development involved compared to the earlier terra-cotta figurines; indeed, these Baroque Ladies, as Wheeler has said, although "sometimes expressive or even decorative, are more like toys or amulets than dignified and sensitive works." India's day in the full sun of conscious artistry had yet to dawn.

The Heirs of the Maurya Dynasty

After ruling for thirty-seven years, Asoka died in 232 B.C.; the Mauryan empire survived him for only a few decades. There were many causes behind the decline of this empire, but one of the main ones must have been the strain on the state organism effected by the most active social groups in the economic field, by now organized into guilds. Yet it seems that the final blow to the dynasty came from an attempt to restore the brahmanic authority. Thus, in 185 B.C. Brhadratha, the last of the Mauryas, was assassinated by his commander-in-chief of the army, Pushyamitra, who belonged to the Shunga family, which according to Panini belonged to the *brahman* clan. The occasion was probably determined by the pressure of external military forces; in any case, we know that the Shunga kingdom included only the central part of the vast territory that had belonged to the Mauryan empire, Magadha. Meanwhile, other regions were falling under the rule of other powers — the kingdom of the Kalingas to the southeast, the Indo-Greeks to the northwest.

Buddhist tradition speaks of Pushyamitra as a ferocious persecutor of Buddhism. He was certainly an orthodox *brahman*, and it is significant that on two occasions he carried out the traditional horse sacrifice (described earlier). However, the orthodox reaction against Buddhism must have been brief, because it was during the Shunga epoch that the first great Buddhist sanctuaries sprang up and that the initiative in the field of monumental architecture extended to broader groups of the population, thus ceasing to be a royal prerogative. The circumstances surrounding the end of the Shunga dynasty (about 75 B.C.) are unknown. It is possible that the last representatives of the dynasty were not officially deprived of power but were put in positions of nominal rule, while the *de facto* ruling dynasty was that of the Kanvas. Yet it seems that the first Kanva, Vasudeva, took power by killing (or ordering the assassination of) the Shunga king Devabhuti. At the end of the Kanva dynasty, about 30 B.C., the fate of Magadha was still not at all clear; it was not to be till the rise of the Gupta dynasty (about A.D. 320) that Magadha returned to the limelight of Indian history.

For all the political disorder, and despite the restoration of traditional social orders, this period became the time when Indian monumental work first took on distinctive forms that have survived. Although Buddhist monumental architecture had made its appearance in the Mauryan age, as we have noted, and although the greatest architecture undeniably belongs to later periods, it was in the Shunga period that in this field — as in the figurative arts — India used for the first time a language all her own, abandoning the Iranian "accent" or placing it in a totally new context. This development can hardly be overestimated.

We have seen how Mauryan art represented basically a court phenomenon. Or better, it was an art based on royal commissions, a manifestation of an ideology according to which the state (and the king)

was ideally identified with the community in its highest expression, with
its welfare, and thus with the social order that surrounds every individual. This was the message that, in the intention of the power commissioning the work, was for all the subjects but which was only passively accepted. Mauryan art ignored every possible counterpart of the king that
did not belong to the monastic community — that is, to the force that the
king wanted to transform into a religious support for his power. The
dialogue thus took place above and beyond the most active social groups
that, paradoxically, strengthened themselves with the support of Buddhism. But this paradox is only apparent, because the king's support was
not granted to the community as a whole, with its free ethical and
theological choices, but only to the orthodox part of the community.
Indeed, Asoka thought of convening a council and condemning the
schismatic tendencies of his time — presumably those who would not
agree with him.

We have also noted briefly how Mauryan official art of a high technical
level was accompanied by a most modest ceramic production that stylistically has nothing to do with the former. They are two currents that
developed side by side and that marked the profound difference between
the court culture and that of the city dwellers who had recently emigrated
from the country and were still by tradition bound to a religiosity associated with agricultural communities. The Shunga period marks a
profound revolution in all these tendencies. The Shunga terra-cottas, for
instance, reveal not only a decidedly better technique compared to the
Mauryan ones but — and this is what counts most — they are perfectly
compatible stylistically with the more ambitious monumental works. And
this despite the fact that the subjects differed: religious in the decorations
of the architectural monuments, and secular (or at least apparently so) in
the terra-cottas found in abundance at excavation sites. When such a
unity in expression has been attained, we may speak of a true "Indian
art."

Following pages:
16.   Sanchi: A close-up of the northern *torana*, showing the central section of this, the
best preserved of the four portals, and dated
to about the beginning of the first century A.D.
The scenes on the horizontal architrave panels
are easily identifiable. On the top is the
Saddanta-jataka, the story of Buddha's incarnation as a six-tusked elephant; full of compassion for the hunter who wounded him, he
helped the hunter to saw off his tusks. In the
middle is a scene of the temptation and
threats used by Mara against Gautama, who is
represented by the pipal-fig tree on the left;
Mara is the seated figure to the right of the
tree, and he is surrounded by his seductive
daughters and the demons of his army. On
the lowest architrave is the second part of the
Vessantara-jataka (the first part being on the
other side of this architrave), the story of the
penultimate incarnation of Buddha as Prince
Vessantara, in whom he realized perfect charity. On the square blocks that separate the architraves are symbolic representations: the
top two, with the vases of lotus flowers,
perhaps allude to the birth of Siddhartha; the
stupa, lower right block, symbolizes the
parinirvana, Buddha's eternal state in nirvana; while in the lower left block is an allusion
to the birth of Buddha. This last carving re-
produces the Hindu iconography of the unc-
tion of Lakshmi, goddess of fortune; but
within the Buddhist context it may be seen as
Maya, seated on a lotus flower and receiving
ablution, thus recognizing the miraculous
birth of Buddha.

The Stupa in Indian Life and Art

When we come to examine the essential characteristics of the more
ambitious monuments, we discover the most typical to be the stupa, the
monument that — perhaps even more than the image of the Enlightened
One — immediately suggests Buddhism. A symbol and a funerary monument at the same time, the stupa seems to have been derived from the
tumulus that had long been erected over the remains of dead notables;
such a custom was not restricted to India any more than it was limited to a
particular form of culture or religion. Covering the remains of the dead
with a heap of stones or earth is a spontaneous gesture whenever one
wants to preserve the memory of the deceased. There can certainly be
symbolic implications — and in many cases these are evident — but they
are not necessarily always the same and they cannot be considered responsible for any continuity in the tradition of the tumulus.

The primitive stupa in India was most likely a simple tumulus, with or
without a cylindrical shaft or column at its center. The oldest stupa was
also without any decorative or crowning elements; we can get some idea
of this by looking at stupas represented on the facade of the Lomas Rishi
cave, although even these represent a relatively evolved stage of the
stupa. Once the transition from simple burial site to symbolic mound
took place, it became essential to have a relic (*sharira*) in the core of the
monument; a little chamber in the center, totally sealed off by the
masonry, held the relic: there was to be no passage between the interior
and the exterior. Other elements, although added later, became essential
components of the "classic" stupa: the *harmika*, a sort of balcony set on top
of the stupa dome (*anda*) and the tiers of discs (*chatras*), like a series of

umbrellas, held up by a central mast *(yasti)* in this balcony. There was also a railing *(vedika)* built around the exterior of the stupa, and this had anywhere from one to four extrance gates or portals *(toranas)*. The space between the stupa and the *vedika* was an area used for the ritual of walking around the shrine, as the stupa was considered; hence this area was known as the *pradakshinapatha*, or "corridor for the circumambulation." Little by little, other elements were added to the stupa, some to come and go in the course of time and according to the circumstances of the individual stupa.

After the stupa, perhaps the most typical Indian religious structure is the chaitya-hall. Originally *chaitya* referred to any sacred enclosure or shrine of the pre-Buddhist worshipers in India; a *chaitya* might be no more than the area surrounding some sacred natural site, such as a tree or rock, or it might have been the simplest wooden hut. As the stupas became points of attraction for the devout, it was inevitable that attendant priests, monks, or other religious officials would take the opportunity to construct places of worship in adjacent structures: these became the chaitya-halls, a clear attempt to associate the Buddhist stupa with the pre-Buddhist world. Eventually the chaitya-hall was transformed into a chapel or temple in which the cult of the deified Buddha developed. But long before that, another development had been underway.

Caves — either natural ones or those cut out by human labor — had long been the site of religious devotions; we have seen those at the Barabar Hills, vaguely reproducing or at least reflecting free-standing architectural forms. But now the entire complex of free-standing structures — including the stupa and the chaitya-hall — would be simulated within the caves by using both the natural stone and some wooden elements. Some of these cave chaitya-halls were to become truly monumental in character, with several naves, free-standing columns, entranceways and roofs, all reproducing in punctilious detail the wooden elements of their prototypes. Later, during the Gupta epoch, the image of Buddha — sculptured out of the same natural rock that formed the simulated stupa — sat on the stupa dome from which he dominated the simulated chaitya-hall.

Meanwhile yet another architectural form had been developing in India — the *vihara*. Originally this referred to a simple monk's cell (although it was also thought of as the habitation of a god), possibly a natural opening in a cliff. But men took to cutting their own little caves out of rocks, and eventually they also took to building monasteries with entirely constructed cells, usually around a courtyard. But then another development took place, parallel to that of cutting chaitya-halls entirely out of rock: *viharas* were cut out of natural rock formations — large caves with many cells facing an inside hall, reproducing the large monastic communities*(samgharama)* with their free-standing cells around courtyards.

It is obvious that all this rock-cutting would, sooner or later, present an unavoidable challenge to certain individuals. The stupas themselves offered little chance for artistic decoration, but the surrounding railings and their gateways provided just such opportunities. So it was that the great figurative-sculptural tradition of India assumed its first important manifestation in the terrace railing of the stupa at Bharhut (in northern Madhya Pradesh). The stupa itself has the original hemispheric shape that will be repeated later in the great stupa of Sanchi (Illustration 12) and that is also found in the northwest region (in Gandhara) with the stupa at Chakpat. Two inscriptions in Brahmi (the earliest Indian script) allow us to place the construction of the Bharhut railing in the Shunga period. (The stupa itself may date from either the Mauryan or pre-Mauryan epoch.)

The sculptured railing at Bharhut — although still clearly derived from its wooden prototypes — provides a firm starting point for observing salient stylistic and iconographic characteristics of Indian art. The sculptures of Bharhut (most of which were transferred to the Indian Museum of Calcutta by the English archaeologist Sir Alexander Cunningham) reveal how in north-central India the essential characteristics of Indian sculpture were already clearly delineated and determined. I

17. **Sanchi: This detail from the eastern portal of Stupa 1, dated to the beginning of the first century A.D., reveals the decorative finesse of the relief carving at Sanchi. There is an almost pedantic precision of detail in the plant parts, but these are counterpoised by the more essential volumes of the human figures. The whole is composed with the rigidity of heraldic symmetry — which, for that matter, even the narrative reliefs of Sanchi tend to imitate.**

THE FUNERAL RITES OF BUDDHA

Then the Mallas of Kusinara said to the venerable Ananda: — "What should be done, lord, with the remains of the Tathagata?"

"As men treat the remains of a king of kings, so, Vasetthas, should they treat the remains of a Tathagata."

"And how, lord, do they treat the remains of a king of kings?"

"They wrap the body of a king of kings, Vasetthas, in a new cloth. When that is done they wrap it in carded cotton wool. When that is done they wrap it in a new cloth, — and so on till they have wrapped the body in five hundred successive layers of both kinds. Then they place the body in an oil vessel of iron, and cover that close up with another oil vessel of iron. They then build a funeral pyre of all kinds of perfumes, and burn the body of the king of kings. And then at the four cross roads they erect a cairn to the king of kings. This, Vasetthas, is the way in which they treat the remains of a king of kings.

"And as they treat the remains of a king of kings, so, Vasetthas, should they treat the remains of the Tathagata. At the four cross roads a cairn should be erected to the Tathagata. And whosoever shall there place garlands or perfumes or paint, or make salutation there, or become in its presence calm in heart — that shall long be to them for a profit and a joy."

Mahaparinibbanasuttanta VI:17

refer in particular to that vision of space peculiar to Indian art up to the Gupta period, in which the figures are included and almost compressed between two parallel planes — the background and the original surface of the stone out of which they were sculptured. In some reliefs, an almost servile transposition of elements typical of Achaemenid relief work is evident. We might mention the small trees in one of the sections of the Bharhut reliefs, so similar in structure and execution to those at Persepolis. But their compositional function, as well as the context in which they — like so many other elements of Achaemenid origin at Bharhut — are used by the Shunga artists, have basically changed.

The Bharhut reliefs are especially valuable for another reason: their accurate representations of architecture in which many of the relief scenes are set. Some of these represent two-story or three-story edifices, with the lower floor, enclosed by a balustrade, articulated into a few spacious rooms and, so it seems, accessible from several directions; the upper floors, not as high, are also sometimes decorated with balustrades and have carinated (keel-shaped) roof coverings with loggias or galleries that are separated from the main body of the edifice. These carvings make it quite clear that the actual structures were made of wood; only this material, with its flexibility, could have been used for solutions that otherwise would have required virtuosity in structural engineering beyond the capacity of that age. One sees, too, how by transferring the traditional wooden architectural repertory to stone, there arises an impression of heaviness caused by the excessive prudence of the artisans working with an unfamiliar material.

Sculpture and the Buddhist Tradition

As we step back a bit from the techniques and details of the Bharhut reliefs, we may begin to see these carvings as expressing something of a broader world. The figures, we note, are usually distributed according to geometrically regular schemes; they are flattened against a background that is left free only in small areas; the superimposed planes offer conventional perspectives that avoid overlapping but still produce effective scenographic effects. The whole is marked by a taste for exaggerated design: the outlines are grooves engraved with slight variations of thickness that define the figures, the objects, and even the most minute details. Every leaf, every tuft of hair, every jewel is clearly singled out and presented in a narrative without pauses, a narrative that remains satisfied with its slightly coarse preciousness, its punctilious minutiae. But if the effect of the whole has its appeal, there is no great ideal that lies at the base of the Bharhut compositions, no ideal that does not belong to a social group (perhaps we might say social class, in this context) that has recently attained a position of economic power and that is still tied to the individual "things" conquered one by one, the signs of well-being and prestige.

Even when the characters of the stories being represented are *brahmans* and *kshatriyas*, the interpreters are clearly men of the new merchant and artisan society. The royal, and at the same time religious, symbols of Mauryan art, reproduced here, take on a more familiar and friendly air; they lose their "grim" aspect; in short, they are more approachable. Man has here taken on preeminence and has a dignity free from the hierarchies of divine origin. Only the symbols of Buddha enjoy a prominent place, but they are still put in a narrative context in which men are the protagonists. Yet there is no attempt at singling out individuals: each character is similar and equal to the others, and they are all practically interchangeable.

Still another reason the Bharhut reliefs are so important in the history of Indian art: for the first time we see scenes of the life of Buddha and the *jatakas* (stories of the preceding incarnations of Buddha), with inscriptions that make their identification certain. Yet from an icono-

18.   Sanchi: The close-up of one of the capitals of the western portal of Stupa 1 reveals two of the four *yakshas* (also to be seen in Illustration 14) that serve as atlantes. In the other *toranas* of this stupa, in place of these *yakshas* are lions (southern portal) and elephants (northern and eastern portals).

graphic point of view, the fundamental feature is the absolute absence of images of Buddha. Since after the attainment of nirvana, Buddha could not be represented except by means of the symbol of the stupa, the various crucial stages of his life had to be indicated by symbols. The *bodhi* tree, for instance, indicates Enlightenment; but it is not only an allusion to the event, it is also Buddha; at the same time, it is the axis of the world, the symbol of the *brahman,* the universal spirit. This complex symbolism, however, made immediate connections, easily understood by the common worshipers, with the tree-sanctuaries that were all over India and that represented one of the most widespread and intuitive forms of religiosity, common to both Buddhism and Brahmanism. The Wheel of the Law *(dharmacakra),* meanwhile, was the symbol of the first sermon of Buddha, but also represented the corporeal vehicle of Buddha; we have already spoken of the great wheel that surmounted Asoka's capital at Sarnath, a wheel that is to be considered almost an image of Buddha. Other symbols that stood for Buddha are his footprints and, more rarely, the horse (a solar animal) and the elephant (as in the Bharhut conception scene) — two animals that, along with the lion and bull, we have also seen represented on the Sarnath capital. So it is that the anthropomorphic image of Buddha is totally missing from a work clearly devoted to Buddha. To compensate, however, the Bharhut reliefs have delightful scenes depicting the previous incarnations of Buddha, the *jatakas,* a kind of compromise with the common worshipers' human desire to see their Buddha in some familiar form.

But if the figure of Buddha was missing from these early sculptures, great importance was attached to other figures, such as those that decorated the end pillars of the Bharhut railing. These were representations of various pre-Buddhist deities and spirits, and included *nagas* (mythical serpent gods symbolizing water), *devas* (a Vedic deity), and *yakshas* and *yakshis* (the pre-Vedic nature-fertility spirits). Such divine or semi-divine personages entered Buddha's sphere in a subordinate position, but, with their solid roots in popular religiosity, they acted almost as guarantors of the cult of the Enlightened One. Among the most characteristic female personages in this pantheon, with its familiar and modest tone, were those standing figures with one raised hand holding a branch of a tree (usually a *sal,* a flowering tree): this motif will later be used for representations of Maha-Maya, the mother of Buddha, at the moment when she gave birth to Siddhartha.

Approximately contemporary with the Bharhut stupa is Stupa 2 (Illustration 7) at Sanchi (Madhya Pradesh). Of much smaller dimensions, the Sanchi stupa displays the same taste for design that tends to isolate the individual figures and their individual parts. Here, too, there appear the decorative elements of Iranian derivation; yet, compared to Bharhut, the balustrade reliefs of Stupa 2 at Sanchi seem more rigid, almost as if they were based on distant models and executed by amateur artisans. It is quite probable — here as well as at Bharhut — that they used painted or ivory models, transferred with difficulty to the less docile medium of stone. Various theories have been advanced by scholars regarding the precise dating of the two monuments — Stupa 2 and Bharhut. Some claim, although they cannot fully substantiate it, that Stupa 2 is older than Bharhut. But the approximate date of 100 B.C. seems to be about the most convincing. (The confused chronology of the ancient sculptural works of India is finally being put into order, thanks to the work of many individuals, among whom the work of Walter Spink is particularly noteworthy.)

During this whole period — the post-Mauryan age that ran from 185 B.C. — the artistic vitality of India rapidly extended over a broader area. The reliefs of the Sanchi Stupa 2, for instance, are echoed in a relief from Jaggayyapeta, near Amaravati (and now kept in the Madras Museum); this relief, which represents a sovereign surrounded by the seven "jewels" of his kingdom, the symbols of royalty, offers also a number of analogies with the reliefs in the Bhaja cave, southeast of Bombay. These reliefs at Bhaja can be dated about half-way between the Bharhut railing carvings and the decoration of Stupa 1 at Sanchi — the former attributed to about

Bharut: Drawings of four of the pillars from the stupa at Bharut. (Calcutta: Indian Museum)

A FIFTH-CENTURY A.D. CHINESE
REPORTS ON PRASENAJIT AND THE
BUDDHA IMAGE

When Buddha went up to the Trayastrimsas heaven, and preached the Law for the benefit of his mother, after he had been absent for ninety days, Prasenajit, longing to see him, caused an image of him to be carved in *gosirsa candana* wood, and put in the place where he usually sat. When Buddha on his return entered the *vihara,* this image immediately left its place, and came forth to meet him. Buddha said to it, "Return to your seat. After I have attained to *parinirvana,* you will serve as a pattern to the four classes of my disciples," and on this the image returned to its seat. This was the very first of all the images of Buddha, and that which men subsequently copied.

FA-HSIEN: *Travels:*XX

100 B.C. and the latter to the period about the beginning of the Christian era. We thus see clearly that although there are some obvious regional variants, India was acquiring a cultural unity; this was in contrast, of course, to the political fragmentation of the post-Mauryan period and the Shungas' short-lived attempts at unification.

As further evidence of this spreading cultural unity, we might look at the caves of Pitalkhora, near Aurangabad (Maharashtra), recently brought to the attention of scholars again, thanks to the excavations and restorations that have produced such fine remains (Illustrations 8-10). The date — based on the style of script used in certain inscriptions — has been suggested as the second century B.C., at least for the more ancient sculptured caves (Nos. 3 and 4). But this seems too early, given the close similarities with the reliefs of Stupa 1 at Sanchi, definitely known to be a later work. Even the splendid image known as the Yaksha of Kanhadasa (Illustration 9), from the name of the goldsmith who sculptured it and probably dedicated it, would seem to date sometime after the second century B.C. Although the comparison of this *yaksha* with the *yakshas* on the western *torana* of the Great Stupa of Sanchi (Illustration 14) shows that this dwarfish figure of the pot-bellied *yaksha* is older, it is difficult to place it before the Bharhut reliefs. And the *yaksha* figure that acted as a *dvarapala*, custodian of the entrance-way, in cave 3 at Pitalkhora (Illustration 10), seems very close to Bharhut; indeed, the greater plasticity of the relief makes us think it should be placed in a still later period.

This period — from the early second century to the early first century B.C. — is also the time where we can place the large group of small molded terra-cotta reliefs that commonly go under the name of "Shunga terra-cottas," even if many are obviously later than that dynasty. Kaushambi was one of the most important centers of production, but the distribution was vast and included an area that goes from Punjab to

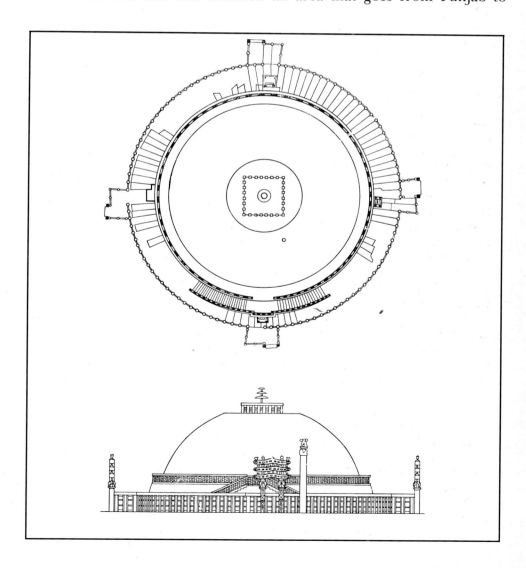

Sanchi: Ground plan and elevation of Stupa 1, the Great Stupa.

Magadha. Some of the terra-cottas (Illustration 11) allow for precise comparisons with the relief sculpture at Bharhut and Sanchi; others could be associated with some reliefs in cave 4 at Pitalkhora (today in the National Museum of New Delhi).

The Great Stupa at Sanchi

Among the architectural monuments that Buddhist India has bequeathed to us, a merited place of preeminence is occupied by the Great Stupa (or Stupa 1) at Sanchi (Illustrations 12-21), both for its architectural complexity and completeness and for the richness of the sculptural elements that make up its decorations. It consists today of an almost hemispheric dome, lopped off at the top where the little balcony (harmika) and umbrella-canopy rise, and surrounded at its base by a high processional terrace, reached on the south side by a double stairway. A second passageway, for the ritual circumambulation, is at the foot of the base's terrace and this is surrounded by a massive railing (vedika). Unlike the Bharhut railing, this was only partly decorated; it was formed by a series of little pillars, connected to one another by three rows of crossbars and surmounted by a continuous coping with its upper surface rounded off. The vedika is divided into sections by the four entranceways positioned to correspond with the cardinal points of the compass. The sculptures and reliefs that have made Sanchi so famous are concentrated on the portals (toranas). An older stupa, made of bricks and then covered by stone facing, is preserved inside the present stupa, although in very bad condition. The English archaeologist Sir John Marshall thinks it also had a roughly hemispherical shape, with a raised terrace around the base and, on the top, a wooden railing and a stone umbrella-canopy. This primitive stupa, which has traditionally been attributed to Asoka, later disappeared under a stone lining executed by filling up, while the construction of the new stupa was underway, the space between the old ruined construction and the new stone facing. Only after the completion of the new dome did they undertake the construction of a terrace around this, so that this base served no supporting function.

It has been suggested that the destruction of the earlier stupa was due to Pushyamitra Shunga, known to have been a persecutor of Buddhism, and that the restoration is the work of Agnimitra or of his immediate successor. Unfortunately, it is not easy to propose a satisfying chronology for the constructions. In any case, the railing and the portals were built later than the domed structure, and the building of the total complex took place over a relatively long period. Such questions of dating, by the way, are not mere technical problems, for their solution could give valuable insights into the social organization of India. In fact, it seems that the railing elements (pillars, crossbars, etc.) were each offered by a different donor, as the inscriptions engraved in brahmi characters reveal. Are we to imagine that the building project moved ahead little by little as the funds arrived for the addition of an element to what was already done? Or perhaps there was a symbolic assignment to each donor of an element, its importance proportional to the contribution and within the context of a project that had been carried out at one time?

A similar problem of dating arises from the four great toranas, but for these a generally accepted chronological succession has been suggested: south, north, east, and west. The priority given to the southern portal is easy to accept if we bear in mind that it opens onto the access stairway to the processional terrace; further confirmation is found at Stupa 3 (Illustration 23) at Sanchi, which has only one portal — also to the south, and also corresponding to the stairway (although there are four entranceways in the railing). In any case, not many years could have passed between the construction of the first and the last toranas; in fact, the donor of the right pillar of the western (or last) portal is the same person who offered the median architrave in the southern torana, while another donor contributed to the construction of both the eastern and western portals.

19.   Sanchi: This detail of the eastern *to-rana* of Stupa 1 shows the traditional motif of a woman-embracing-tree (a *dohada*), here used as a corbel support of an architrave. This figure might well be compared with that of Illustration 20, which originally served a similar function; but note that this figure has been conceived more in two-dimensional terms, an impression enforced by the figure's blending with the tree and leaves.

Although all four *toranas* of the Great Stupa at Sanchi deserve a detailed analysis, we must limit ourselves to a more general description of the characteristics of these portals (and let the photographs support individual analysis). Each *torana* consists of two square pillars surmounted by figured capitals (as of *yakshas* or elephants or lions) which hold up the superstructure including three gently curved architraves that end in volutes (Illustration 15). The architraves are separated from one another by cubic blocks aligned with the capitals and by two rows of three small pillars that divide the space between into four areas; these resultant areas are filled with small sculptures in the round (Illustration 16). On a level with the capitals, some *yakshis* serve as corbels connecting the top of the pillars to the volutes of the lowest architrave (Illustration 19). Similar female figures appear between the outer ends of the architraves (Illustration 16), while the volutes may have lions or elephants on top of them. On top of the uppermost architrave, crowning the entire portal, there was often a *dharmacakra,* or Wheel of the Law, flanked by two guardian *yakshas;* also on the top architrave, but aligned with the pillars, were two *triratnas,* symbols of the Buddhist trinity: Buddha, the Law *(dharma),* and the monastic community *(samgha).*

Virtually every square inch of these *toranas* is thickly covered with reliefs that represent *jatakas,* stories of Buddha's life, episodes after he attained nirvana, and other symbolic motifs. The Enlightenment, the First Sermon, and nirvana are the fundamental recurrent episodes, especially in the cubic blocks and on the pillars between the architraves. Other scenes, somewhat more lively in content, adorn the architraves and other elements of the *torana.* The narrative aspect of these carvings assumes an increased importance over the previous carvings of the Shunga period: the scenes strike the onlooker not so much because of the symbolic meaning of the event that took place in the past as for the sense of the choral participation of the characters in the edifying episode. But as at Bharhut, Buddha is never portrayed anthropomorphically but is represented by symbols.

From a stylistic point of view, the reliefs at the Great Stupa of Sanchi, compared to the ones at Bharhut, reveal the artists in possession of greater knowledge of the possibilities offered by the medium of stone. And if the vision of space is basically the same — if anything, the tendency to "crush" the figures between two planes is accentuated — the distinctive plastic character of Indian sculpture manifests itself here in an evident way. Probably, however, the artistic experience that lies at the root of the Sanchi works was still sculpture in a different medium — wood or ivory. Although evidence of such work is practically non-existent in India, an inscription refers to the role of a guild of ivory-carvers in the execution of some panels on the south portal at Sanchi. The stylistic convention that conceives of figures between two parallel planes is here so solidly established that the horsemen represented in the spaces between the uprights set between the architraves (Illustration 16) are two-sided figures, so that they can be seen frontally from either side of the *torana.* However, in some of the figures carved in the round, especially if we look at them separately and not in their decorative context, we note a new interest in a less traditional plastic vision.

This is particularly true of the *yakshis* that function as corbels between the abacus of the capitals and the volute of the lowest architraves. Among these, the one easiest to analyze, although damaged (Illustration 20), comes from the western (or possibly southern) *torana* (and now is in the Boston Museum of Fine Arts). In this *yakshi,* the two-dimensional plastic vision of Bharhut is completely surpassed; this change is particularly appreciable in a slightly off-frontal view, which emphasizes the importance of the torsion of the bust and the powerful plasticity of the breasts, the hips, and the swollen thighs. These surfaces seem to be taut as if from internal pressure, and they define only convex volumes, according to patterns still to be traced in Indian work done a thousand years later (such as the *virkshaka* in the Gwalior Museum). However, this analysis must be carefully integrated with the observation of the other similar figures still *in situ* — as that of Illustration 19. A more complete critical

THE YAKSAS ATTEMPT TO SLAY THE BODHISATTVA

Once upon a time when Brahmadatta was reigning in Benares, the Bodhisattva came to life as the son of his chief queen. And when he was of age, he was instructed in all the arts; on the death of his father, he was established in his kingdom and governed it righteously.

At that time men were devoted to the worship of the gods and made religious offerings to them by the slaughter of many goats, rams and the like. The Bodhisattva proclaimed by beat of drum, "No living creature is to be put to death." The Yaksas were enraged against the Bodhisattva at losing their offerings, and calling together an assembly of their kind in the Himalayas, they sent forth a certain savage Yaksa to slay the Bodhisattva. . . .

*Ayakuta-Jataka:*347

Four typical yakshas *or* yakshis, *fertility spirits*
A. *A* yaksha *from Parkham (Mathura: Archaeological Museum)*
B. *A* yakshi *from Didarganj (Patna Museum)*
C. *A* yaksha *from Patna (Calcutta: Indian Museum)*
D. *A* yakshi *from Besnagar (Calcutta: Indian Museum)*

appreciation of these *yakshis* forces us to realize that the compact mass of foliage was inextricably involved with the effect of the figure. But at least the isolation of the figure is useful for allowing us to see to what extent the artist commanded his technical medium.

Just as for so many works of figurative art in India, different dates have been suggested for the Sanchi reliefs. The first suggestion, that the *toranas* of the Great Stupa date from the second century B.C., was later rejected; the consensus of scholars accepted a date about the second half of the first century B.C. But the current tendency has been to lower the date to the first decades of the first century A.D., and this date now seems to offer the best guarantee of probability.

There remains still another stupa at Sanchi, of a slightly more recent date, and indicated in archaeological literature as Stupa 3 (Illustration 21). It was in this one that Cunningham discovered the relics of two famous disciples of Buddha, Shariputra and Mahamogalana, whose names were engraved on the stone boxes that housed the reliquaries, set in a chamber at the center of the structure and on a level with the upper floor of the terrace. Leaving aside Stupa 3's dimensions, so much smaller than those of Stupa 1, we may note that the only elements that differentiate the two monuments from one another are the presence of but one *torana* at Stupa 3 and the more swollen shape of the dome of Stupa 3. Otherwise Stupa 3 can almost be considered a replica of the Great Stupa. Today almost the entire outside railing is missing, but even in ancient times it got broken up (so much so that some of its elements were found in the foundation of Temple 45); the lotus flower was the sole decorative motif used on this railing. Stupa 3's *torana,* replete with reliefs, gives us no new insights compared with those of Stupa 1's portals; it was definitely made later than the stupa itself. The gate is off-center with regard to the axis of the staircase (but then the same holds true for the Great Stupa's southern portal) because the "elbow" entrances to the *pradaksinapatha* were created in such a way as to block the sight of the corridor to the onlooker standing outside.

Yaksha and Yakshi Figures in Indian Life

Before we leave this period, we should examine somewhat more closely certain figures so typical of Indian art and life, the *yakshas* and *yakshis* that provided such inspiration for Indian sculptors. A representative selection is illustrated (on page 59) and just to trace the problems of dating these works would be to get a glimpse into the progress of Indian art history in the past century. Thus, with the yakshi (B) from Didarganj (in the Patna Museum), the idea that highly polished surfaces — so evident in this work — was an exclusive characteristic of Mauryan art, once greatly influenced the date suggested by various scholars. Today few authorities place this figure before the first century B.C. The same is to be said of the *yaksha* (C) from Patna (in the Indian Museum of Calcutta), which was once even considered pre-Mauryan by some scholars. This is a massive figure, wearing a *dhoti* (a cloth wrapped around the waist) but not in the customary fashion — that is, with one end drawn between the legs and ending up on the back — but with the edge falling over the feet; a belt tightens the cloth against the hips and then hangs loose, ending in a large knot. A work like this, as we shall see later, allows us to make comparisons with some Gandhara sculpture (as in Illustration 30), comparisons that would hardly be justified if we did not date this *yaksha* at least to the first half of the first century A.D.

On the other hand, I would not hesitate to place the *yaksha* from Parkham (A) much earlier in time, both because of the manner of treating the folds — which connects it with the Bharhut reliefs — and because of the almost absolute lack of connection between the front and rear views. Just such a connection was emerging in the Patna *yaksha* and with the *yakshi* corbels at Sanchi, evidently marking a different relationship between the

worshiper and such images. The stylistic difference between the Patna *yaksha* and the one from Parkham may also be partially due to the distance between the two sites. However, there is no reason to believe that the Mathura region — in which Parkham is located — should be considered backward in such matters. We should remember that the Bharhut and Sanchi "schools," far from being phenomena limited to just a few centers, extended for quite a vast area to the west and into the northwest; the reliefs from Amin (Haryana) and some terra-cotta plaques probably from the Peshawar area (Illustration 11) are worthy examples of this widespread activity.

This group of *yakshas* and *yakshis* is also important for the light it sheds on the question of representing the form of divinity. Although the first approach to the problem of the anthropomorphic image of Buddha (proposed by the pioneering Indian scholar, A. K. Coomaraswamy) has been vitiated by the erroneous chronological attributions of the figures now under discussion, the connection between them and the older images of Buddha remains valid. It is especially important not to make the ingenuous mistake of believing that the anthropomorphic representation of the Enlightened One is a foreign, Graeco-Roman contribution. It is quite true that in Gandhara, as we shall see, Buddha was dressed in Hellenistic clothes, but this does not mean that the abandonment of the anti-representational tradition ("aniconism" is the technical term for this) was due to an influx of foreign cultures. Nor does it imply that the Indian artist, bound by religious prejudices, was shut off from the most complete expression of himself, realizable only in the anthropomorphic image of Buddha. In reality, India in this crucial period was undergoing a phase of cultural leveling that affected large layers of its population; in particular, there was a crisis of political power and of the state mechanism. It was for this reason, in my opinion, that the Mauryan and Shunga aniconism, in which was reflected the ideology of the king who identified himself with the state, gave way to a more affable vision of the king himself and hence of Buddha: this remote being in nirvana now became a deified figure who could be approached and whose will could be influenced by the intensity of personal devotion.

The *yaksha* lent itself to this profound modification of the figure of Buddha. A semi-divine personage, who lived in woods, on trees, in cliffs, the *yaksha* (and his female counterpart, the *yakshi*) was a force of nature who could be rendered benevolent; his cult provided for a direct relationship between the devout and the divine. The *yaksha* would have found it hard to find a place in the official religious iconography of Mauryan India, although the *yaksha* cult was certainly firmly established among the people by that time. But in the post-Mauryan period, the cult found relatively easy access in an India that was politically unstable and territorially divided. At the same time — and in iconographic forms analogous to those of the *yaksha* — the Bodhisattva cult was also making headway. This personage was no longer conceived of only as the imperfect Buddha in the narrative context of the aniconic tradition, where the Bodhisattvas inevitably were seen as mere "stages" of the Enlightened One. Now the Bodhisattva was being venerated as a divine personage in his own right, benevolent, a source of compassion, one who could be invoked directly. It thus follows that Buddha himself would take on a more human form.

And it is no coincidence, either, that in this period there appear the first images of Indian sovereigns. Among these were the reliefs on Nanaghat Pass near Puna (Maharashtra) — now unfortunately lost — accompanied by inscriptions indicating the names of the various personages represented. Among these were Queen Nayanika and King Satakarni of the Satavahana dynasty, together with the founder (during the first century B.C.) of the dynasty, King Simaku. If the Nanaghat reliefs are to be assigned to Satakarni's time — about A.D. 15–30 — they provide the perfect transitional image from the traditional India we have been exploring to the more heterogeneous India that was to come.

CLASSIC AND MEDIEVAL INDIA: THE REVIVAL OF HINDUISM

The Foreigners Invade India

On the southern *torana* of the Great Stupa of Sanchi there is a votive inscription that mentions a donation made by Vasishthiputra Ananda, the head of King Satakarni's artisans. This is not proof, to be sure, that the Satavahana dynasty had taken over Malwa, the region where Sanchi lies, because it may be that Vasishthiputra only visited Sanchi as a pilgrim. Nor, for that matter, is it clear that the Satakarni mentioned in the inscription was the first Satavahana ruler of that name or one of his successors. Indeed, the dynastic history of the Satavahanas, the succession of rulers who followed the Shungas, presents several difficulties. To begin with, we do not know the exact relationship between the name "Satavahana" and the other one, "Andhra," used in the *Puranas* (those sacred books of the Hindus of a cosmologial and historical-legendary character) to indicate the family name of the first of the Satavahanas, Simuka, and his successors. Nor do we know how many sovereigns were in this dynasty, since the Puranic tradition itself oscillates between nineteen and thirty kings.

The problem of marking out the territory that the Satavahanas actually ruled is equally confused. The first testimony of the dynasty comes from central India and northern Deccan, not from the Andhra region that has often been assumed to be their place of origin — and so has given its name to the period in some texts. Meanwhile, an inscription of the king of Kalinga, Kharevela, probably a contemporary of Satakarni I, speaks of the Satavahanas as those who protected the west. It is possible that their original homeland was the region immediately south of Madhyadesa and that the name Andhra ended up being attributed to them in a later age when — the territories to the north and west having been lost — the Satavahanas found themselves ruling only the region around the mouth of the Kistna River.

The range of time covered by this Satavahana-Andhra dynasty is also in dispute; we place it between the first century B.C. and the third century A.D. But finally more important than this particular dynasty and its origins is the fact that this was the period in which India was most profoundly subject to direct foreign domination and influence — by the Yavanas (Greeks), the Shakas (Scythians), the Pahlavas (Parthians), and the Yueh-chih (the Kushans). If it at first seems a surprise to be encountering these peoples in a history of India, we must realize too that they had all been interacting among themselves for various periods in the territory north of India before they spilled down into India itself. We should also realize that at this stage in history, these peoples were not all that far removed from one another — nor from the Aryan-Indians: all shared in speaking Indo-European languages; without getting into any biological-racial issue, all were Caucasoid peoples who had probably shared a common cultural tradition; and perhaps all even shared common ancestors only some 2000–3000 years back.

Among the various Shaka groups, the one known as the Kshaharata ruled in Maharashtra and in other adjacent areas of western India, probably with Nasik as its capital; but it seems that the first monarch of this dynasty, Bhumaka, was merely the satrap of the region of Kathiawar.

22. **Karli: A relief carving of a divine couple from the chaitya-hall of the caves at Karli. These caves, which include only the one chaitya-hall and several monastic chambers (*viharas*), are situated on the road from Bombay to Puna. This is only one of many such couples who decorate the walls of the vestibule to the chaitya-hall; they must have been seen as members of the retinue of Buddha, who was represented by the stupa within the hall. A certain heavy plasticity characterizes these figures, bringing them near to the mature Kushan works of Mathura; they are dated to the first quarter of the second century A.D.**

The greatest of these Shaka satraps was Nahapana, who, ruling about A.D. 119–124, enlarged his dominion in Maharashtra at the expense of the Satavahanas; but in 124, Nahapana was defeated by Gautamiputra of the Satavahana dynasty. The point is that the Satavahanas' fortunes in the central-western regions were closely linked to the stronger or weaker force of the neighboring Shakas, both the Kshaharata and the satraps of Ujjain, to whom the Satavahanas were also connected by matrimonial ties. Ties, by the way, that did not prevent conflict between the two powers: thus, there was the link of noble marriage during the reign (about A.D. 130–150) of the Shaka king Rudradaman, whose daughter married a Satavahana king. It was about this same time that the Satavahana king Gautamiputra destroyed the power of the Shaka king Nahapana.

What is equally interesting to note is that the Satavahanas, who evidently did not hesitate to enter into marriage with foreigners such as the Shakas, presented themselves as the defenders of the *brahmans* and enemies of contamination among the Indian castes. This was not, however, a question of simple discrepancy between theory and practice dictated by some open-minded *Realpolitik,* but rather an elasticity within the caste system itself, which worked essentially to preserve class privileges and thus adapted itself from time to time to the socio-economic realities of the nation. On the other hand, the Hindu Satavahanas were known as protectors of Buddhism — that is, of a religion that, at least in theory, rejected the validity of the caste system. It should not be surprising that exactly in a fluid system like this — in which groups of different origins, meeting on a level of common activity (for instance, artisans in the same guild), gave birth to mixed castes — there were attempts to impose a rigorous orthodoxy from above. Instances of this are seen in the propaganda of the Satavahanas, who declared themselves the defenders of the *brahmans,* in the drawing up by the sage Manu of the code of social laws (the *Manavadharmashastra*), which occurred in the early centuries of the Christian era. It was, in fact, quite understandable that the need to

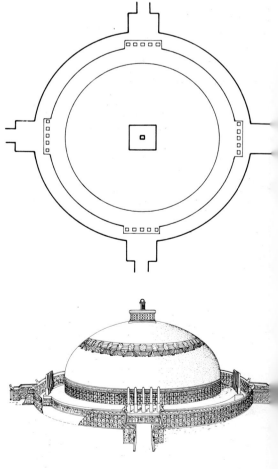

Amaravati: Ground plan and elevation of the Great Stupa.

23.   Amaravati: Left: A relief from the railing *(vedika)*, showing scenes from the life of Buddha; it is dated to the second century A.D. The slab (some 9 feet 3 inches long and 2 feet 7 inches high) was part of the crowning piece of the railing and was sculptured on both sides, although the side not shown had only genii holding up garlands. This side shows Buddha's return to Kapilavastu, his hometown. On the left is the procession of his father, King Suddhodana, leaving the city; in the center, Buddha performs the miracle of lifting himself off the earth; then Buddha is depicted seated and preaching the Law to his father; on the right, Suddhodana gives Buddha an evergreen grove. The presence of the stupa is, of course, anachronistic in the literal, realistic sense of time. (London: British Museum)

24.   Amaravati: This carved relief once decorated the drum, or tambour, of the Great Stupa; it is carved on both sides, although each side was done at quite different times. The older carving, not seen here, shows the Illumination of Buddha and was done according to the aniconic convention (that is, without representing Buddha's human form); as such it belongs to the oldest phase of Amaravati. This side, however, is considered to be the work of the late, or third, phase, the third century A.D. (It is 2 feet 9 inches wide and 4 feet 1 inch high.) It gives us an approximate idea of the appearance of the Great Stupa of Amaravati; note that it was heavily decorated on the dome itself with scenes from Buddha's life. (London: British Museum)

codify a social system was felt just when it was undergoing a crisis and being threatened by new emerging forces.

We have already spoken of that characteristic class of architecture, or if one prefers, "pseudo-architecture," represented by the monastic and cult chambers cut into natural rock formations. A whole group of these rock-cut sanctuaries, conspicuous in number and importance, created to meet the devotional needs of Buddhists, was constructed over an extensive period in the Bombay region of western India. For some time now the basic evolution of the stylistic patterns of this monumental complex has been recognized. For example, in the oldest of these chaitya-halls, Bhaja and Kondane — about 50 B.C. — the interior columns are simple octagonal shafts with no decoration; in later monuments — for example, Karli, about A.D. 120 — the columns are much more elaborate. And even between Bhaja and Kondane, one can distinguish an evolutionary process in the lesser use of wood; at Kondane there was already demonstrated a step toward total independence from the original construction techniques — that is, the wooden prototypes. However, the absolute dating of these works remains one of the most controversial points in Indian art history, and unfortunately the erroneous interpretation of certain documentary elements has greatly influenced this state of affairs; only recently have steps been taken to put this delicate matter in order.

For example, an inscription at Karli refers to the great chaitya-hall as having been founded by a banker from Vaijayanti called Bhutapala, whom scholars about a century ago identified with the last king of the Shunga dynasty, Devabhuti, who ruled around 80 or 70 B.C. It has since been demonstrated (by Spink) that this attribution was entirely fantastic; as a result, there has been a complete redating of Karli and related sites (Bhaja, Kondane, Nasik). Today we place Karli (Illustration 22) with greater exactitude at the time of the satrap Nahapana — that is, the first quarter of the second century A.D., a few years before his defeat at the hands of Gautamiputra. In fact, Nahapana is mentioned in an inscription engraved under the threshold of the central window of the Karli chaitya-hall, while inside other inscriptions bear the names of his followers and one of his grandsons, represented as the donors of some pillars. Since we know that, at the time of his defeat, Nahapana bore the title of mahaksatrapa ("great satrap"), it is clear that the Karli chaitya-hall, already completed when the inscription was executed, must date back some years before A.D. 124. And since Nahapana was already a grandfather when the Karli inscriptions were undertaken, one can deduce that the completion of the chaitya-hall took place toward the end of his reign.

It was by means of such considerations that Spink reached the conclusion that the great rock edifice at Karli was finished about A.D. 120. And it is a significant fact that the Kshaharata-Shakas committed themselves so thoroughly to the support of Buddhism; this is demonstrated both by the numerous inscriptions at Karli in which persons defined as "Yavana" — evidently those who belonged to the conqueror's entourage — are mentioned, and by the relatively large numbers of caves cut out of the rock (e.g., at Nasik and Junnar) that can be attributed to the Kshaharata period, itself rather brief. And it is also interesting to note that everyone — Yavanas, "natives," and members of the royal family — appears as a donor on the same level, with the sole exception of the king, who held a position of supreme eminence.

Unfortunately, we do not have sufficient documentation concerning the position of the king in the society of this time. However, we can reasonably assume that the evolution already observed in the post-Mauryan period continued along the same lines that had led to a leveling within the power groups and a more familiar "approach" by the king to his subjects. There is certainly no trace of a concept of royalty such as that to be found at the same time in the northwest, as we shall see. But for all that, the Kshaharatas did not basically represent anything revolutionary compared to the Satavahanas, at least as far as their attitude toward religious groups was concerned. As we have seen, the Satavahanas themselves, despite their professions of Hindu faith, protected Buddhism, as is demonstrated by the oldest chaitya-halls at Bhaja, Nasik, and Kondane. If for no other reason than that no single individual or group possessed the power to impose a unity over India at this time, a pragmatic tolerance and diversity were the order of the day.

Amaravati as a Center of Trade and Art

Nor was the religious aspect the only one that the Satavahana culture had in common with that of the Hellenized Scythian conquerors — as we might best think of these Kshaharata-Shakas. In the Deccan, in fact, there seems to have been an actual importation of terra-cottas from the Mediterranean that left their stylistic and even technical imprint on the local production of ceramics. M. N. Deshpande, the scholar who called attention to this phenomenon, put forth the hypothesis that both the importation of little Hellenistic-Roman terra-cotta pieces as well as the local imitations were placed directly under the control of the Satavahana kings: it must be significant that one of the centers of the production of imitations was their western capital, Pratishthanapura. Even the southeastern coast of India engaged in considerable maritime trade with the

25. Vengi Region (Andhra Pradesh): This is a detail from a limestone relief depicting Buddha's bath in the Nairanjana River; it is dated to the first half of the second century A.D. and measures 63 inches by 40 inches. The slab is sculptured on both sides. That not seen here has a relief typical of the mature style of Amaravati (which also happens to be in the Vengi Region, the delta area of the Kistna and Godavari rivers). The relief seen here has a style suggesting a later period. The serpent-king Kalika (the center figure at the bottom), with his two wives, watches Buddha taking his bath in the Nairanjana before his Enlightenment. Above them, arranged in a pattern typical of Indian sculpture of the first centuries A.D., are four river divinities. Not appearing in this detail are Indra and the symbolic representation of Buddha, his footprints. (Boston: Museum of Fine Arts, Ross Collection)

26.   Guldara: Left: The large stupa of Guldara, in the Lugar Valley of Afghanistan.

27.   Shevaki: Below: Stupa 1 at Shevaki in the Kabul Valley of Afghanistan.

Stupa 1 at Shevaki lies in an isolated spot about six miles from Kabul, the capital of Afghanistan, and is the best preserved of the four stupas in its group. Its lower part has been irremediably damaged not only by local inhabitants but also by a German doctor, Martin Honigberger, who went treasure-hunting there around 1835. The upper part, with its characteristic row of keel-like arches on the drum and the dome, is in fair condition, with large sections of the original plaster cover intact. Contemporary, or slightly later, to this is the stupa of Guldara, which lies a short distance from the Shevaki group of stupas, just beyond the mountain range that separates the Kabul Valley from the Lugar Valley. The Guldara stupa, which has a staircase on its front side, is located within a fortified monastic complex. UNESCO recently sponsored a major restoration of this stupa, but further examination of it and other similar monuments in Afghanistan is required, especially to establish proper dates. Both of the two stupas pictured seem to date from the Kushan period, sometime in the early centuries of the Christian era.

Gift of a stupa pillar with a relic, near the southern portal, from the merchant Kuta, together with his wife, his sons, his daughters and grandchildren.

Inscription on a pillar fragment
from Amaravati
(Museum of Madras)

Mediterranean; excavations have documented the importation of a type of Roman ceramics in the port of Arikamedu-Virapatnam and — perhaps more surprising in such a remote spot — local pottery that imitated the Mediterranean types.

When we turn to more ambitious works, the Satavahana period has left its greatest traces in the "Oriental" Amaravati school of sculpture, connected — as is to be expected in India — with the construction of large stupas, such as those at Amaravati and Nagarjunakonda. The son and successor of Guatamiputra, Vasishthiputra Shri Pulumavi (who ruled about A.D. 130 to 158), left epigraphs of himself on the Amaravati stupa; his coins, found in Andhradesa, also testify to the consolidation of Satavahana power in the southeastern region of India. (Although the vital part of the Satavahana kingdom had by this time been reduced to the Andhra region, even as late as the time of Yajna Shri Satakarni, A.D. 175–203, the Bombay region seems to have been under Satavahana influence, as inscriptions of this king at Kanheri and Nasik demonstrate.) The great stupa at Amaravati has been completely destroyed because of the way in which it has been investigated over the years; the researches were not always carried out by trained archaeologists, and in one case, the enthusiastic "research" of a Madras governor virtually destroyed the monument in 1880. However, D. Barrett was able to make a graphic reconstruction of the stupa on the basis of the reports of certain excavators, comparisons with other contemporary stupas in Andhra, and the representations of the stupa itself that appear on the decorative reliefs from Amaravati (Illustration 24).

The best documented part of the monument is the *vedika,* or railing (Illustration 23). It had a diameter of some 190 feet and is the richest Buddhist stupa railing to have survived. It was formed of uprights adorned with a lotus-shaped medallion in the center and half-medallions, also lotus-shaped, on the ends, all of these being connected by three rows of crossbars, also shaped like medallions; this balustrade was completed and held together by a coping with a rounded top. A sort of compact wall was thus formed, by elements that could be said to form a paling (from which in fact the *vedika* form was derived) but which in practice did not afford any view of the interior. Four entranceways set at the cardinal points of the compass, afforded access to the inner precinct, but they had no *toranas.* In the decoration, a clear hierarchy between the outside and the inside is recognizable, the latter being more important than the former, because it was visible only to the worshiper who had already entered the shrine; in fact, the inside of the coping bears relief carvings of stories of Buddha's life and *jatakas* (Illustration 23), whereas the outside part has only a garland decoration. Also, the crossbar medallions have stories of Buddha only in the middle row and on the outside part; the uprights are an exception, in that, although richer on the inside, their outside also have representations of religious motifs, such as the worship of the tree, the wheel, and the stupa.

The stupa dome sat on a drum, or tambour, that had a diameter of about 160 feet, was about six feet high, and had four jutting platforms corresponding with the *vedika* entranceways, on each of which there rose up five pillars. The dome itself rose almost vertically from the tambour and then receded in a rather abrupt curve so that it assumed a slightly "crushed" profile: elements for this reconstruction can be obtained both from the stupa reconstructions on the Amaravati reliefs (Illustration 24) — which, however, ought not to be taken too literally — and from what remained of other stupas in the region, such as the one at Bhattiprolu. The sweeping curve began only above an ample band covered with decorative sculptured slabs; at this same point also began the plastered part of the dome — of which almost nothing remains — this part being decorated halfway up with a stucco frieze. An octagonal pillar rose up at the center of the balcony on top of the dome. On the basis of stylistic elements of the sculptures on the Amaravati stupa, Barrett has distinguished three chronological groups ("Early," "Middle," and "Late" Phases), which also correspond to a typological evolution of the uprights and crossbars of the railing. Whereas the characteristic style of the second

phase seems to assert itself completely in the third quarter of the second century A.D., the transition between the second and third phases is placed by Barrett around the end of the second century. The Amaravati style then finds its natural continuation in its immediate successor, the Nagarjunakonda style.

As for the beginnings of the Amaravati style, it has been pointed out that it was already established in that region in the early years of the first century B.C. This Amaravati style is characterized by the clear vertical development of the figures, by the nervous detachment of the limbs, and by the conspicuous weightiness of the details derived from the greenish nuances of the soft limestone without any need for figurative retouching. Nonetheless, the works of the early phase of Amaravati art remind us of the Bharhut and Bhaja reliefs more than of those from Sanchi (once again confirming the need for the "short" dating of the art of this period). A relief (now kept in the Boston Museum of Fine Arts) from the Kistna-Godavari delta area, is of the utmost interest because both sides are sculptured and reveal two different styles, much like a palimpset. One of the two faces represents a stupa in the typical mature Amaravati style. The other (Illustration 25) — which depicts Buddha's bath in the Nairanjana before his Enlightenment — is certainly older and suggests comparisons with the portals of the Great Stupa at Sanchi and with some of the celebrated ivory pieces attributed variously to the Mathura school or to the Satavahana sphere (sometime, that is, between the first century B.C. and the first century A.D.). In the Late Phase of Amaravati art, we note a tendency toward the flattening of the relief and the emergence of a taste for strong figurative elements. The figures are even more elongated and thin, and lose the touch of composure they had in the preceding period; the movements are brusque, unnatural; the composition becomes a knot of broken lines that are set above geometrically rigid patterns, with an extraordinarily striking effect of abstraction.

Graeco-Roman Influences on Northern India

We have been noting occasionally the influence that trade relations with the Mediterranean peoples had on the India of the Satavahanas. And when we shift our attention to the northwest of the subcontinent, we notice that certain offshoots of Mediterranean culture took quite strong and extensive roots, so much so that various commentators on the art of the region have gone so far as to include the Buddhist sculpture of the region among "the non-Mediterranean descendants" of Greek art. The tendency today, however, is to accept that it is a more specialized and localized phenomenon, that it is not to be confused with the early impact made by the Greeks in the wake of Alexander the Great, and that if anything it should be called "Graeco-Roman" rather than Greek or Hellenic. Which is not to diminish the importance or extent of relations between the two cultures — merely to recognize the complexity while making relevant distinctions.

The colonies of Greeks in Asia, originally formed in Bactria (a part of Afghanistan) under the Achaemenids as part of their general tendency to "internationalize" their empire, had been successfully reinforced by

32.   Tepe Shotor: This is a section of the stucco decoration of one of the smaller stupas, stupa 19, in the sanctuary found at this site, near Hadda, Afghanistan (and recently excavated by the Afghanistan Institute of Archaeology). In the center is Buddha, flanked by two worshipers — a monk on the left, a woman taking vows on the right. Her distinctive hair style, by the way, is clearly of Sassanian derivation. The little pillars on both sides, however, reflect classical Graeco-Roman models, if greatly modified.

erected at Besnagar (Madhya Pradesh) in honor of a Hindu god associated with Vishnu. So Greeks were indeed becoming assimilated to that extent. And at Taxila and elsewhere (in Punjab and Gandhara) the Indo-Greeks did not bring about any great change in the administrative system, which must have basically been that of the old Achaemenid satrapies. It is reasonable to suppose, however, that these Indo-Greeks exercised an influence in the field of arts and crafts; these Indo-Greeks, to the extent that they looked over and back to the Mediterranean culture, must have been a relatively limited elite but no less jealous of its tradition.

And yet, up to recent times, the art of these Indo-Greeks was seen through quite blurred and even prejudiced eyes. The very term "Indo-Greek" confused matters by being used to refer to both the early Bactrian people and to the later development in Punjab and Gandhara. Its documentation was at first limited to coins, which although perfectly "Greek" in type and workmanship were too limited to support a whole superstructure of Indo-Greek art, a structure that was to climax in the art of Gandhara. Recently, however, and thanks in great part to the work of the French Archaeological Delegation in Afghanistan, more substantial evidence has been brought to light. The excavation of Ai Khanum (near Qunduz) on the Oxus River (present-day Amu Darya), has revealed the existence of a veritable Hellenistic city with an acropolis, whose remains

allow us to understand better those works that have been attributed to Graeco-Bactrian art.

Among the several monumental constructions brought to light at Ai Khanum, we shall mention briefly the one that may most justly be considered the product of a local culture open to suggestions from diverse origins: the so-called *temple à redans* (*redans* being the large indentations or stepped niches cut into the exterior wall of the edifice). The temple sat at the end of a courtyard that opened directly onto the main road; square in plan, about 62 feet long on each side, it had a vestibule set crosswise and a smaller cella flanked by two sacristies. The interior, on a higher level than the courtyard, was entered by a stairway. The construction was of unfired bricks, but stone was used for the floors; the walls were especially thick. Three jutting bases ran along the inside walls of the cella; of these, the most important is the end one, which held the plinth for the cult statue; only a few fragments of this last-named object have survived, but enough to give some idea of the quality of the work.

33.   Tepe Shotor: This is all that remains of a niche with figures, made of unbaked clay, that once adorned a structure at this site near Hadda, Afghanistan. The feet belonged to a colossal Buddha (whose original height is estimated as 15 feet or more); he was flanked by a donor who was dressed in a classical Graeco-Roman robe but wore a pair of boots typical of the Kushan aristocracy. The dating of this work is extremely difficult, but it has tentatively been assigned to the fourth century A.D.

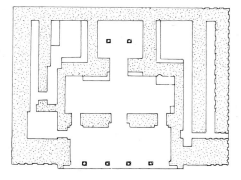

Khalchayan: Plan of the "little palace" at this site in Uzbekistan, U.S.S.R.

TAXILA SEEN BY APOLLONIUS OF TYANA IN FIRST CENTURY A.D.

Taxila was about the size of Nineveh, walled like a Greek city, and was the residence of a sovereign who ruled over what of old was the kingdom of Porus. Just outside the walls was a temple of near a hundred feet, of porphyry and in it a shrine, small, considering the size of the temple and its many columns, but still very beautiful. Round the shrine were hung pictures on copper tablets, representing the feats of Alexander and Porus. In these tablets the elephants, horses, soldiers, and armor, were portrayed in a mosaic of orichalcum, silver, gold, and tinted copper; the spears, javelins, and swords in iron; but the several metals were all worked into one another with so nice a gradation of tints, that the pictures they formed, in correctness of drawing, vivacity of expression and truthfulness of perspective, reminded one of the productions of Zeuxis, Polygnotus and Euphranor. They told too of the noble character of Porus, for it was not till after the death of Alexander that he placed them in the temple, — and this, though they represented Alexander as a conqueror, and himself as conquered and wounded, and receiving from Alexander the kingdom of India.

FLAVIO PHILOSTRATO: *Life of Apollonius of Tyana* II:XX

34. Khalchayan: Above: Head of a Bactrian personage, possibly from the first century B.C.; it is 9½ inches high. (Tashkent Museum of Art)

35. Khalchayan: Below: Head of a warrior; possibly the first century B.C; it is 10½ inches high.

These two heads, made of unbaked clay, were found along with much other similar sculptured material in the "little palace" (excavated by the Russian archaeologist, Miss G. A. Pugachenkova) at a site in Uzbekistan. They document one of the first phases, if not the first, of the adaptation of the classical Graeco-Roman artistic currents to the central Asian milieu. (We exclude the sculptures of Ai Khanum, which are more a case of Hellenism transplanted than adapted.) The palace measures 121 feet by 85 feet, with its facade facing the east; both these heads came from the decoration of its central hall.

The plan of the temple has been compared to certain Mesopotamian precedents, but the statue was typically Greek in both style and technique. It was thus a sculptor working in the Greek manner and, judging from the perfection of the work — or so suggests the French archaeologist who discovered it — "he could only have been a Greek." The largest fragment of the statue is the front part of a shod foot of a colossal size (from two to three times life size); this was an acrolith, in which the cheapest part was of unfired clay held together by a wooden frame. It is difficult to say which god was represented, even if the decoration of the sandal reveals an element, the thunderbolt, that gave rise to a hypothesis that it may be a statue of Zeus; it may also be that the image represented a Greek god (whether Zeus or another) assimilated by some Oriental divinity. The assignment of this work to the third century B.C. seems acceptable, and this would be the same date for the limestone statuettes of males found in the same temple. A separate problem is posed by the two heads (a female in unfired clay, a male of stucco) that belonged to decorative images for the temple vestibule. Although because of their style they can be included in the tradition of Greek statues, comparisons with other material from Afghanistan and from the Central Asian Republics of the Soviet Union require us to withhold judgment on their dates.

Naturally the traces of the Hellenization of Bactria recognizable at Ai Khanum do not end with these remains. There are, for example, the many Greek inscriptions. The continuation of what is among the most important excavations in the Indian cultural realm will eventually lead to a much more articulate knowledge of the phenomenon of Hellenization in this Graeco-Bactrian sphere and its consequences in later times. Taxila, for instance, already bore witness to the Greek contribution to town-planning. In fact, the Indo-Greeks were responsible for the founding of the second town at Taxila, known as Sirkap and built — unlike the chaotic site at Bhir Mound, previously mentioned — on a rectangular-geometric pattern. The same sequence that occurred at Taxila took place at Charsada (Pushkalavati), where the living quarters were moved from the original settlement, Bala Hisar, to the adjacent site, Shaikhan Dheri.

The excavation of this last-named site has furnished, among other things, a most interesting confirmation of the date of distribution toward the east of "Hellenized" artistic products. Among the terra-cottas, in fact, the Hellenistic types characterize the Scythian-Parthian levels (of about 50 B.C. to A.D. 50) as well as successive periods; the sole major exception is represented by a Cupid figure obtained from a double mold and found in a Graeco-Bactrian level. For the rest, in the Graeco-Bactrian period the dominant type of terra-cotta figurine is what we have already met, the Baroque Ladies, which continue — if only as vestigial forms — up to the Kushan period, the early centuries of this era. In Swat, however, we meet (as at the partial excavation at Udegram, Pakistan) a continuity of life from Alexander's conquest to the fourth century A.D.; this might be explained by the fact that Swat was to some degree set apart from the events that involved the two metropolises of the plain, Taxila and Charsada. But the Udegram excavation is still too limited to allow for any such far-reaching conclusions.

Among the most significant architectural monuments of this period of Hellenization — due, it should be said, as much to the Scythians and the Parthians as to the Bactrian Greeks themselves — we should mention one of the most singular edifices in Taxila and the entire subcontinent, the Fire Temple at Jandial, which can perhaps be identified with the temple described by Philostratus in his *Life of Apollonius of Tyana* (a neo-Pythagorean philosopher who lived in the first century A.D.). This temple has several remarkable affinities with Greek temples, not only because of the Ionic columns but also because of the very plan: in place of the open peristyle, it had a wall with large windows; a pronaos, or vestibule; a naos, or cella; and an opisthodomos at the rear. A basic difference with Greek temples, however, was the presence at Jandial of a block of brickwork between the naos and opisthodomos; its huge foundations suggest it was once a tower. What cult practiced here is not known for certain; the generally accepted hypothesis that it was a Zoroastrian temple is con-

36.   Tepe Sardar: Top, left: Head of a man, possibly a Bodhisattva, from this site near Ghazni, Afghanistan; it is 7 inches high. (Ghazni: Italian Archaeological Mission)

37.   Tepe Sardar: Bottom, left: This fragment of a head of a warrior is 4½ inches high. (Ghazni: Italian Archaeological Mission)

38.   Tepe Sardar: Right: This head, possibly of Buddha, is 6 inches high. (Ghazni: Italian Archaeological Mission)

These three heads exemplify the terra-cotta production of the first phase of this site in Afghanistan; the fragments were found in a large deposit of "waste" materials, and seem to have been destroyed on purpose. The warrior (Illus. 37) is the closest to the Graeco-Roman prototypes, and is probably the portrait of a Kushan or a noble related to the Kushan dynasty. (During the 1971 excavations, the upper part of the head was found; it has a cone-shaped headdress similar to one in a portrait found at Dal'verzin Tepe, in Uzbekistan, and dated to about the second century A.D.). The head of the Buddha (Illus. 38) is perhaps closest to the style of Gandhara, both in the use of stone and stucco. The head of the man (Illus. 36) suggests a later date: the elongated eyes, the exaggerated lower part of the face, and the sharp arching eyebrows are elements that place it at least in the fifth century A.D.

Taxila: The ground plan (top) and the base and capital of an Ionic capital from the "Fire Temple" at Jandial.

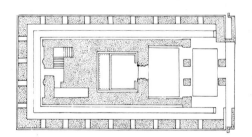

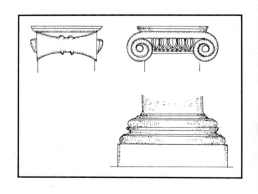

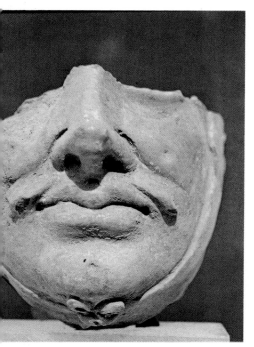

THE WISDOM OF THE MOTHER-
COUNTRY

These wise words of ancient men, sayings of
celebrated men, are consecrated in holy
Delphi; from there Clearchus copied them
with care and placed them in the sanctuary of
Cinea, resplendent from afar.

Greek Epigram (on base from Ai Khanum)

sidered less because of any precise determinants than because there is a
lack of other identifying remains. Moreover, if we accept the view that
the Jandial temple is the one described by Philostratus, it still remains a
difficult task to explain the presence in a Zoroastrian temple of reliefs
narrating the events of Alexander and Poros.

A more "provincial" aspect of Hellenistic culture at Taxila is represented by the "Shrine of the Double-headed Eagle" at Sirkap. This once
contained a stupa, and the main interest of the monument now is the base
of this stupa: it was divided by Corinthian, or at least composite, pilasters;
between these were niches with sculptured reliefs representing architectural elements such as a pedimented aedicule, an Indian *torana*, and an
arch from a chaitya-hall. Some birds — perhaps eagles, one of which
seems to be two-headed — are perched on the top of the arch and in the
niche of the *torana*. The various motifs, so different in origin, epitomize
the composite character of the Taxila culture during the Scytho-Parthian
age, a culture that is also well documented by the jewelry found at Sirkap.
As the great Russian historian Rostovtzev clearly saw, this jewelry has

obvious Scythian elements mixed with Hellenistic and Indian ones, often with excellent results. We cannot venture to diagnose the social structure in a period so rich in disparate elements. Despite the extensive archaeological research carried on in northwestern India and in Afghanistan, we have such scanty and uncertain literary and epigraphical documents that we must admit that too many aspects of this society still elude us.

39. Surkh Kotal: This photograph shows the exterior wall of the cella — with its pilaster moldings clearly demonstrating their Graeco-Roman derivation — of the "Fire Temple" at this site in Afghanistan. The Surkh Kotal sanctuary was evidently quite important, and its founding was due to Kanishka, the Kushan king of the northwest; this is confirmed by a long inscription in cursive Greek (at the foot of the hill where visitors began to ascend the large stairway to the temple).

Art Under the Kushans: The Gandhara School

In any case, it seems evident that the Hellenized artistic production, originating among Greek or strongly Hellenized ethnic "outposts" in Bactria, became — along with expansion due to military conquest — characteristic of a class that was probably military but certainly merchant as well, a class capable of taking over the artistic culture by imposing itself on what is still difficult to imagine as a cultural vacuum. But still, we should realize that the spread of Hellenistic modes and iconographic themes outside Bactria and among the largest strata of the population was due more to the Scythian and Parthian conquerors in the first century B.C. and the first century A.D. than to the Graeco-Bactrians themselves. Naturally, as the distribution of this culture expanded, it was

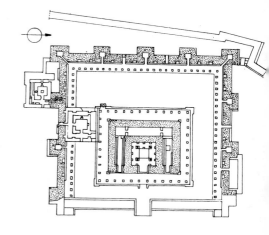

40.   Kapisa: The exact origin of this relief is unknown, but the area is clearly Kapisa, Afghanistan. The schist slab, 17½ inches by 9 inches, portrays a Bodhisattva flanked by donors wearing non-Indian dress; they are probably persons who belonged to the Kushan aristocracy. Although some elements serve to place this relief in the Gandhara "school," there is also expressed here a taste different from most of the Graeco-Buddhist reliefs, a taste that can be attributed to the dynastic art. (Rome: National Museum of Oriental Art)

Surkh Kotal: Ground plan of the "Fire Temple" and the surrounding fortifications.

accompanied by a movement away from "classical" models, a qualitative impoverishment from the point of view of Hellenistic aesthetic canons. At the same time, the artistic tradition of those stylistic modes and iconographic themes took deeper root and ended by being absorbed into the indigenous reinterpretations that left little of the original intact. (This, in effect, was what was happening to Hellenism in the age of Rome; Rome's role in transmitting Mediterranean culture to India should not be forgotten, either; to do so is to make as serious an error as in attributing some direct, unbroken line from Indo-Greeks back to "classic" Greeks.) This last phase within the Indian cultural sphere was to take place during the domination of the Kushans, those Indo-Scythians who ruled during the flourishing of the so-called Gandhara art in the northwest and its contemporary "school" to the south, centered around Mathura.

Nomadic people of uncertain origin, but probably Scythians who had originated in the northwestern fringes of China, the Kushans were known as the Yueh-chih by Chinese historians. By the first half of the first century B.C. they had evidently settled in Transoxiana where they had been driven by pressure from other tribes. (The claim transmitted by the eleventh-century Arab historian, Al-Biruni, that the Kushans were of Tibetan origin refers to the later kings of Kabul, whose Kushan descent has never been established.) From what can be judged of the archaeological data, the Kushans were bearers of a culture similar to that of other Iranian nomadic populations, although some indications suggest other possibilities.

But the problem of the origin of the Kushans is one we shall not try to solve, and we shall furnish only a brief account of what seems to be certain about the chronology of the kings of this dynasty. The first Kushan to reign in the Punjab seems to have been Kujala Khadphises, in the first part of the first century A.D. There then seems to follow a "nameless king," known as Soter Megas (evidently a title: "great savior"), who might have been merely a vassal of Kujala's successor, Vima Khadphises. But a recent examination of the numismatic and epigraphic evidence has led a British scholar (D. MacDowall) to recognize "Soter Megas" as Kujula's successor and Vima's predecessor, making him the first Kushan to extend his dominion greatly north and south of the Hindu Kush, the man who built his Indian empire by defeating the Pahlava dynasty of Gondophares, which had taken possession of the lands conquered by Kujula in Punjab. There then followed Kanishka, Huvishka, and Vasudeva, the best known kings of the Kushan dynasty, known to us especially because of the gold and copper coins that replaced the silver coinage of the Indo-Greeks, the Shakas, and the Parthians who had dominated the northwest. The most controversial chronological problem is

41.   Butkara: This torso of Buddha, in red sandstone (5½ inches high), is one of the few art objects of the Mathura "school" found in the northwestern regions; it was found in the Butkara I sanctuary, the only Mathura object found in Swat up to that time. (Rome: National Museum of Oriental Art)

The Hindus had kings residing in Kabul,
Turks who were said to be of Tibetan origin.
The first of them, Barhatakin, came into the
country and entered a cave in Kabul, which
none could enter except by creeping on hands
and knees. . . .

Some days after he had entered the cave, he
began to creep out of it in the presence of the
people, who looked on him as a new-born
baby. He wore Turkish dress, a short tunic
open in front, a high hat, boots and arms. Now
people honored him as a being of miraculous
origin, who had been destined to be king, and
in fact he brought those countries under his
sway and ruled them under the title of a
shahiya of Kabul. The rule remained among
his descendants for generations, the number
of which is said to be about sixty.

AL-BIRUNI: *India* XLIX

**42.   Kankali Tila: This red sandstone
figure, with its distinctive features, has been
proposed as a portrait of a Kushan by some
scholars, but it seems more likely to be a portrait of Surya, the sun god. The cult of this
sun god, although based on *a posteriori* justification in the *Vedas,* was certainly popular
with the Kushan conquerors and was probably taken under the wing of the ruling
dynasty. The Shahiya kings of the northwest
were also associated with the Surya cult (as is
demonstrated by a sixth-seventh century A.D.
figure found in the temple of Khair Khana,
near Kabul). Note the "northern" costume,
including the high boots, which will remain a
characteristic of Surya figures in medieval
Indian works. (Mathura: Archaeological
Museum)**

that concerning the ascension to the throne of Kanishka — fixed between
A.D. 78 and 144; this is important because it marked the beginning of an
era — "the Kanishka era" — used in dating inscriptions; perhaps the
most reasonable date is A.D. 128 as the beginning of this reign.

But what concerns us is less some specific date and more the general
fact that it was under this Kushan dynasty that the Indian arts thrived,
particularly in the northwestern region known as Gandhara. The art of
Gandhara also presents various problems, two of which remain preeminent: its dating, and the nature of the "classical" (i.e., Graeco-Roman)
elements present in it. At first it may seem difficult to understand how the
first matter remains unsolved (over a half century after the publication of
Alfred Foucher's fundamental study, *L'art greco-bouddhique du Gandhara*).
But this is partially due to the still fluctuating dates for Kanishka's reign;
it is also due to the difficult task of analyzing excavations that yield "Gandharan" material, because in many cases these are monuments whose
reliefs have been utilized again, and not even necessarily for decorative
purposes. However, there are indications that suggest earlier dates for at
least some groups of Gandhara relief carvings: for example, some sacred
images found at Butkara (Illustration 30) in the Swat valley (by the Italian
Archaeological Mission in Pakistan) cannot be understood if they are not
compared with works from the Ganges region such as the *yakshas* of
Patna, the date of which has been opportunely lowered (as mentioned, to
possibly the first half of the first century A.D.). This does not mean,
however, that other excavations cannot indicate still earlier dates, as is the
case with the "Gandhara" schist lid with a lotus decoration, found in a
layer of Tall-i Takht of Pasagardae (Iran), whose latest date is established
at 280 B.C. Now we certainly cannot imagine such an early date even for
the very first Gandhara works, especially since objects like the Pasargadae
lid have been found both at Taxila and Charsada in the Scytho-Parthian
strata, but not in older layers. The same can be said for the so-called
cosmetic trays, which have proto-Gandhara stylistic characteristics but
which also reveal close contact with certain Iranian works of the Parthian
age but of Graeco-Roman inspiration. In any case, it is probable that most
Gandhara works are to be placed in the Kushan period, between the first
and fifth centuries A.D.; indeed, the great works of Gandhara sculpture
were probably done before the end of the third century.

The problem of the nature of the "classical" elements present in Gandhara art may be approached from two different angles, both valid
within their limitations. In particular, this is a question of deciding which
specific contacts with the Mediterranean world can justify stylistic
"influences." One thing seems certain: trade relations with the Roman
Empire represent the thread along which the rich "classic" morphology
of Gandhara culture was laid out. The northwest region and eastern
Afghanistan — that is, the area where the "school" of Gandhara
flourished — were, because of their geographic nature and political circumstances, extremely important crossroads through which passed the
road that linked Bactria to Punjab and hence to India. Thus Kushan
coins, partially modeled on their Roman counterparts, with their use of
gold (compared to the exclusive use of silver in the coinage of the Parthian empire), demonstrate how Kushan India looked toward the Mediterranean more than toward Iran for its commercial exchanges.

Put another way, we must exclude the interpretation that tends to
explain Gandhara classicism solely by looking back to Graeco-Bactrian
precedents — an interpretation, we should say, that no longer commands
serious support. An examination of the iconographies disproves this
connection, while at the same time it reveals that many can be traced
directly to precedents in the Roman period. On the other hand, it seems
that trade cannot be considered a sufficient explanation for this
phenomenon of cultural influences. In fact, we could well ask why there
was this Hellenization on the frontier areas of India — but no "Indianiza-
tion" on the Mediterranean coasts. From this point of view, we may
accept that Graeco-Bactrian and Scytho-Parthian Hellenism played some
part in the development of Gandhara classicism. Two significant facts still
remain to be considered. The art of Gandhara, compared with the pre-

ceding Hellenized works in this area, is much richer in quality and quantity (if we leave aside the Bactrian coinage and the few "Greek" works of Ai Khanum). Moreover, its contents are new, and with this we come to the crux of the issue: the art of Gandhara is distinguished by its Buddhist subject matter.

"Graeco-Buddhist" or "Romano-Buddhist" art? These two terms reflect two different schematic formulations of the same problem. For this reason, we prefer to remain with the term "Gandhara art," even knowing that this art flourished in an area much larger than ancient Gandhara and that the presence of the Mediterranean elements is crucial. But the real problem is not that of distinguishing the Greek or Roman, or even "classical" or "Hellenistic" influences in the art of Gandhara, although this task is certainly a preliminary necessity. Rather the problem is one of understanding the factors and causes within the social structure of Gandhara that allowed trade relations to determine another phenomenon: the partial cultural "subjection" of one region by another. For this goal, the examination of the iconography is most useful.

43–44. Mathura: This column from a stupa railing is 28 inches high and dates to the second century A.D. Like the rest of the art from Mathura, it is made from the reddish sandstone from Sikri. On one side (left) is the standing, haloed Buddha making the gesture of *abhaya mudra* ("have no fear"); on the other side are large lotus flowers. (Paris: Guimet Museum)

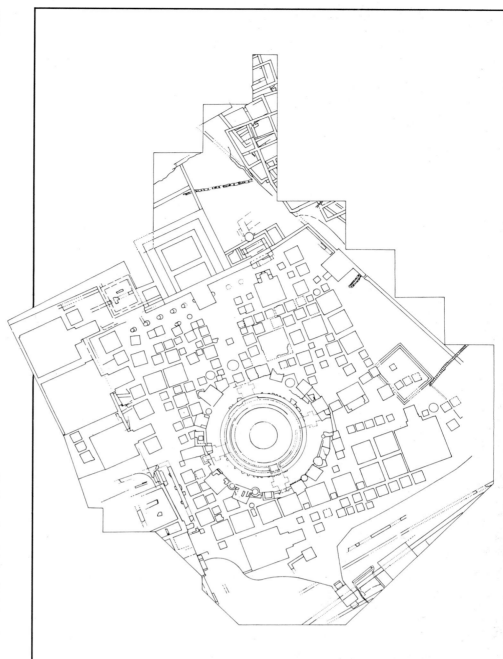

A RELIQUARY OFFERING AT TAXILA

Anno 136, on the 15. day of the first month Ashadha, on this day were established relics of the Lord by Urasaka, of the Imtavhria boys, the Bactrian, the resident of the town of Noacha. By him these relics of the Lord were established in his own bodhisattva chapel, in the Dharmarajika compound of Takshasila, for the bestowal of health on the Great King, the King of Kings, the Son of Heaven, the Khushana, in honor of all Buddhas, in honor of the Pratyekabuddhas, in honor of the Arhats, in honor of all beings, in honor of mother and father, in honor of friends, ministers, kinsmen, and blood-relations, for the bestowal of health upon himself.

May this thy right munificence lead to Nirvana.

Inscription on a Silver Scroll (Corpus Inscriptionum Indicarum II, 1:XXVII)

The Gandhara schist reliefs, found in surprisingly large quantities in the region extending from Taxila to Swat and to Kapisa, had practically one use: decoration for the stupas. These stupas were either isolated structures, or located in the interior of monastic complexes; in this latter situation, they often were surrounded by small stupas that ended up being crowded together and set one against the other without even the suggestion of pattern. The form of the characteristic Gandhara stupa, by the way, was not basically unlike that of the earlier stupas. Some of the large Gandhara stupas are still in a good state of preservation in the mountains of the Northwest Frontier (Pakistan) and in Afghanistan. Particularly worthy of mention are the ones at Shankardar, Abhasahebchina, Barikot, and Tokardara in the Swat region; those at Daruntah near Jalalabad, at Shevaki (Illustration 27), and Guldara (Illustration 26) near Kabul. Others existed until a few decades ago, and still others have been discovered during recent archaeological expeditions; of the latter we might mention the stupa at Butkara (Illustration 28) in the Swat region, the one known as Dharmarajika at Taxila, and finally the stupa at Tepe Sardar, near Ghazni (Afghanistan).

The Architecture and Sculpture of Gandhara

The Great Stupa at Butkara merits particular consideration. In the center of a sacred area that underwent long and complex building changes, the stupa itself reveals various construction phases, each incorporated into the succeeding one, so that the entire history of this monument can now be clearly "read." The first phase has been attributed to the third century B.C., a date that seems confirmed by the epigraphic evidence; that would allow the Butkara stupa to qualify for the name "Dharmarajika," the name given to Asoka's foundations. The second phase, datable between the end of the second and the beginning of the first century B.C., with its cylindrical base, its niches and moldings, was an interesting precedent of the Gandhara type of stupa. This type was fully realized in the stupa's third phase (the end of the first century B.C. to the beginning of the first century A.D.) and was taken up again in the fourth phase, in the "high" Kushan period. By that time, the stupa consisted of two elements set one on the other, the lower of which (a diameter of some 57 feet) had a base and a molded cornice. Built with blocks of soapstone, this stupa had sixteen niches or panels, later modified, that must have contained reliefs, of which only a few have survived; behind the panels were sixteen reliquaries, which yielded 107 coins. The stupa seems to have collapsed in the seventh century A.D., but religious life was taken up again with the construction of a new stupa, this time set directly over the preceding one.

Butkara's minor monuments either are now lacking decorative details of any appreciable quantity or else have a type of decoration without any organic connection with the architecture because they were taken from decorative elements from earlier destroyed edifices. Nevertheless, among

45.   Mathura: A *yakshi* figure that formed the corbel of a *torana;* it is 20 inches high and dated to the second century A.D. Although the figure decorated the portal of a Jain stupa, it reveals no characteristics of any particular religion. The dynamic sense of the figure is somewhat like that of the *yakshi* at Sanchi (Illus.19); but the Mathura artist repeated the figure completely on the other side of the corbel (the two parts have been separated but are both kept in the same museum), rather than, as at Sanchi, represent the figure in the round. The material is the same reddish sandstone associated with all Mathura works. (London: Victoria and Albert Museum)

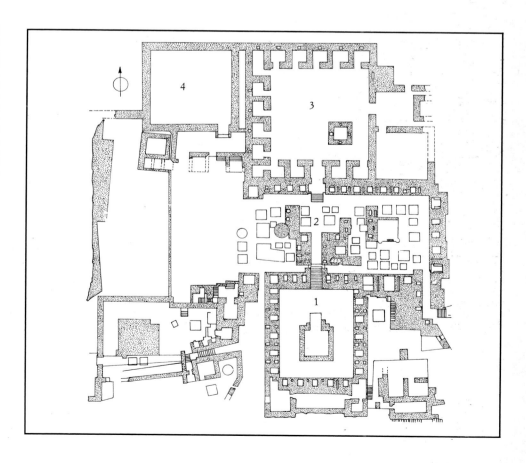

Takhti-i Bahi; Plan of the monastery
1.   *Courtyard with chapels and main stupa*
2.   *Courtyard with chapels and votive stupas*
3.   *Courtyards with monastic cells*
4.   *Assembly hall*

them there stand out some stupas chronologically linked with the third phase of the Great Stupa. Stupa 17, the best preserved of this group, has two quadrangular levels; the lower one has walls divided by Corinthian half-columns, with pilasters on the corners; the upper cornice is made up of fillets and various moldings, as well as a series of lion heads that alternate with eagles, cupids, lotus flowers, etc. Our ability to date, with some degree of certitude, such a monument to the outset of the Christian era, is a most useful fact in itself, for the art of Gandhara needs as many dates and excavation sites as possible if its isolated works are to be placed in context.

Another well-preserved stupa, this time with figurative decoration, is the one at Sikri (north of Mardan, Pakistan). This monument is enormously important because it documents the position of the reliefs (although these are now in the Lahore Museum) in their architectural context. However, its date is obscure, the proposals being extremely divergent, ranging from those that would make it one of the oldest documents of Gandhara art, to those that place it in the third to fourth centuries A.D. In my opinion, the Sikri stupa is definitely later than Stupa 17, which makes it no earlier than the first century A.D. As for the monastic complexes of the Gandhara period, one at least should be mentioned — that of Takht-i Bahi, in Pakistan. Its central nucleus consisted of three courts: the lowest is surrounded by the monks' cells; the middle one was crowded with stupas and surrounded by chapels; and the upper one was marked off by a row of chapels on its four sides while in the center was a stupa, with a stairway on its front side.

A comprehensive examination of the monumental complexes of Gandhara would reveal a rather obvious evolution of the structural plans that may be summarized as follows. At first a group of stupas and other small monuments (pillars, chapels) develops around a large isolated stupa, the smaller structures being distributed with regularity; later the minor monuments, of a votive nature, become denser and their construction no longer follows a set plan but seems quite casual: the stupas are erected wherever there is a bit of available space, and no attempt is made to avoid hiding portions of preceding stupas. Often this multiplication of votive edifices in a restricted space corresponds to a lowering of the qualitative level of the buildings, at least from a technical point of view. This suggests that the ability to initate buildings (even if at a modest level) was spreading among larger and larger groups in society, a phenomenon that easily conforms with an increase in trade and with the merchant class's substantial independence from the state authority. The multiplication of stupas in a limited area and the resultant loss of a coherently unified vision of the sacred area was also accompanied by a practice, begun long before but now becoming exclusive: the use of stucco instead of schist for the decorative sculptures.

The first examples of Gandhara stucco work — among which are those found at Sirkap (Taxila) — are certainly contemporary with the schist reliefs, and yet the latter end up being entirely replaced by stucco for sculpture. This substitution seems to have been finally realized by some time in the fourth century A.D. The use of stucco is not, *per se,* proof of the existence of new economic conditions, because it can legitimately be attributed to the non-availability of other suitable material in certain areas. Such might be the case, for example, for certain works, not yet precisely datable, in stucco or unfired clay, in Afghanistan, especially at Surkh Kotal, as well as at Hadda (Illustrations 32–33), Tepe Marandjan, etc.; after all, the use of limestone along with schist at Hadda shows an adaptation to the possibilities offered by the territory. The use of stucco (or of other moldable material, such as unfired clay) becomes, however, a significant development when it means the mechanical reproduction of the entire decoration or of part of the same. In any case, compared to stone, stucco permits much more rapid execution, and is consequently much less wasteful in terms of material and labor. Stucco is also a much more rapid and less expensive means of making votive works; stone must be carefully connected to the masonry, whereas stucco decoration covers such masonry in such a way as even to cover up possible flaws.

46. **Bezwada: Below: A figure of Buddha, from Andhra Pradesh; it stands 20 inches high and is dated to the sixth century A.D. (Boston: Museum of Fine Arts, gift of the Madras Government Museum)**

47. **Sarnath: Opposite: A head of Buddha; it is 8 inches high and dates from the fifth or sixth century A.D. (New Delhi: National Museum)**

The stylistic and iconographic elements of the bronze figure (below) are typical of the art of the Gupta period, and a comparison with the Sarnath stone head is revealing. An element of "frozen" expression in the face and the hand gesture, as well as the simplified surfaces that are poorly connected, suggest a later date for the Bezwada statue than for the head. Besides the characteristic signs of Buddha — such as the whorl of hair between the eyebrows (urna), the protuberance on the head (ushnisha), the elongated ear lobes, and the folds in the throat — the two figures can also be understood as carrying on a tradition of portraying Buddha as described in the Arthaviniscaya: ". . . the limbs round, pure, regular . . . the hips round, developed, straight, a thin belly, a deep navel . . . the face not too long . . . a prominent nose, large and long eyes . . . a broad and full chest. . . ."

succession and through real moral actions. And around this Buddha there gravitates a whole series of persons, differentiated by categories (monks, *brahmans,* "nobles," gods, etc.), all participants in the edifying event, personages in a dramatic action that is made to occur really in a precise, unrepeatable moment. This explains the lack of interest displayed by Gandhara toward the *jatakas,* events in the former incarnations of Buddha: these might be edifying, but the episodes were too slightly connected to an ideal path that leads to the total realization of the individual Buddha: this could be more easily followed in the narration of the "historical" episodes of the life of Buddha himself.

In a succeeding stage of Gandhara relief sculpture, some isolated scenes of particular symbolic value took on a preeminent character, especially those that represented exceptional moments in Buddha's "career." A special position of honor was occupied by the Great Miracle of Shravasti, in which Buddha became the moment of synthesis of the universe, the center from which radiated the infinite Buddhas in all directions, the source of fire and water. The Buddha-hero vanishes through the process of deification in these figures loaded with symbols; the man Siddhartha, the performer of moral actions, disappears, leaving in his place an epiphany; the action itself becomes timeless, repeatable, and in fact repeated every moment. Well-known examples of the two moments of the Shravasti miracle are the great stelae at Paitava and at Shotorak (Kapisa), and those from northwestern India (most of which are now in the Peshawar and Lahore museums).

With the transition to stucco work, we witness a further reduction of the Gandhara iconographic repertory. Now only the image of Buddha or of the Bodhisattvas (Illustration 32), seated or standing, occupy the walls of stupas (at Taxila, Butkara, Hadda, and elsewhere); these figures are repeated again and again. The gestures of the hands are particularly conventionalized and have taken on a precise meaning; they are *mudra* (literally, "seals"), which summarize the entire scene in which the sole interest lies in the attitude of the Enlightened One: *abhaya mudra,* the invitation to have no fear; *dhyana mudra,* meditation; *bhumisparsa mudra,* the call to the Earth to testify to the Enlightenment; *dharmacakra mudra,* making the wheel to turn — that is, preaching. The scenes — when they are preserved, as are some of the stucco decorations at Hadda — were created with a view toward ornamentation, often reduced to essential elements and without those surroundings of landscape and minor characters that decorate the stone-carved reliefs. In addition to the images of Buddha that decorate the stupas, however, there appear gigantic figures, also in stucco, inside the chapels or under the porticos of large monastic complexes.

49–50: Mirpur Khas: These decorative bricks are from the stupa at Mirpur Khas in Sind (Pakistan); the upper (Illus. 49) shows a wild cat; the lower (Illus. 50) an abstract, maze-like design. They date from the fifth century A.D. The Graeco-Roman influence in this part of ancient India has yet to be fully studied, but such objects as these, together with objects from Rajasthan, provide interesting subjects. (Bombay: Prince of Wales Museum of Western India)

Art Under the Kushans: Mathura School and Elsewhere

It should be understood that these aspects of Gandhara iconography are not to be viewed as rigidly successive phases; they were probably also contemporary aspects, their divergencies due at least partially to different persons' commissioning the works. Thus, one of the characteristic features of the art of the Kushan period — both that of the Gandhara region and that centered at Mathura to the south (in Uttar Pradesh) — was the existence of a "dynamic" art parallel to Buddhist art. This was work with its own unmistakable characteristics, not only formal but also

51–52:　　　Ajanta: Over the winding bed of the Waghora River, a small tributary of the Tapti, sixty miles northeast of Aurangabad, in western India, extends a rocky hill, some 260 feet high. Cut out of its sides along a stretch of 540 yards are some thirty caves (including the unfinished ones). Five of them (9, 10, 19, 26, 29) are chaitya-halls; the others were used as monasteries. The oldest of the caves are numbers 8, 9, 10, 12, 13, and 15A; after the creation of this first group, there was about a four-century interval until, in the fifth century A.D., most of the rest of the Ajanta caves were cut out. Today they are world famous, especially for their magnificent paintings. Yet despite the grandeur of the complex, it was "discovered" only in 1819 by some of the officers of the British army in Madras. One of them, a certain John Smith, cut his signature into the rock in cave 10. The first report on the Ajanta caves was sent to the Royal Asiatic Society by Lieutenant J. E. Alexander, who visited the site in 1824.

contextual. We cannot get involved in the problems of its style and rich iconography here; we are interested, rather, in seeing if this dynastic art was a uniform phenomenon or whether it underwent an evolution over the course of time also from the point of view of its function in India and the northwestern region.

The oldest monument to be considered from this viewpoint is the "palatial" edifice at Khalchayan, in Transoxiana (southern Uzbekistan), brought to light in 1959–63 by the Soviet archaeologist, G. A. Pugachenkova. This was a structure with a rectangular plan, whose largest chamber, on the front, was a hexastyle portico, or loggia; this led through three passageways to an elongated central hall; this then led to a room with two columns; three rooms around this were connected with each other and with the front loggia by means of corridors, with the exception of one, which seemed to have access only to the outside. The stone bases of the wooden columns on the front are still preserved; their form, plus an examination of the complex of the architectural and decorative elements, allow us to link Khalchayan with Ai Khanum. This connection becomes more legitimate when extended to the sculptured decoration of the loggia and the central hall, whose remaining fragments (Illustrations 34–35) are the most important aspect of the excavation and can be compared to the clay and stucco heads found in the *temple à redans* at Ai Khanum. These clay fragments from Khalchayan, with their strong Hellenistic connotations, have invited comparison to certain divinities either of classical or of indirect classical inspiration (Athena, Apollo, satyrs, etc.); the suggested reconstruction of the decorative complex reminds one more of Gandhara taste than of that of the other early medieval work from Soviet central Asia. Moreover, one of the heads with a distinctive skull form has been identified as an early Kushan leader, Heraos, who lived a little before the beginning of the Christian era, or a member of his family. (The identification depends on portraits of Heraos on coins.) Thus the Khalchayan sculptures are placed in an intermediate phase between the older Graeco-Bactrian art and that of the Kushan period; but we must also keep in mind that this type of work, with its strong Hellenistic echoes, must have undergone a long development.

Well to the south of Khalchayan, at Ghazni (Afghanistan), in the lower strata of the Buddhist sanctuary of Tepe Sardar, some fragments of terra-cotta sculptures have been brought to light. Although in the same artistic tradition (but certainly more recent) as the Khalchayan works, they have been found in association with others that would appear to be of a later age (Illustration 36); however, before this problem can be resolved, the Tepe Sardar site must yield more finds.

It does seem, though, that the decorative complex at Tepe Sardar belonged to real cult edifices, and is thus to be connected with other works from Uzbekistan — in particular, ones from Dal'verzin Tepe, which have been dated to the second century A.D. The Khalchayan edifice, meanwhile, has the character of a palace, and the figures that decorate it cannot be considered cult images, even if they were placed there to glorify the reigning dynasty.

The sanctuary of Surkh Kotal in the southern part of Bactria (Afghanistan), which stands on a hill with an imposing brick and stone staircase, presents quite different problems. The type of cult practiced there has not yet been identified, but it was certainly one connected to the dynasty; we cannot exclude the hypothesis that the term "fire worship," so widely used in the scholarly literature on Surkh Kotal, is consistent with the "dynastic" character of the sanctuary (Illustration 39). The figures found at Surkh Kotal link this site with the Kushan sanctuary, also of a dynastic nature, at May, near Mathura, the eastern capital of the empire (Illustration 42). At both sites we find princely figures, standing or seated and always rigidly frontal, who even in their dress reveal their foreignness to Indian artistic culture and the Buddhist tradition. The same figures are to be found in the Kushan coins and they appear only rarely, as donors (Illustration 40) and always in a subordinate position, in some Gandhara Buddhist reliefs, especially at Kapisa (Begram, Shotorak, etc.). There thus takes place in Kushan India a clear-cut break between the court milieu and the rest of society.

In fact, despite some trends toward a revival of the imperial Mauryan ideology, which must have been sympathetic to a Kushan king with the ambitions of Kanishka, the position of the king had by this time changed greatly. The merchant class, with its initiative and firmly acquired economic power, elaborated an ideology of its own, profiting from the Hellenistic tradition it inherited from the Bactrian experience. With the rise of Kushan power, the Hellenized elite probably gave up its military power but kept all the economic strength in its hands. The sovereign no longer stood for the entire state, nor was he any more a personification of the good of the community. The king, the dynasty, due in part to their "barbarian" extraction, found themselves to some extent set above a world that had culturally pushed them to one side. The king needed to be deified to justify his power by strengthening those features that distinguished him from his subjects — features such as ethnic characteristics and supernatural magic powers, as various sources (among them, Al-Beruni) tell us. In Gandhara — and Mathura as well — Buddha could no longer be identified with this new type of sovereign; on the contrary, he was in a certain sense his antagonist. It was this ideological opposition

53. Ajanta: This is one of the two *yaksha* figures that flank the "skylight" on the facade of Cave 19. The reliefs carved in the niches, left, represent isolated images of Buddha; in the bottom niche is Buddha between two Bodhisattvas. The little heads set in the horseshoe-shaped arches along the base are characteristic of the period, too. Cave 19, which is a small chaitya-hall of elegant proportions, is rich in its decoration, both paintings and sculptures.

54–55.   Ajanta: These are two views of the
interior of Cave 19. Above: The front of the
stupa (itself cut out of the rock) has a large
figure of Buddha making the gesture that in-
vites the faithful to have no fear *(abhaya
mudra)*. Opposite: The capitals have a central
panel with an image of Buddha, while the jutting corbels are decorated with elephants,
fantastic animals, flying couples, ascetics, and
musicians.

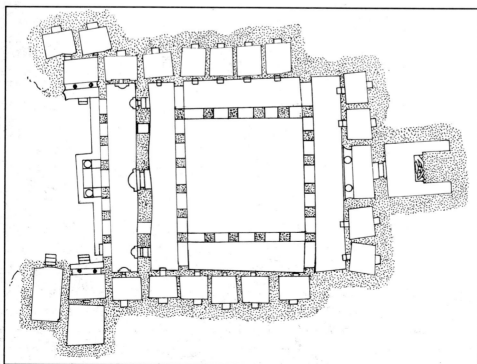

*Ajanta: Plan of Cave 1, an example of the Ajanta caves
used as monasteries (as opposed to those like Cave 19
used as chaitya-halls).*

that justified both the overt non-Indian images of the rulers and the very rise of the anthropomorphic representation of Buddha.

This isolation of dynastic art under the Kushans — hardly diluted by the presence of stylistically "intermediate" works, especially in Kapisa — also took place at Mathura, one of the most important artistic centers in Kushan India. Yet at Mathura, the dynastic-type images (Illustration 42) adapted themselves in a certain sense to their immediate environment, exalting the very characteristics that must have belonged to their northern prototypes. It has been claimed that we cannot assume any direct relationship for the images of Kushan India and those of the Parthian kings and Sassanian emperors of Iran; we are to assume, rather, a common descent of prototypes belonging to a particular type of nomadic culture. Thus it becomes interesting to note that Iranian works developed just that "baroque" exuberance (as seen in the drapery, for instance) that Mathura — perhaps even more than Gandhara — suppressed to the advantage of more rigorous but no less expressive vol-

56.   Ajanta: Another detail from the interior of Cave 19. The Buddhas in the upper panels are portrayed in the attitudes of (left) the first sermon *(dharmackra mudra)* and (right) of charity *(varada mudra)*.

This youthful form, whose bosom's swelling
  charms
By the bark's knotted tissue are concealed,
Like some fair bud close folded in its sheath,
Gives not to view the blooming of its beauty.
But what am I saying? In real truth, this bark-
  dress,
Though ill-suited to her figure, sets it off like an
  ornament.
The lotus with the Saivala entwined
Is not a whit less brilliant: dusky spots
Heighten the luster of the cold-rayed moon:
This lovely maiden in her dress of bark
Seems all the lovelier. E'en the meanest grab
Gives to true beauty fresh attractiveness.

KALIDASA: *Sakoontala* Act I

umetric effects. The remains of Mathura are distributed uninterruptedly from the Maurya to the Islamic period, through the Shunga, the Kshatrapa-Shaka, and Kushan periods. This fact is amply documented by the excavations (carried out since 1936) in the numerous hills scattered in the countryside around Mathura. These have yielded a great number of sculptures and fragments made of red sandstone from Sikri, typical of the Mathura "school," works that continue to be made with the same material at least into the Gupta age.

From the stylistic point of view, the contrast with Gandhara is generally evident. Gandhara art saw the figure immersed in a space that is the same space the spectator moves in. (Consider, for instance, those continuous running reliefs in which only a row of small columns serves as a kind of screen for the scene.) In the art of Mathura, the space was a limited, closed volume, whose form and compactness were reproduced in the different elements that go to make up the scene. This latter treatment of space was most consonant with the artistic tradition of India, the one which India would develop coherently (Illustrations 43–44).

But this should not start us thinking of Gandhara and Mathura as two worlds isolated from each other; in fact, we see in the one "school" reflections of the stylistic modes of the other. Moreover, at least one Gandhara sculpture was found at Mathura (a female figure, perhaps a donor, now in the Mathura Archaeological Museum), while red sandstone (Sikri variety) sculptures, most certainly executed at Mathura during the Kushan age, have been found at Taxila, Charsada, and Butkara (Illustration 41). But the fact remains that the art of Gandhara — for all its Buddhist-Indian subject matter — remained apart from the mainstream. It was the art centered at Mathura during the early centuries of our era that drew upon and then fed back into the true sources of Indian art.

India Under the Guptas: Moving Toward Feudalism

The developments we have been observing under the Kushans, both from a political as well as an artistic point of view, represent an India extremely receptive to outside influences. We have seen, moreover, how this ability to receive had characterized India since the Maurya epoch, although we cannot fail to have observed its converse — that India never lacked the capacity for reworking foreign models into new forms. But there is no denying that some Western scholars have attached a perhaps excessive weight to the cultural contributions from foreigners — above all, to those of the Graeco-Roman world, inevitably triggering a reaction on the part of Indian scholars. With few exceptions, the latter evince only meager interest in such foreign "imports" as Gandhara art. (It is certainly no accident that the bibliography of this art is made up almost entirely of works written by Westerners.) This is understandable, but at the same time deplorable, for certain artistic phenomena of ancient India have an equally pressing need to be contemplated by eyes different from those traditionally focused on them. No less understandable is the satisfaction with which Indian scholars see in Gupta art — India's own "classic" art — the conquest of full cultural independence, or in other words, the "reaffirmation of India's tradition." The classical quality of the Gupta period is at the same time recognized in other aspects of Indian society of the time, from the political to the economic to the literary.

Territorial unity, prosperity, the flourishing of Sanskrit literature — these are only some of the aspects that never fail to evoke excitement when Indians view their Gupta period. Here is how a widely used (in its thirtieth edition) history text, designed for Indian university students, presents the beginning of the dynasty: ". . . the rise of the Guptas marks a transition from darkness to light, from an unsettled, anarchical state of things to well-ordered progress and civilization. Almost the whole of northern India was unified under a strong enlightened rule. The foreign rulers, the Parthians and Kushans and other non-Aryan dynasties were

rooted out . . . in short, free from foreign domination, the country felt a new pulsation of life and displayed remarkable activity in science, art, and literature. Hence the Gupta period has been aptly described as the Golden Age of northern India." (Only at first might it seem odd that the same assessment of the Gupta period had also been presented by the British "scholar-administrators" who considered it a prefiguration of the British Raj.) We certainly will not try to pronounce a final judgment on the Gupta period or any other period of Indian history. But we shall endeavor to determine whether the "classical" quality of Gupta art — generally accepted on all sides — is always a positive aspect or whether it does not at times represent an artificial arresting of tendencies that Indian culture had shown earlier and was later to take up with success.

The origin of the Gupta family is by no means clear. The fact that they were not of royal strain is more than probable, in view of the importance that their own coins attach to the marriage of the first sovereign of the dynasty, Chandra Gupta I, to Kumaradevi, a princess of the Lichchhavi tribe — a tribe, by the way, known from centuries earlier, when it was defeated by Ajatashatru, a ruler in Magadha. But if Chandra Gupta (and do not confuse this sovereign with the Mauryan of the same name) sought in marriage aristocratic backing and a consolidation of his power, he must certainly have obtained his power in some other way, since he succeeded in advancing Magadha once again as the leading political and territorial power of India. The theory that the Guptas — before Chandra Gupta I ascended the throne about A.D. 320 — were no more than a family of wealthy landowners should be seen in the light of what the term "landowner" might have meant in India at that time, when the economic power appears to have been primarily in the hands of guilds.

The dynastic history of the Guptas reveals a fairly rapid extension of their dominions from the original nucleus of Magadha along the Ganges into the eastern part (Uttar Pradesh) under the reign of Chandra Gupta I. This spread of Gupta power was sustained by his son and successor, Samudra Gupta (A.D. 335–375), who conquered all the most fertile and populous regions of northern India between the Brahmaputra and the Yamuna rivers, the Himalayas, and the Narmada River. Scholar, poet, musician, and warrior, Samudra Gupta appears to have embodied all the qualities of a refined epoch, and his reign sustained what was probably the most flourishing period of the Gupta dynasty. But the greatest territorial expansion was reached by his successor, Chandra Gupta II (375–415), known by the title Vikramaditya. (Still obscure is another son of Samudra, Rama Gupta, who is thought to have been the legitimate heir but who was quickly unseated and put to death by Chandra Gupta.) A contemporary of the great poet Kalidasa and of the Chinese pilgrim Fa-Hsien, who visited his kingdom, Chandra Gupta II added to the empire inherited from his father the western regions (Malwa, Gujarat, Kathiawar), taking them away from the Shakas. Many other territories, from the Indus to south of the Godavari River, in addition to Nepal and Assam (Kamarupa) in the north were tributaries of the Guptas.

The decline of the empire began with Kumara Gupta (circa A.D. 415–454) under the impetus of external forces: the invasions of the Huns, a tribe from central Asia, who also made things extremely difficult for his successor, Skanda Gupta (circa 454–467). Little by little, the Gupta dynasty lost its territories until it had ceased to be a power of any importance. This was in the early decades of the sixth century A.D. But long before this, it was evident that the domestic policies of the Guptas had succeeded only superficially in restoring the centralized system that the Mauryas had set up. In reality there had been a definite administrative decentralizing. The Gupta sovereigns, sitting in Pataliputra, represented the supreme power; but in practice, a large portion of this power was delegated to the governors of the provinces and to the administrators of the various districts. At the same time, the villages saw an affirmation of their autonomy as conducted by councils of their more elderly inhabitants. And finally, although the authority of the sovereign remained intact on questions concerning common policies, the exercise of power took

57. Ajanta: These are details from the painted pillars of Cave 17, one of the Ajanta caves with the most paintings. An inscription engraved on the outside wall of this monastery-cave informs us that the cave was initiated by a feudatory of King Vakataka Harisena; the cave is thus contemporaneous with Cave 16 (also a monastery-cave), dedicated by Varahadeva, Harisena's chief minister. The paintings are dated to the last quarter of the fifth century A.D.; such pillar decoration was typical of the Gupta age.

THE KING LONGS TO BE WITH SAKOONTALA

Beautiful! there is something charming even in
  her repulse.
Where'er the bee his eager onset plies,
Now here, now there, she darts her kindling
  eyes:
What love hath yet to teach, fear teaches now,
The furtive glances and the frowning brow.
Ah happy bee! how boldly dost thou try
To steal the lustre from her sparkling eye;
And in thy circling movements hover near,
To murmur tender secrets in her ear;
Or, as she coyly waves her hand, to sip
Voluptuous nectar from her lower lip!
While rising doubts my heart's fond hopes de-
  stroy,
Thou dost the fulness of her charms enjoy.

                    KALIDASA: *Sakoontala* Act I

**58–59.   Ajanta: These are details from the
paintings in Cave 17, and are dated to the last
quarter of the fifth century A.D.**

place in a special form of collaboration between the state officials and the city "bourgeoisie," (as has been pointed out by the Indian scholar, Buddha Prakash). A great many documents illustrate this state of affairs. Not the least interesting of them is the passage from the *Mrichchha-Katika*, a drama of the fourth–fifth century A.D., in which the banker sits in the court of justice alongside the judge. The position of importance assigned to representatives of the guilds (bankers, merchants, etc.) on a level with the officials of the administration is explained by the need for direct control of the productive agricultural forces, which would guarantee the utilization of surpluses to the advantage of that "bourgeoisie" whose corporative organizations in some instances could even mint money.

The Gupta dynasty therefore represented a guarantee of law and order that was particularly useful in assuring the systematic exploitation of the peasants by the bankers and merchants who, after the grave crisis of the Roman empire in the third century A.D., could once again count on extensive exchanges with the West. At the same time, the bankers and merchants backed up the dynasty economically. All this shows how greatly the economic and political realities of the Gupta period differed from those of the Mauryan period, even though some of the propagandistic themes of the latter were now once more pressed into use. During the decisive years that witnessed the progressive consolidation of Gupta domination in India, another social class was coming to the fore, running counter to that of the merchants; this latter group may be seen as the urban "bourgeoisie" that enjoyed an alliance with the state power, while the new group was the landowner class, which tended de facto to break away from the central power. This gave rise to the so-called feudalism of India, a subject that still remains to be studied in the light of the particular forms that "ownership" of land took on in the period.

The interests of the traditional merchant class that handled wide-ranging transactions had no doubt received an initial blow at the time of the crisis of the Roman Empire in the third century A.D., and the rise of the Gupta dynasty can be explained precisely by a resumption of these transactions. The expeditions of the Huns, the decreased availability of western markets, the growing vigor and initiative in trade toward the east and toward the south — the area of the Coromandel ports — during the reign of the first Pallavas (the people who were to become a power in southern India after the decline of the Guptas); all these were elements that may have made it necessary for northern India to recast the nature of its trade. The expedition of Samudra Gupta toward the south may well have been a bid to counter the irksome competition of the Pallavas. An examination of the paleographic phenomena has also led to the conclusion that there must have been close, steady contact and regular maritime communication between the Coromandel region and its overseas territories to the east and south (namely, Ceylon; now Sri Lanka) beginning about the year A.D. 300.

The circulation of money was to reach particularly high levels during the Gupta period; the bankers obviously played an important role in this, but the monastic Buddhist community itself carried on banking operations and lent money for interest. Nevertheless, the concession of lands became an ever more coveted privilege, albeit in theory ownership did not actually pass from one person to another. This was particularly true at a time when the difficulty of carrying on trade over large distances rendered the availability of cash less necessary. On the whole, one can see a more marked tendency on the part of the Brahmans to tie themselves to the land, while the Buddhist community, traditionally linked to the "bourgeoisie" of the cities, preferred to devote itself to business and financial enterprises. This may also have stemmed from the fact that *brahman* orthodoxy made it virtually impossible for the upper castes to leave Indian territory, to make contact with "impure" foreigners, or to run the risk of not being able to abide by caste rules.

The granting of land to Brahmans and officials, when it became widespread, ended by representing a genuine breaking away of vast areas from the central authority. We are left with the impression, however, that the juridical control of the land remained the traditional one, so that it

60.   Ajanta: This detail of a painting from Cave 17 is part of the *Vessantara-jataka* painted on the left wall of the central chamber. It is dated to the last quarter of the fifth century A.D.

Following pages:
61.   Ajanta: A detail of a painting in Cave 17, dated to the last quarter of the fifth century A.D. The painting depicts Buddha's sermon. In the center (not included here) Buddha sits with his hands in the gesture of preaching. What we see here is one of the groups of worshipers, formed of monks and nobles, listening to the Master's words.

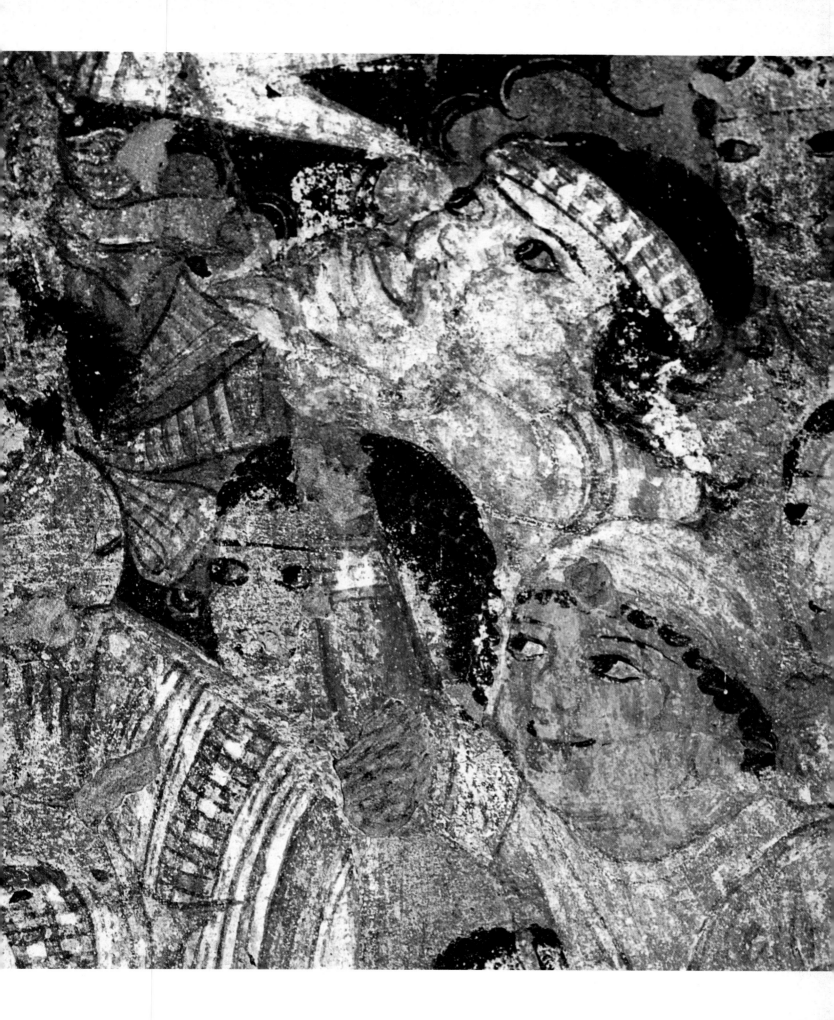

was not easy to come by large land holdings, not even when the granting of land was of a hereditary nature. In a broad sense, therefore, the "proprietors" of land continued to be administrative officials, often at odds with the central authority and ready to set up a new ruler whenever the pressure from this authority no longer seemed tolerable.

Religious Life and Art Under the Guptas

The Guptas were at one and the same time protectors of Hinduism, Buddhism, and Jainism. Leaving aside the last-mentioned group, whose ascendancy was in practice confined to the merchant classes of western India, Hinduism and Buddhism were evolving toward an ever greater

62.   Ajanta: This is part of the facade of Cave 1, the only monastery-cave at Ajanta that has its facade decorated with sculptures. (See its plan on page 98.) This work — now partly damaged — is dated to the last quarter of the fifth century A.D. The capital on the far right has its central panel decorated with an image of Buddha in the attitude of preaching. Note, too, the decorative richness of the various elements of the column and capital.

63. Ajanta: This is a close-up of a medallion carved on a pillar in Cave 23; it is dated to the last quarter of the fifth century A.D. It is worth comparing this with the decorative details of the facade of Cave 1 (Illus. 62). The ostensible subject here is a person opening the jaws of a crocodile. But the body of the monster has been turned into a web of intricate forms that have become purely decorative: the artist has lost all interest in the subject itself.

mitigation of the differences between the two religions and toward a stressing of the aspect the two religions shared. This may be summed up in "devotionalism" — a more personal sense of the relationship between the individual devotee and the divine. This aspect was essentially new, having belonged neither to Buddhist nor to Brahman orthodoxy, although it began to emerge several centuries before the Guptas. This tendency was also unquestionably present in the Gupta epoch, but it was not officially accepted by this dynasty, which attached primary importance to the establishment of a religious peace based on an equilibrium between the prevalently Buddhist and city-dwelling merchant class and the *brahmans,* who tended to be tied to the land.

The devotionalistic tendency with a strong vocation for syncretism, which was to develop freely later on and which could already be seen in the Gandhara of the Kushan age, is known in India as *bhakti,* a religious movement that affected especially Vishnuism and Buddhism and which

A SECOND-CENTURY BUDDHIST THINKER EXPOUNDS THE NATURE OF THINGS

Separate elementary form, taste, smell, touch, and sound are not found outside the four elements of Matter. And it is a fact that a cause of Matter apart from matter cannot be found.

Conception of matter in a form that is devoid of the cause of Matter becomes illogical. So for the fallacy of causelessness, the conception of matter, devoid of cause of Matter, is not proper.

If Matter as cause is imagined without any reference to Matter as an effect, then a cause becomes effect-less, but an effect-less cause cannot exist.

The conception of cause of Matter becomes improper both in cases of existence and non-existence of Matter.

In the absence of cause, a causeless Matter as effect is not possible. Therefore, no person with philosophical foresight should conceive of Matter as obstructed or unobstructed.

An effect is neither like the cause nor unlike the cause.

The non-existence of other so-called existing things — like feelings, consciousness, and such — may be proved by applying the same sort of logic.

The non-existence of other things like feeling may be proved like the non-existence of Matter, which has been proved through the medium of the Void.

Even it can be shown that the imaginings and other conceptions in the form of words that are done at the time of explaining all these things, to the students by the teachers, are also non-existent if judged in the light of the Void.

NAGARJUNA: *Madhyamaka Karika* IV

64.　Ajanta: A detail from a painting in Cave 1, dated to the last quarter of the fifth century A.D. It is from a scene of the *Mahajanaka-jataka*, in which Prince Mahajanaka announces his decision to abandon the world.

could perhaps be considered responsible for some of the less orthodox iconography of Gandhara art, particularly those images of a "dionysian" spirit. It has been argued that *bhakti* represented the ideological basis of India's "feudal" society: the exclusive devotion to a divinity — the total abandonment of oneself to it, entrusting oneself to its benevolence — corresponds to the loyalty demanded by a feudal lord of subjects. The Gupta sovereign found himself in a position of having to resist this by now irreversible tendency of Indian culture; he preferred to lean on the orthodoxies, although these were also pervaded by the new spirit. The iconography had once again become a telling symptom of the political will; this was particularly true of Buddhist iconography.

The Gupta period witnessed the triumph of the Mahayana ("Greater Vehicle") sect of Buddhism: simply put, what this branch of Buddhism offered was an easier path to liberation than the orthodox Buddhism of the Hinayana ("Lesser Vehicle") sect. The severe, laborious road that the faithful had to travel to achieve the condition of *arhat*, with its morality that conceded nothing to human weakness, no longer appealed as a possible ideal: that which a man cannot attain alone can be reached only through Buddha's benevolent concern for the suffering of all living beings. The rational commitment was replaced by an easier devotional impulse, within reach of all. The effects of a meritorious deed could be directed toward loved ones, to one's fellow men in general, to all men of noble feelings. Clearly surfacing in Buddhism at this point was the contradiction ever-present in Indian thought between the ethic determinism of *karma* and the potential for individual devotion, the latter finding its clearest expression in *bhakti*.

It should not be thought, however, that the passage from the Lesser to the Greater Vehicle is a phenomenon that can be placed in a precise moment in the history of India. "As a literary expression in some texts," the Italian authority Tucci has written, "and as a doctrinal expression of some theories and dogmas [the Mahayana] no doubt came after the canon of the Lesser Vehicle; but as a living, popular expression of the Buddhist experience, it is contemporary with it." The emergence of Mahayanic devotionalism on the level of official iconography, therefore, marked not the birth of the Greater Vehicle but rather its acceptance on the part of the classes wielding power. Precisely through its theoretical elaboration, these classes reserved for themselves the right to its most complete use, curbing the original innovating thrust of its popular origin. However, it should be admitted that it is not always easy to distinguish between Hinayanic and Mahayanic images; for example, it is still being debated whether the Buddhism mirrored in the art of Gandhara was Hinayana or Mahayana. In fact, the Buddhas of the Gupta age could have issued from either of these religious sources, if the inscriptions, some of them carved into images of Buddha (for example, those at Sarnath), did not provide obvious indications that the nature of Buddhism had changed. But beyond the distinction between Hinayana and Mahayana Buddhism, the iconography can demonstrate the role of various religious impulses in Indian society.

During the Gupta period, the image of the Enlightened One took on a numerical and hierarchical preeminence over all the other iconographies of Buddhism, a phenomenon we have already encountered in the contemporary works of the northwestern region. The two principal centers of the production of these images in the central region were Mathura and Sarnath. At Mathura it is understandable why we find a greater adherence to the figurative and iconographic conventions of the Kushan period, given the greater importance that Mathura itself had in those days. A celebrated image (now in the Nelson Gallery at Kansas City, Missouri) dated to the fifth century A.D., shows — in the words of Benjamin Rowland — "the massive and heavy proportions of the Kushan Buddha; the drapery has been reduced to a schematic convention of quilted ridges falling in repeated loops down the median line of the body, so that it appears as a nude seen through a network of cords." This Buddha is missing its head, but we can complete it in our mind by think-

65. Ajanta: A detail of a painting on the
east wall of Cave 1. We see, on the right,
Bodhisattva Avalokitesvara, one of the companions of Buddha.

66.   Ajanta: The facade of Cave 26, dating
from the second half of the fifth century A.D.
The facade of this chaitya-hall was damaged
due to the fall of the pillared veranda. However, the beauty of the sculpture may still be
appreciated: they are images of Buddha and
Bodhisattvas arranged in a composition of a
calm, rhythmical pattern.

67. Ajanta: An image of a Bodhisattva in Cave 26, dated to the second half of the fifth century A.D. The Bodhisattva, who is making the gesture of reassurance, has a rosary in his right hand and a flask in his left. The simplification of the body's volumes, so characteristic of Gupta art, reaches its extreme in such a work.

When a century and fifty-four years of Gupta rule had passed [A.D. 474], on the second day of Jyaistha [May–June], when the earth was under the protection of Kumara Gupta, this image of the master, which has no equal in merit, was executed for the cult at the request of Abhayamitra, a monk whose mind has been subdued by means of devotion. Through the acquisition of this religious merit may the multitude of animated beings, including parents and preceptors, obtain the desired passing from worldly existence.

Inscription on an image of the Buddha (Sarnath)

ing back on other images restored to us from the earth around Mathura: the perfect oval of the countenance, the hair frozen in a schematic array of snail-like curls, the eyes with their half-closed lids resembling petals of the lotus flower, the brows forming the vigorous profile of an arch. Such heads are perfect abstractions; we are no longer looking at the Buddha-hero engaged in, nor even capable of engaging in, human enterprises, but at the representation of a benevolent divinity, far from men in his essence, near mankind in his act of compassion.

Not dissimilar is the type of image characteristic of Sarnath, the place where Buddha proclaimed the Law for the first time. In the Buddhas of Sarnath, however, the process of abstraction was carried still further, and the monastic vestment no longer has even the conventional indication of the folds, but adheres perfectly to the youthful body of Siddhartha. Consider in particular what can be judged as one of the masterpieces of Indian art, the head of Buddha found at Sarnath (Illustrations 47, now in the National Museum of New Delhi). It represents a wise combination of abstraction and adherence to the reality of the body, to the human element; there is a rigorous discipline in the geometrical arrangement of the countenance, whose message only a few can grasp fully, but of which all can become aware by intuition, thus feeling that they are participating in a benign order. It has been rightly observed, however, that the Sarnath images of Buddha, universally recognized as the most typical products of Gupta art, are to be attributed — judging by epigraphic documentation — to a fairly late moment of the dynasty, about A.D. 475, whereas previously it was thought that the highest moment of the "school" had been reached at the time of Chandra Gupta II and Kumara Gupta I — that is, from A.D. 375 to 454. The two sovereigns mentioned in the Sarnath inscriptions, Kumara Gupta II (A.D. 474) and Buddha Gupta (A.D. 477) already bear witness to the complete decline of the empire. The "golden age" of Gupta art, therefore, can by no means be explained as coinciding with the political apogee of the empire. Rather, we might say that the Sarnath images, although of an exceptionally high quality, represent a phenomenon extremely limited in scope, a perhaps brief revival owing to a propagandistic commitment, justified in a city of the importance of Sarnath. It has also been observed that the works produced only a few miles from Sarnath, precisely at the time of Buddha Gupta (A.D. 478), whose name appears on one of the loveliest Buddhist stelae in the Sarnath Museum, are on a much lower level of quality. This is also the case with the Vaishnite pillar of Rajghat at the Bharat Kala Bhavan of Benares, which is in the same stylistic current as the Buddhas of Sarnath but lagging far behind in quality.

The Emergence of Hindu Art in Gupta India

Among the oldest works of sculpture of the Gupta period is the celebrated cave of Varaha (named after one of the avatars, or incarnations of Vishnu) at Udayagiri (Madhya Pradesh). Represented on the wall is Varaha — much larger than all the surrounding figures — with the head of a boar, trampling on the *naga* king (a snake deity) and lifting Prithvi, the personification of the Earth, with a tusk, drawing her up from the depths of the ocean. An inscription enables us to attribute this colossal relief to the time of Chandra Gupta II (circa A.D. 400). In addition to such works of an artificial nature, Gupta India also offered some that might be called "popular" works, like the terra-cotta sculptures of Ahicchatra (Uttar Pradesh). Fine examples of these include the splendid heads of Shiva and Parvati, and the reliefs with mythological scenes, generally attributed to the fifth century A.D. The use of clay in place of stone was unquestionably indicative of a different milieu, although we should not describe this difference in terms of religion alone.

68. Ajanta: This is a close-up of a sculpture in Cave 26, dated to the second half of the fifth century A.D. It shows Buddha in the traditional pose of *parinirvana* — dead, but eternally reigning. The figure is about 23 feet long and is shown as if sleeping; around him are men and gods, all quite small compared to the Enlightened One. This scene, so familiar in reliefs of the Kushan period — particularly in Gandhara — was often carved in such colossal dimensions, not only in India but in the other regions where Buddhism was adopted, from Afghanistan and central Asia to Ceylon.

69.   Sigiriya: This is a painting on the cliff-wall at Sigiriya, Ceylon; it is dated to the second half of the fifth century A.D. After Ceylon had been governed for about 27 years by a member of the Indian royalty from Madras, a Ceylonese leader called Dhatusena got rid of these foreigners and made himself lord of the island. That was in A.D. 460, but his reign was interrupted in 478 by a revolt led by his son Kassapa; he then ruled for 18 years, until Moggallana, another son of Dhatusena and the legitimate heir, took over the throne with the aid of Indian troops. The defeated Kassapa committed suicide. But during his reign he had left the traditional capital of Anuradhapura to settle in Sigiriya, a gigantic cliff that rose up some 200 yards over the surrounding plain; he there set about to turn this into an impregnable fortress. (Moggallana was to return to Anuradhapura, allowing Sigiriya to fall into neglect and oblivion.) But, as has been observed, in erecting his fortifications, Kassapa not only thought of his defensive needs but was also concerned to design the entire complex with a view toward the cosmic pattern and the myth of the holy mountain, Kailasa, home of the god Kuvera. Kassapa wanted to be identified with this god, and thus we see that behind the beauty of the paintings that enhanced the usurper's residence there was a clear attempt at absolute despotism. These paintings, although they reveal some similarities with painting on the Indian mainland, also have certain distinctive features.

Another aspect of Gupta art, still largely to be placed in its exact chronological position, is the output of western India, where a number of recent excavations have begun to confirm the fairly close relations linking this region with the northwest. Such relations had been hinted at by the terra-cottas of Mirpur Khas (Sind) (Illustrations 49–50: now to be seen at the Prince of Wales Museum of Western India in Bombay), which have recently been brought back to the attention of scholars as one of the most interesting manifestations of Gupta art. The antecedents of these contacts in the Kushan period have been further clarified by the excavations of Rang Mahal (Rajasthan). Of considerable importance for what it reveals of the Gupta period itself was the excavation at Devnimori, near Shamalaji (Gujarat), revealing a stupa and a monastery (of the fourth to fifth centuries A.D.), whose sculptural attributes were extremely similar to those of Mirpur Khas. Of exceptional interest at Mirpur Khas, as at Devnimori, are a number of fragments from the architectural decoration: for example, the capitals, which are clearly derived from the "Corinthian" prototypes of Gandhara but reinterpreted and reduced to

70.   Sigiriya: This painting from the cliff-wall of Sigiriya, like the one on the preceding pages, adorned the access gallery. It has been noted that the top of the cliff could have been reached more easily, and with less expense, without this gallery. But here, too, Kassapa's desire to shape the complex in the form of the sacred mountain Kailasa guided the architect. The female figures in these paintings are evidently heavenly spirits, and are shown as emerging from clouds.

71.   Northwest India: The head on the left is that of a Buddha and is in the Gandhara tradition; the head of the female on the right (about 5 inches high) shows more of the influence of Gupta art. They are both tentatively dated to the seventh century A.D., and may be compared to similar heads found elsewhere — in Ushkur, Kashmir, and at Fondukistan, Afghanistan. (London: British Museum)

their essential elements, in keeping with a taste that calls for the breaking down of architectural forms and the covering of available surfaces with naively grotesque vegetal motifs. All things considered, I judge the Devnimori reliefs as slightly older than those from Mirpur Khas.

The importance of Shamalaji as an artistic center of considerable magnitude was made clear some years ago by Umakant P. Shah with his catalogue of the Hindu sculptures from this site in Gujarat (and now preserved in the Baroda Museum). The Indian scholar had found a clear Gandharan influence in some of these sculptures; recent excavations have brought to light elements that, in this respect, are even more significant. As for the proposed dating, it seems to me that some of the sculptures that Shah assigned to the end of the Kshatrapa period or the beginning of the Gupta period (at the time of Chandra Gupta II, that is) should be given a later date. Otherwise we would have to accept that the Gupta age saw a revival of the motifs of the northwest after a beginning that fits perfectly (aside from the unquestionable regional variations) into the development of the most typical Gupta art; or we would have to think

72.   Avantipur: This is the Temple of Avantisvami-Vishnu in Kashmir. The *Rajatarangini*, a twelfth-century Kashmir work, tells us that this temple was erected by Avantivarman (who reigned from A.D. 855 to 883) before he ascended the throne. It has a large precinct enclosure, whose exterior decoration is concentrated on the west side, where the entrance and its stairway lie. The main temple rises at the center of the court, which is 174 feet by 148 feet; other smaller temples are set at the four corners. This photograph shows part of the interior of the precinct wall, with the characteristic trilobate arches that frame the access-ways and form little cells all along the four sides. (See plan, opposite.)

73.   Kafirkot South: In the Dera Ismail Khan district of Pakistan, near the large village of Bilot, on the right bank of the Indus, lie two monumental complexes, both known as Kafirkot. This is a temple-tower at the southern complex; it is dated to the eighth century A.D., and is typical of Indo-Aryan architecture of the period. Although not as important as Kafirkot North in the totality of documentation of the development of architecture in the northwest, Kafirkot South is a major center for this regional architecture.

Avantipur: Plan of the precinct and Temple of Avantisvami-Vishnu.

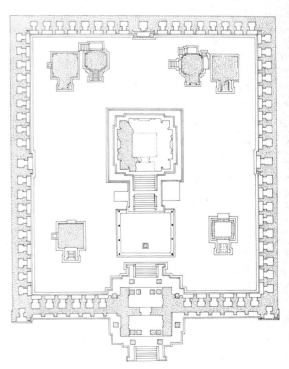

74.   Swat: This haloed figure of Buddha, with silver-leaf eyes (and for those of his attendants) and with the *urna* (the whorl between the eyebrows, the sign of a superior being) is a bronze work of the eighth or ninth century A.D. It is 11 inches high. It is considered an example of the Shahiya art of the period, but its exact origin is unknown. But on the basis of comparison with similar figures, it may be assigned to the Swat region, although objects of the same type have been found in Kashmir and even in Afghanistan. (Rome: National Museum of Oriental Art)

75.   Afghanistan: This marble fragment (14 inches × 10 inches × 7 inches) is known as the "Scorretti marble," after the Italian who first obtained it in Kabul. It is dated to the eighth century A.D. When in 1955, D. Schlumberger reported this valuable example of Shahiya art, he thought he could identify it as a form of the taurochthonic Mithra. But since then it has been given a more probable identification: it is the great goddess Durga, killing the demon Mahisa. Other findings in Afghanistan have since demonstrated that this form of the goddess was especially popular in the region. (See the figure at Tepe Sardar, Illus, 76–77.) (Rome: National Museum of Oriental Art, on loan)

that the Buddhist sculpture of Devnimori was produced by artisans of a culture different from that which is at the basis of the Hindu statuary of Shamalaji. This would be the exact opposite of what we found around A.D. 475 in the Sarnath-Benares area, where the Buddhist output was at its highest cultural level and the Hindu works appear in a certain sense to have been relegated to a secondary concern.

At this time, too, Hindu temples appear alongside the stupas. Unlike the sanctuaries carved out of rock and even unlike the stupas themselves, because the latter lack an accessible internal area, the temples are free-standing structures built with blocks of stone. While their design was extremely simple at the outset, it soon underwent a far-reaching evolution that enriched them with roofs studded with spires (sikhara), which would later be tremendously successful in medieval Indian architecture. Among the oldest examples in central India we may mention the temple of Nachna-Kuthara and that of Shiva at Bhumara. This latter consisted of a cella (garbha-griha) with a flat roof of stone slabs; a door was carved with images of river gods on the posts and with a bust of Shiva on the architrave. Around the cella, which contained a lingam (the phallic emblem of Shiva), ran a large walled circumambulation (pradak-shinapatha), also covered, while a portico (mandapa) opened out in front. A still simpler type, lacking the open corridor for its pradakshina, is represented by Temple 17 at Sanchi and the temple of Kankali Devi at Tigowa.

Recently added to the group of older Gupta temples of central India was that of Vamana (another avatar of Vishnu), discovered in 1968 at Marhia. With its step-like roofing, this temple represents a halfway stage in the development of the Hindu temple, with the later type represented by the celebrated Vishnu temple at Deogarh (Madhya Pradesh), sur-

76–77: Tepe Sardar: This sculpture of unbaked clay is in the sanctuary at Tepe Sardar, near Ghazni, Afghanistan; it is dated to the eighth century A.D. and once represented the great goddess Durga killing the demon Mahisa. All that remains is the pedestal with the fallen and decapitated body of the buffalo-demon, the head of Durga (opposite) and fragments of lesser importance. The torso and legs of the goddess have been lost, but it is known she had at least four arms that held her attributes; one of the right hands must have held the trident with which the goddess struck the buffalo's body; the other one — which has been found — held the thunderbolt. The splendid head (at present kept by the Italian Archaeological Mission in Ghazni) is 25 inches high. Note the third eye in the middle of the forehead. The ambiguous smile is the perfect visual realization of this goddess's character, for Shiva's wife, in the words of Robert C. Zaehner, "is terrifying in her beauty and her grace lies exactly in her terrible nature." This image is one of the most important discoveries from this period, because it is the first time in Afghanistan that a Shaivite image has been found in a context in other respects purely Buddhist.

mounted by a *sikhara*. It is still uncertain whether this latter monument, of exceptional geometrical design (probably contemporary with the Sarnath images of Buddha and reflecting an identical vision), had a portico on each of its four sides, as it is almost unanimously presented in archaeological literature. A suggested alternative is that the temple, built on a terrace, was surrounded by four minor temples at the corners. In any case, the relief panels decorating the walls of the temple are considered among the most significant of the Gupta period, with their balanced arrangement of volume harmonizing with the compositional patterns (although we may be left with the impression of an excessively calculated equilibrium smacking of "good manners," to use the apt phrase of Goetz). The subject of one of the Deogarh panels, certainly the best known of them, is Vishnu reclining on the cosmic serpent Sesha, the same subject that appears on a terra-cotta relief of the almost contemporary (fifth century A.D.) temple of Bhitargaon, near Kanpur (Uttar Pradesh). But what a difference between the two. In the Deogarh work, the disproportionate limbs of the god, which almost extend beyond the frame of the panel, while losing nothing of the effective abstraction of the most cultured Gupta art, are contracted in a dynamic pattern that reabsorbs in itself the nervous coils of the serpent and embraces the entire composition. It is a full-fledged "alternative culture" confronting the official culture with a popular-expressive charge, although it remains the expression of the dominant class (see the terra-cotta of Illustration 48).

The Ajanta Caves and Indian Painting

During one period of the Gupta empire — from the outset of the fourth to the end of the fifth century A.D. — a large part of central India was under the dynasty of the Vakatakas, who replaced the Satavahana in the work of making these lands into a unified state. Open to direct Gupta

78.   Tepe Sardar: A demon's head, from the eighth century A.D. (Ghazni: Italian Archaeological Mission)

79.   Tepe Sardar: Head of Lokapala, from the eighth century A.D. (Ghazni: Italian Archaeological Mission)

These two clay heads are from the Buddhist sanctuary at Tepe Sardar. The demon's head (top) was part of a group that had Buddha seated on a lotus flower emerging from the water, in a rocky setting populated by Bodhisattvas, gods, demons, and animals. The Graeco-Roman "classical" inspiration of the group is evident, the inspiration being based on a long tradition and manifested in various forms, of which Gandhara art is only the most noted. The Lokapala (below) was a custodian of one of the four points of the compass; he is here represented in a warrior's garb; he decorated one of the small clay stupas set along the back and sides of the Great Stupa. This head was made slightly after the head of the demon, and is in a different style. We would have to look to central Asia, particularly to Chinese Turkestan (for example, at Tumshuq) to find an exact comparison with such a head.

THE ROLE OF PLEASURE IN INDIAN LIFE

Objection
Those who are inclined to believe that Artha is the chief object to be obtained argue that pleasures should not be sought because they hinder the pursuit of Dharma and Artha, both of which are more meritorious than Kama, which is looked down upon by the virtuous. Pursuit of pleasure brings man into distress and into the company of low persons who lead him to unrighteous acts and make his life impure. This also makes him rash, encourages irresponsibility and levity. The result is that he is disbelieved by all, is welcomed nowhere and is the object of contempt for everybody.

Answer
This objection cannot be sustained because Kama is as necessary for human existence and wellbeing as food. Moreover, Kama is a direct consequence of Dharma and Artha. Besides it has always to be pursued with moderation and caution. No one refrains from cooking because there are beggars who may steal it. Nor do men hesitate to sow seeds for fear of the animals who may destroy it when it ripens.

Thus a man who pursues Dharma, Artha, and Kama enjoys happiness both in this world and hereafter. The virtuous perform those acts which do not jeopardize their welfare in this world and also do not compromise their future. Any action conducive to the pursuit of Dharma, Artha, and Kama together with any one or two of them should be encouraged but with the only caution that the practice of neither is at the cost of the other two.

VATSYAYANA: *Kamasutra* I, II:40–48

influence, even of a political nature, under Chandra Gupta II, the reign of the Vakatakas was always closely linked to the Gupta empire to the north. Yet it would not be fair to consider the Vakatakas as mere tributaries of the Guptas as far as cultural activity — artistic, literary, and philosophical — is concerned; indeed, the so-called Hindu renaissance may be largely attributed to the Vakatakas, a family dynasty that was centered in central India. And whatever the political and cultural currents, Buddhism managed also to leave monumental traces of its presence in the Vakatakas' territories, especially in the western region. Ajanta is the undeniable proof of that.

Ajanta has by now deservedly reached a fame that outstrips the restricted milieu of the specialist. Along the sides of a rugged valley (Illustrations 51–52) north of Aurangabad (in present state of Maharashtra), a community of Buddhist monks began as early as the second century B.C. to excavate sanctuaries and monastic complexes out of the natural rock. Cave 10 was probably the oldest chaitya-hall at Ajanta, and the paintings surviving in this cave are among the most priceless remains preserved in India, although their condition makes any attempt to "read" them a desperate undertaking. The documentation Ajanta offers for later periods, however, certainly consoles us for the loss of the most ancient works. It is a complex of sculptures and paintings (Illustrations 53–68) whose dates had long been placed between the fourth and seventh centuries A.D., during the reign of the Vakataka and Chalukya dynasties in this part of India. Recently, however, Walter Spink, using arguments that are hard to ignore, questioned whether any form of artistic activity can be seen at Ajanta that dates to after A.D. 500, thus confining it to the Vakataka period. It appears difficult to date some of the paintings in Cave 2 to before the sixth century, but in general Professor Spink's theory appears acceptable. The stylistic affinities between the paintings, for example, of Cave 1 (Illustrations 64–65) with Gupta sculptural art of the fifth century are so evident that it is not easy to continue to accept the previous notion that they come much later than those of Cave 17 (Illustrations 57–61) — also now assigned to the fifth century, of course.

The murals of the Ajanta caves appeal to us on many levels, of course, including the nature of their technical execution. They are not full-fledged frescoes — painted while the surface layer of plaster is still wet — but works carried out with a technique comparable to our tempera and "dry-fresco" painting (the *fresco buono*, or "good fresco," of Italian Renaissance treatises). The design of each plays a crucial role in the working out of the volumes within, while shading and gradation of tones are used with ingenuity. The compositions are complex, and at times somewhat mechanical, but they are always skillfully controlled, never casual. All available surface is filled with paintings; only a few spaces are left free between one figure and another. "In this mass of personages and details," Jeannine Auboyer has written, "the viewer can scarcely distinguish a guideline, at least at first sight. Little by little, however, the eye becomes accustomed to making out different groups. Led from one gesture to another and through scarcely perceptible levels of depth, [the eye] ends by learning how to isolate them and to pass from one to another without difficulty. . . . An attitude, the orientation of a gesture, the curve of a figure caught off balance, the direction of a face turned outward from the scene, all this links these personages to the action of the group to which they belong and also to the group alongside." Inside the individual groups of figures as well, we can recognize rigorous compositional patterns, but these patterns have been achieved with an apparent freedom of movement, a constant converging toward an ideal center, a preoccupation with a rhythmic equilibrium that aims at suggesting the harmony of a society in which every activity, every gesture, every fulfilled desire has its precise place in a vision of the world without perturbation. The subjects are religious scenes of Mahayana Buddhism, scenes similar in content to those that, in another spirit, we have seen narrated at Bharhut, at Sanchi, in the northwest. Here everything has shifted, though, into a courtly milieu where the Bodhisattvas are no longer the thoughtful Siddhartha of Gandhara or that of the tumultous gestures of

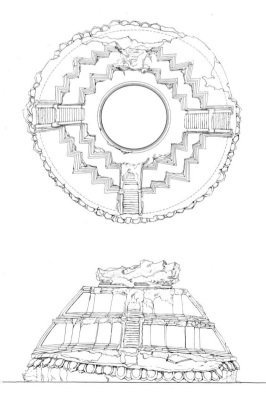

Tepe Sardar: Plan and elevation of one of the clay votive stupas in the sacred area around the Great Stupa.

Amaravati, but refined youths whose loveliness of form appears (Illustration 65) to make them lean more toward the arts of the *Kamasutra* than toward reflections on the suffering of living beings. But this is precisely where the originality of classical India lies, in this equilibrium between the three component parts of man's activity: *dharma, artha,* and *kama* — the moral law, the quest for prosperity (or, in a broader sense, power), and the pleasure of the senses. All such concepts were precisely classified, in keeping with the taste of the Indian literature of the time, but a great degree of freedom was left to the individual, to his desire to seek out his own way, albeit within the impassable frontiers of the sacred texts. It is not surprising that this refined urban society of the privileged should find its most complete expression in painting, which enjoyed greater social prestige than sculpture. Nor was there anything extraordinary in the fact that works of such profane beauty should adorn the walls of religious chambers. It stems from the alliance between the class of wealthy merchants and bankers, particularly strong in India's western regions, and the Buddhists and the court. The court in question could proclaim its brahmanic orthodoxy (both the Guptas and the Vakatakas practiced the traditional sacrifice of the horse, the *asvamedha*), but it was unstinting in its support for the Buddhist community that was still the expression of the ruling class.

80. **Bamiyan: West of Kabul, Afghanistan, situated in a valley between the Kuh-i Baba peaks, is Bamiyan, today but a modest bazaar. What remains of the monastic complex cut out of the long wall of the cliff is enough to give an idea of the importance of this site in antiquity. Madeleine Hallade has written of it: "The Sassanian conquests and a brief Ephthalite occupation in the fifth century A.D. did not obstruct the development of this Buddhist center of Bamiyan, situated in a region where local rulers preserved their independence. From the second century A.D. on,**

the monasteries multiplied in this relatively fertile valley, a resting place after the difficult crossing of the Hindu Kush for the caravans that came down from the north, or after a long trek for those who came from India." Different religious and artistic currents mingled at Bamiyan, and ended by co-existing; the stylistic comparisons possible for the works at this site range from Iran to the Ganges plain, from the northwest of the subcontinent to Chinese Turkestan. The major centers of attraction at Bamiyan today are the two colossal images of Buddha; visible at the center of this photograph is the smaller of the two.

Echoes of the art of Gupta India, as we know it through the paintings at Ajanta, are also to be found in Sri Lanka, where the walls of the Sigiriya rock-cliff — once the fortress of King Kassapa I (A.D. 478–496) — still hold images of female divinities marked by bursting vitality (Illustrations 69–70), although they have been heavily restored. And although we must be cautious in speaking of "echoes" or "influences" of Gupta art, the fact remains that certain iconographic canons may be applied to discriminate between pre-Gupta art and that which followed. Even here, though, one can speak of "canons" in a strict sense only for a part of the sculptural output, particularly in the post-Gupta period. Perhaps chief among these canons was the characteristic way of conceiving the very quality of forms and volumes and their relationships, a refusal to consider the image as if immersed in space, an insistence on seeing the image as a container of space itself, pressing toward the outside. This way of conceiving will distinguish India's entire post-Gupta artistic production, constantly and inevitably prompting a comparison with the art of the Gupta period. At the same time, the canons required a balancing of volumes suggesting a perfect equilibrium, a form of motion — even when rapid or positively violent — that did not aim at a different state, but at a continual cyclical re-emergence of the same moments, a relationship with empirical reality that is one of abstraction

81.   Bamiyan: This is the larger of the two Buddhas; it towers some 175 feet high and is dated to about the fifth century A.D. The colossal Buddhas of Bamiyan were sculptured — or better, rough-hewn — in the limestone conglomerate that forms the cliff extending for a few miles, in which were also cut the numerous monastic caves. The figures are set in deep niches, the sides of which still have traces of paintings. The outer form of this larger Buddha was shaped by means of a thick layer of plaster, still partly preserved. To keep the folds straight, large ropes were used; these gave the required bulge to the stucco and helped to hold it. The work was then completed by an application of colors and gilding. This was a different technique from that used in the shorter — 120 feet — Buddha, on which the folds were modeled in clay mixed with straw. In both images, Buddha was represented with his right hand raised in the gesture of reassurance (the *abhaya mudra*), while the left hand held on to his cloak.

THE HYMN TO THE INCOMPARABLE ONE

O incomparable One, homage unto Thee, who knowest the truth that phenomena have no essence of their own! Thou art eager of the benefit of this world, misled by different theories.

Nothing is seen by Thyself with the eye of the enlightened One. Sublime, O Lord, is Thy view which perceives the truth.

From the standpoint of metaphysical truth there is neither knower nor thing to be known. Oh! Thou knowest the reality very difficult to be known.

Thou dost neither create nor destroy anything; having perceived the sameness of everything, thou reachedst the most sublime condition.

Thou dost not take *nirvana* as the suppression of *samsara;* since thou, O Lord, dost not perceive any *samsara,* thou obtainedst quiescence.

Thou knowest that the defilement of passion and the purification of virtue have the same taste; since no discrimination is possible in the reality thou art completely pure.

Thou, O Master, didst not utter a single syllable, and yet the entire mass of people fit to be converted was gratified with the shower of the law.

Thou art not adherent to the *skandhas,* to the *dhatus,* or to the *ayatanas.* Thou art mind only as infinite and pure as the ether, nor dost Thou reside in any contingent thing (*dharma*).

The notion of being does not occur to Thee at all, and yet Thou art exceedingly compassionate towards all beings tortured by sorrow and pain.

Thy mind, O Lord, is not attached to those multifarious opinions as regards pleasure and pain, existence of an ego, non-existence of an ego, affirmation of some eternal being, negation of some eternal being.

Thy belief is that things do not go changing into some other condition, nor do they come into existence by the agency of some force: nor dost Thou admit that there is a whole as the conglomeration of many parts. Therefore Thou knowest the absolute truth.

Thou art followed everywhere, but Thou art born nowhere; oh great ascetic, Thou art beyond our thought, as regards attributes of birth and corporeity.

Thou, the irreproachable One, didst understand that this world is neither unity nor multiplicity; it is like an echo, it is subject neither to changing into other forms nor to destruction.

Thou, my Lord, didst know that the cycle of existence is neither eternal nor impermanent, that in it there is no predicable nor predicate, since it is similar to a dream or to a magic play.

All defilements which have their root and their fruit in the faculty of projecting new karmic series have been completely overcome by Thee, immaculate One. By realizing the nature of the defilements thou obtainest immortality.

O Thou, firm in thy resolve, Thou didst see the world of material appearances as devoid of any predicate and like the immaterial. Still in the material sphere Thou appearest with a body shining with the thirty-two marks of the great man.

But even if Thy appearance has been seen, it cannot be said that Thou hast been seen. When the object has been seen, Thou art well seen, but reality is not the object of vision.

Thy body has not the nine holes as mortal beings have, it has no flesh, no bones, no blood; still Thou manifestedst a body which is a mere reflex just as the rainbow in the sky.

Neither disease nor impurity are in Thy body; it is not subject to hunger or thirst and still in order to comply with the world, Thou hast shown a worldly behavior.

O impeccable One, no fault whatsoever caused by the obstruction of the actions can be found in Thee; still on account of thy pity for this world Thou hast shown an apparent diving into *karman.*

Since the reality cannot be differentiated, there are no different vehicles of liberation; only in order to convert living beings according to their different tendencies and maturity Thou preachedst the three vehicles.

Thy body is eternal, imperishable, auspicious. It is the very law, it is the Victorious one. Still on account of the people to be converted to the path of salvation Thou showedst Thy passing away into *nirvana.*

In the infinite universe Thou art now and then beheld by those who have faith in Thee, and are anxious to become Buddhas and to imitate Thy descending upon earth, Thy birth, Thy illumination, Thy preaching, Thy entering into *nirvana.*

No feeling, O Lord, no ideation, no motion are in Thee. Thou art accomplishing in this world the duty of a Buddha, without participating in it.

I have spread over the perfect One, who is beyond our thoughts and any limitation, the flowers of his very attributes. Through the merit which I have begot may all living beings in this world participate in the extremely deep law of the sublime ascetic.

NAGARJUNA: *Catuhstava* II

Pandrethan: The facade of the Temple of Shiva. Characteristic of this and other medieval temples of Kashmir were the pilasters of Graeco-Roman origin, the portal with the trilobate arch, and the triangular tympanum.

but not of negation. All this helps to give rise to an aesthetic concept that, despite its readily discernible regional variants, left its mark on all the cultured art of post-Gupta India, particularly sculpture.

Indian Influence in Kashmir and Afghanistan

There are several directions in which we might look at this point as we begin to bring together the various strands of ancient Indian art. But we start with the northernmost regions and the adjacent territories, now belonging to other nations but once within the cultural sphere of India. There was Kashmir, for instance, which had produced a particularly lively art — as testified by the terra-cotta slabs of Harwan, dated to the fourth or fifth centuries A.D. — work that probably was closely rooted in the nomadic populations then ominously confronting India. And then, in the post-Gupta period, Kashmir supported a flourishing of stucco and terra-cotta works in the late-Gandhara tradition. These included the fragments, tentatively dated to the seventh century A.D. from Ushkur, near Baramula (Illustration 71), which can be compared with the stucco works of Jaulian (Taxila) and with several works from Afghan territory.

In the eighth century, the kingdom of Kashmir turned not only toward India but also toward China, to which, at least nominally, it appears to have been subject. But Kashmir remained relatively independent, and the Kashmir king Lalitaditya Muktapida (A.D. 724–760) extended his sphere of influence to the bordering regions. If we are to believe the *Rajatarangini* (a chronicle of the Kashmir kings written by Kalhana toward the middle of the twelfth century) his vassals included the Shahiya of Kabul, who were said to have reigned in the Hund area (Udabhandapura, near Attok, at the confluence of the Kabul and the Indus rivers) up to the time of their defeat at the hands of Mahmud of Ghazni, at the outset of the eleventh century. Worthy of mention among the works sponsored by Lalitaditya is the stupa of Parihasapura. Surrounded by a vast courtyard (128 feet along each side), the stupa itself was a square structure with stairways that formed a cross-shaped design; this design was to be repeated frequently not only in Kashmir but also in Afghanistan (for example, at Tepe Sardar), in central Asia, and Tibet. The Sun Temple of Martand, also erected during the reign of Lalitaditya, gains its interest from its mixture of elements of Graeco-Roman origin (pilasters, capitals, triangular tympana) with others more typical of India, such as the trefoil arch. This style of arch was widespread in the architecture of Kashmir, as witness the temple at Avantipur (Illustration 72).

Meanwhile, northwestern India — possibly at the very time of Lalitaditya — was marked by an architecture similar in ways to that of Kashmir. What is lacking, however, is the coincidence of enough elements to enable us to speak of a "Kashmir art" transplanted to the Punjab. The Dutch archaeologist J. E. van Lohuizen-deLeeuw has rightly confined to the temple of Malot (Salt Range) a true derivation from the architecture of Kashmir; the other temples of the Salt Range area (Amb, Kalar, Katas, Nandana) are attributed to a different school, which she suggests be called "medieval architecture of northwest India"; this would also include the two splendid groups of North and South Kafirkot (Illustration 73), near Bilot, in the Pakistani district of Dera Ismail Khan.

The affinity between Kashmir and the regions of the northwest appears evident, however, in the sculptures — especially in the small Buddhist bronzes (Illustration 74), dating from the seventh to the tenth centuries; these works imply a sort of artistic *lingua franca,* which probably had its principal centers of production in Kashmir and Uddyana (Swat) but whose area of diffusion also included Afghanistan. The presence of Hindu temples similar to those of Kafirkot in Afghan territory is documented by the discovery of architectural fragments at Chiga Sarai in

82–83. Bamiyan: Two details of the paintings inside the niche of the larger Buddha; they are dated to about the sixth century A.D. Both portray Buddha within an arched frieze. In the one at left, we can just make out a stupa with a niche at the top of the staircase — this is at the right of the photograph, in the space between the arch of the niche. The influence of Indian painting on the Bamiyan artists is evident: this might be seen by comparing these images with the paintings at Ajanta. But a strong Sassanian-Iranian cultural component is to be seen in such elements and conventions as the jewels or the arrangements of the edges of the drapery.

the Kunar Valley (eastern Afghanistan), attributed to the eighth or ninth century, and by the temple on the Khair Khane Pass (north of Kabul), which has given us the sculpture representing Surya — the old Aryan sun god — on a chariot (and now in the Kabul Museum). This last-named work is a marble relief that probably dates from some time after the fifth century; it can be considered one of those rare works, produced in the post-Gupta era and relatively near in time to the Islamic conquest, that — distributed between Afghanistan and Pakistan's Northwest Frontier Province — make up the ideal catalogue of Shahiya art.

The Shahiyas were the people who ruled the Hund area, and also belonging in such a "catalogue" of their works would be various fragments of Shaivite images (in the Kabul Museum) and the so-called Scorretti Marble (from the name of the man who bought it in a bazaar in Kabul; he has since given it on loan to the National Museum of Oriental Art in Rome). The Scorretti Marble (Illustration 75) is a fragment of a group depicting the Shaivite goddess Durga Mahisasuramardini. Another work of signal importance is the group of Shiva and Parvati, with strong reminiscences of Gandhara in its style and iconography, discovered at Tepe Iskandar (north of Kabul). Worthy of being mentioned with these works are those in clay found at Tepe Marandjan (Kabul), at Surkh Kotal, and at Fondukistan (between Bamiyan and Begram); the sculpture of this last-named site is, it seems, more recent than the work of strong Gandhara inspiration from Tepe Marandjan and Surkh Kotal.

The recent excavation of Tepe Shotor (Hadda, near Jalalabad) has yielded both the clay sculptures of the oldest type (associated with the Gandhara stucco creations, which were also found at Tepe Shotor), and a group much closer to the works of Fondukistan, the so-called fish-niche, one of the most important figurative complexes of the entire northwestern sphere of Indian art. It is not easy to assign a precise date to these architectural and sculptural works of Buddhist Afghanistan. At Tepe Sardar, near Ghazni, excavations still underway have restored a notable group, even quantitatively speaking, of clay sculptures (Illustrations 76–79), stylistically associated with Fondukistan. The stratigraphy shows that

these sculptures are without question more recent than those of the Tepe Marandjan type. Among the more recent works of Tepe Sardar was an important decorative complex in unfired clay. At the center was a Buddha (now lost), probably seated on a lotus flower emerging from the water and supported by two *nagas* (Illustration 78); a similar iconography has been found at Fondukistan. Added to the sides, probably soon afterwards, were (on the left) a standing image of Buddha, adorned with jewels (of a type also known from Fondukistan) and (on the right) a sculptural group (Illustrations 76–77) representing Durga slaughtering the buffalo demon. This latter subject is identified only on the strictly iconographic level, and it may well be that the Durga of Tepe Sardar had, in the Buddhist context here, connotations different from those of the Durga of the Hindu cult. The presence of this image, however, shows how greatly the religious climate in Afghanistan had changed in the eighth century, even on the level of the dominant social class, to which the sanctuary of Tepe Sardar doubtless belonged. The path taken by Buddhism here in Afghanistan was the same that would lead later to the forms of open syncretism in Tibetan Buddhism; it was also the road taken at an early date in the northwest of India, although at the beginning only timidly, as is shown by the art of Gandhara and particularly at the level of popular religiosity.

84–85. Mamallapuram: The temples (*raths* — literally, "chariots") that the Pallava king Narasimhavarman I Mamalla had built in the seventh century A.D. Mamallapuram was an important port on the Coromandel coast many centuries before, but it was this king who gave it the monumental character it is known for today. The first report by a European on this locality was made by an Italian, Gasparo Balbi, in 1582; at this time it was known as "Seven Pagodas." Not until the end of the seventeenth century did another Italian, Niccolo Mannucci, show any interest in the monuments — and he claimed to find similarities with Chinese art. Reports were more frequent in the eighteenth century, and in 1788 there appeared (in the first volume of *Asiatick Researches*) the first detailed de-

scription "of the sculpture and ruins of Mavalipuram" by W. Chambers. The five *raths* were actually cut out of the natural rock. They now carry, by tradition, the names of the heroes of the *Mahabharata*. In the photograph above, we see, from left to right, the Dharmaraja-rath, the Bhima-rath, the Arjuna-rath, and the Draupadi-rath (Draupadi being the wife of the five brothers). In the photograph at right, we see, in the foreground, the back of the Arjuna-rath with Indra on the elephant Airavata (in the center of the reliefs on the base). In the background is visible part of the Nakula-Shadeva rath, which takes its name from the twins who were the youngest of the five sons of Pandu, King of Hastinapur.

North of the Koh-i Baba, which is the western extension of the Hindu Kush, one finds the town of Bamiyan (Afghanistan), located on the caravan track that led from Bactria to Taxila and to India. Buddhist monasteries had been built at Bamiyan since the time of Kanishka; various monastic and cult chambers were soon being carved into the craggy sandstone cliffs above the Bamiyan Valley (Illustration 80) and in some side valleys (Foladi, Kakrak); this activity appears to have continued up to the middle of the seventh century, continuing in a lower key up to the time of the Moslem conquest in the eighth century. The Chinese pilgrim Hsuan-tsang visited Bamiyan in A.D. 632, finding a large number of monks, all of them followers of the Lesser Vehicle, or Hinayana Buddhism. But a century later, in 727, another pilgrim, the Korean Hui Ch'ao, also found followers of Mahayana there. Today the fame of Bamiyan is based on two colossal images of Buddha, respectively 120 feet and 175 feet high (Illustration 81); they were mentioned by Hsuan-tsang (who also spoke of a reclining Buddha about 1000 feet long — nowhere to be seen today). Paintings and sculptured decorations in relief (formed of clay mixed with straw) adorn the niches of the two Buddhas and the other chambers carved out of the rock. Bamiyan is an architectural and decorative complex that still awaits definitive chronological placement. Indian and Iranian elements, influenced in some ways by the Gandhara

tradition, are unquestionably present, but they constitute a rather solid and homogeneous local form that was later to produce the paintings, unfortunately all too few in number, of Fondukistan (at present assigned to the seventh century A.D.) and those, perhaps a bit later, recently discovered at Tepe Sardar. The largest of the two Buddhas at Bamiyan is probably to be assigned to the fifth century A.D., and is the most recent. The paintings adorning its niche (Illustrations 82–83) are considered to have been added later.

In addition to the decorative details (vegetal scrolls, rows of miniature arches, animal foreparts) the chambers carved from rock in the Bamiyan Valley are fundamental documents for the study of the ancient architecture of the region, which otherwise might have been lost altogether. Here we find rock-cut reproductions of wooden architectural elements such as the so-called lantern roof and others in which the various details are so well executed that they permit a precise reconstruction of the wooden originals: it seems virtually certain that these elements were part of the building patterns common in the regions of Kashmir, the Hindu Kush, the Himalayas — indeed, from eastern Turkey to central Asia. The relationship between "architecture" carved from the rock and genuine architecture is not, nevertheless, as immediate as one might think. In fact, in the broadest sense the entire area of the northwest — from Kashmir to Afghanistan — presents recurring technical solutions in its religious architecture, solutions typical of a lost wooden architecture that, if one can

86–87.   Mamallapuram: The Shore Temple, from the late seventh or early eighth century A.D., unlike the five *raths*, was constructed out of cut stone blocks. It was built by Narasimhavarman II Rajasimha (circa 690–715) and is dedicated to Shiva. Next to the temple is a large sculpture representing the lion of Durga (opposite); the goddess Durga is seated on the animal's hind leg. An image of Durga is also inside the niche in the lion's chest. (The preservation of this Shore Temple, exposed to the wind and salinity of the sea air, is one of the most urgent problems for our time.)

Preceding pages:
88.   Mamallapuram: "The Descent of the Ganges," the relief carved out of the natural granite; it is dated to the seventh century A.D.

89.   Mamallapuram: Opposite: A detail of this relief carving; it should be realized that all these figures, as well as the elephant (on preceding pages) are life-size.

The subject represented on this enormous rock relief has been the subject of discussion among scholars ever since 1914, when V. Goloubew put forth the hypothesis that it represented "The Descent of the Ganges," not the generally accepted "Penitence of Arjuna," which had been proposed back in 1798 by J. Goldingham (in the fifth volume of *Asiatick Researches*). This interpretation — of the descent — has since had the most supporters, although the old hypothesis is still accepted by some prominent scholars. But the "descent" theme seems to be more consonant with the grandeur of the relief; moreover, certain essential elements are inexplicably absent if this were the "penitence" that Arjuna, the hero of the *Mahabharata*, had to endure in order to gratify Shiva. In any case, scholars and everyone agree on one point: with the relief at Mamallapuram, India has given the world one of the great works of all time.

imagine them present as models in Kashmir or Bamiyan, cannot be justified in areas with a completely different climate — for example, at Kafirkot. Although the connotations here are completely different, the phenomenon typical of Gandhara architecture is produced once again: the loss of usefulness of the architectural elements and their crystallization in a decorative function.

The Great Age of the Hindu Temple

But finally it must be said that the regions of the northwest represent (even in relation to the greater resistance of Buddhism) a cultural world that is largely independent from that of the rest of India. There one finds the Hindu temple is the form that concentrates in itself the greatest effort to speculate on art as a religious factor: the *shilpashastras,* or art treatises, describe in detail both the plan of the edifice, with the relationships among the various parts of the temple according to very specific symbolic needs, and the smallest details of the structure itself. The symbolism of the world axis, for instance, is found once again in the spire *(sikhara)* as also, inside the temple, in the lingam. The temple itself was a reproduction of the cosmos in which the worshiper, through the mediation of the priest, found a place for himself.

"In such an architecture as that of India," Benjamin Rowland has said, "an emphasis on the vertical is not determined by any aesthetic or structural necessities as in the skyscraper, but because this vertical, the sikhara or spire, is literally meant to point to God, to be the very embodiment of that magic axis that pillars apart heaven and earth and is variously symbolized by the mountain, the tree, or the Universal Man, Purusa." These words of the American scholar may be true as far as they go, but it remains to be demonstrated that the needs of verticalism in the skyscraper are merely aesthetic and structural and not, for example, dictated by considerations of prestige. Moreover, behind all aesthetic, structural, and even symbolic solutions there is the need of functionality in the broadest sense: in the case of the works of the ruling classes aimed at the community, this function is to be construed as the more complete control over the lower classes. The various components of such works — architecture or major works of "official" art — are always so closely connected and interdependent that it is pointless to claim a subordination of the aesthetic imperative to other factors as a phenomenon typical of India or, for example, of medieval Europe. This subordination is in a sense true even when the ideology upholds the autonomy of art: "art for art's sake." The Hindu temple was first and foremost the reproduction of a cosmic order that was also a social order, in which the individual found the confirmation of his condition and the hope of a better one. On the next level, it was also the ideal center in which the Brahman, who monopolized the rites, controlled the activities of the lower classes, particularly the tillers of the soil, adding to the percentage tax on production that other tax that was the compensation for the performance of the rite and for the care of the divinity. It was a mechanism of the "divine benevolence market," which operates in a similar manner in different socioeconomic formations and which is hardly exclusive to ancient India, but which nevertheless deserves to be stressed and to be compared with that in effect in the sanctuaries of other areas and times.

It was in the centuries that followed the end of the Gupta dynasty (from about A.D. 600) that the Hindu temple and related monumental structures moved into a truly expansive period. Politically it was a time of disunity, with a whole succession of dynasties, people, and regions competing to control parts of India. But it was also a time when the Hindu religion experienced such a revival that these centuries are sometimes described as a time of the Hindu renaissance. Somewhat confusing is the fact that the art — particularly the temples — of these centuries is referred to as that of India's "medieval period"; as we shall see, the works

cannot be compared literally to the works of Europe's Middle Ages, but there is no denying certain superficial resemblances to the general phenomenon of "cathedral building." In any case, we must confine ourselves to the essential references to the better known monumental groups and leave the illustrations to support more detailed explorations.

From the typological point of view, the Indian temples can be divided roughly into three groups, on a basis of the forms of their roofs, or coverings. These are the *nagara, vesara,* and *dravida* temples, distributed respectively in northern India, the Deccan (central India), and in southern India. The *nagara* type is characterized by the presence of the conical-convex *sikhara,* or spire, usually surmounted by an element in the form of a rain-vase *(kalasa);* the *vesara* temple was derived from the Buddhist chaitya-hall and has a roof similar to the barrel vault; the *dravida* type is based on a succession of terraces rising in pyramidal form. We must realize, of course, that this classification is only approximate; not only were there many variants and intermediate forms, but the areas of distribution cannot be that rigorously defined. But as long as we do not

90–91.   Ellura: The Temple of Kailasa, dating to the second half of the eighth century A.D. Above, the relief representing Shiva as a great ascetic; opposite, a view of a section of the central court. Ellura is a village about 13 miles northwest of Aurangabad in western India (and not far from Ajanta). It is still the seat of the Ghrshnesvara cult, whose sanctuary is one of the most important pilgrimage sites for Hindus. The central attraction of the pilgrimage was evidently once within the caves carved at Ellura, but the site lost much of its prestige when it was desecrated by the Mogul Emperor Aurangzeb (1658–1707), so much so that the cult and

image of Ghrshnesvara had to be moved into the village. The monuments cut out of the wall of the mountain extend for a little more than a mile and are divided into three groups: the southern caves are Buddhist (the oldest being from the Chalukya period); the northern ones are Jain; and the ones in the middle section are Brahman. The Temple of Kailasa is situated along with caves 14 and 15, at the southern edge of the central group of Brahman caves. Strictly speaking, it is not a cave but a temple; but instead of being constructed, it was entirely cut out of the natural rock on the site — similar to the *raths* at Mamallapuram.

expect to find complete consistency, we may keep these types in mind as points of reference.

If we start with southern India, where we would expect to find the *dravida* style, at once we find a variety of styles in the temple erected under the Pallavas, the successors of the Andhras in southeastern India from the fifth to the ninth centuries A.D. The Pallavas left abundant manifestations of their monumental building activity, especially during the period of the Mamalla dynasty (630–700) and in that of the Rajasimha dynasty (circa 700–731). The most important group is that of Mamallapuram, known also as the "Seven Pagodas," on the Coromanel coast, south of Madras. The celebrated five *raths* (literally "chariots," but here meaning temple-vehicles) are copies of various contemporary architectural types, all cut out of the natural rock formations on the spot; technically speaking, therefore, these works are sculptures (Illustrations 84–85). Executed — as were the bulk of the monuments at Mamallapuram — by order of Narasimhavarman I Mamalla (circa A.D. 630–668), they are particularly important because of their influence on

92-93.   Ellura: These are both details of
relief carvings in the Temple of Kailasa, and
date to the second half of the eighth century
A.D. The one opposite is in the sanctuary of
Lankesvara, a part of the Kailasa complex; it
shows Shiva doing the cosmic dance *(tan-
dava)*, the movements of which have the
power to keep together, as in a sort of rhythmical pulsation, the subtle energies of all creation. Although damaged, this relief, with the
god represented with six arms, was one of the
first Indian works to arouse the admiration of
Europeans. In the photograph above is a ce-
lestial being in flight, with part of the painted
plaster still remaining.

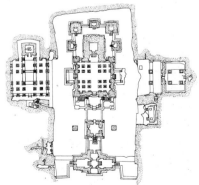

*Ellura: Plan of the upper story of the Temple of
Kailasa.*

the succeeding evolution of the architecture in south central India. The Bhima-rath, for instance, documents the survival of forms typical of Buddhist monuments, such as the chaitya-hall. Also characteristic is the type of the Draupadi-rath, a square plan with an overhanging sloping roof evidently derived from the hut with a straw roof. Another Pallava sovereign, Narasimhavarman II Rajasimha, was responsible for building the so-called Shore Temple at Mamallapuram (Illustrations 86–87) and the Temple of Kailasa at Kanchipuram; these were both full-fledged structural architecture. At the latter, the pyramidal covering (already present in the Arjuna-rath and in the Dharmaraja-rath at Mamallapuram) is flanked by the roof derived from the chaitya-hall, while the Shore Temple has two pyramidal towers.

In all these temples, the carved figures and decorative elements are not to be seen as a superimposition; on the contrary, the relationship between architecture and sculpture is one of the most organic to be found at any time or place in India. It was the result of a long formal elaboration, which began with the Andhra period and was influenced only generally by Gupta art. This is also demonstrated by the most singular artistic expression of the Pallava period, perhaps also the work of Narasimhavarman I: the great rock at Mamallapuram, carved with the representation of "The Descent of the Ganges from the Himalayas" (Illustrations 88–89). It is actually not so much a representation as a re-production of this mythical event: the fissure of the rock, through which the collected rainwater once flowed from a basin above, mystically becomes the sacred river itself, the Ganges. The images, reminiscent of the art of Amaravati in their nervous but agile arching of limbs, cover with a thick texture the upper portion of the great mass of rock, while in the lower part the life-size figures of elephants express in the shape of their bodies the convexity of the mass.

All the Pallava architecture and sculpture of the Mammala period excite admiration for the cautious, wise intervention of the artist in the natural environment. In the period of the Rajasimha dynasty, the Hindu temple took on an independence from the environment and began to build a space of its own, separate from that outside the sacred precinct, a technique that will be fully developed in the great temples of Madura, of Tiruvannamalai, of Kanchipuram. A significant example of this sense of independence is offered by the Vaishnite temple of Vaikunthaperumal at Kanchipuram; begun in the eighth century, it was later completed at the time of the Vijayanagar kings (in the fourteenth to sixteenth centuries). But it was the cliff sculptures of the Mamalla period (which also include numerous cave temples) that became most significant, particularly in the case of the "sculptured" rath, a type of monument that implied a symbolism that was to some extent new in India: the sanctuary that, rather than being carved into the mountain or erected to represent the mountain, became part of the sacred mountain itself.

After Mamallapuram, we find this type of symbolism at Ellura, not far from Ajanta, in the Temple of Kailasa, a reference to a sacred mountain of Hindu mythology (Illustrations 90–93). The arrangement of the various parts of this sanctuary, which aimed at suggesting the peaks of Kailasa, the dwelling place of Shiva, is more or less in the form of a cross; the pattern is repeated in the principal temple, whose center — also the exact center of the entire complex — is marked by a pillared hall that precedes the cella and opens onto three porches. Distributed around the sanctuary (the cella) are five minor shrines, while on the temple axis itself, between the temple and the entrance, one finds the canopy with an image of the bull Nandi, the *vahana,* or "vehicle," of Shiva; the image of the god in the form of a lingam is located inside the sanctuary. This splendid complex, which can be dated between the eighth and ninth centuries, at the time of the Rashtrakuta dynasty, although now free-standing, was entirely carved out of a massive rock formation — like its predecessors at Mamallapuram. Although Buddhism had similar monuments — that is, entirely carved out of rock (for example, the stupa of Haibak in Afghanistan) — it cannot be denied that it was Hinduism that gave this type of monument a more precise and conscious symbolic impact.

94.   Ellura: A relief carving from Cave 15, showing the struggle between Vishnu —in his incarnation as the lion-man, Narasimha — and the titan Hiranyakasipiu. It is dated to the second half of the eighth century A.D.

Cave 15, also known as Dasavatura ("the ten incarnations of Vishnu"), contains a lovely series of reliefs with both Vaishnite and Shaivite subjects.

Another monumental complex of the Maharashtra region, and also of the eighth century, provides still better clarification of the hidden significance incorporated into a Hindu temple: the rock sanctuary of Elephanta, an island lying just off Bombay. This sanctuary contains Shaivite reliefs and images, including the celebrated one of the Trimurti, or Trinity of Hinduism — that is, Shiva Mahadeva in triple form: Tat-purusa at the center, Aghora and Vamadeva at the sides. Disturbing in its impassive aspect, at once benign and terrifying, the god appears as if emerging from the solid rock with his broad youthful breast, a genuine theophany in a setting that, thanks to the light that barely filters in from the outside, embraces the worshiper in a luminous aura that is both frightening and reassuring. Here perhaps more than anywhere else in India one understands the drama of the individual in a society that crushes him and that leaves him the sole resource of finding a place for himself, miniscule as he is, in the universal unity represented by the god.

95. **Ellura:** This relief from Cave 14, dated to the second half of the eighth century A.D., shows Varaha, the incarnation of Vishnu as a boar-man, resting his foot on a serpent as he holds Prithvi (the earth) up from the depths of the ocean. Cave 14 — also known as Ravana-ka Khai, after one of its reliefs — is perhaps one of the oldest of the Brahman caves at Ellura and is also one of the oldest caves of the Rashtrakuta period.

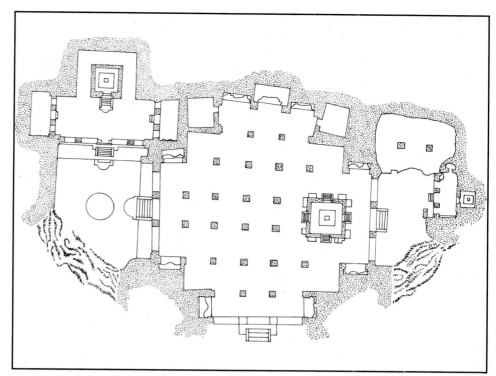

Elephanta: Plan of the Temple of Shiva. The image of the god is located in the niche opposite the entrance of the temple.

Pattadakal: Plan of the Temple of Mallikarjuna. Access to the temple is through all of the three small porticoes.

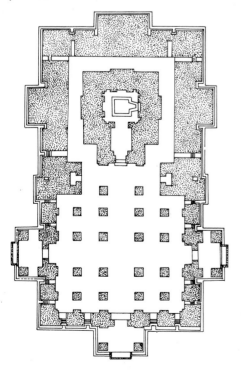

Survival and Revival of the Buddhist Tradition

To the Chalukya period (roughly A.D. 600–750) belong the celebrated complexes of Aihole (Illustration 96) and Pattadakal (Illustration 97), where we can follow the evolution of the Hindu temple from the transition period of the Guptas to the Chalukyas and up to the eighth century A.D., when this last-named dynasty was replaced by that of the Rashtrakutas in the Deccan region. While the Pallavas in the southeast and the Chalukyas in the west led India onto the road of a return to orthodox Hinduism, Buddhism was making a stiffer resistance in the northeast. This did not mean, however, that there was a religious war in Bengal and Magadha. On the contrary, in line with the peaceful cohabitation mentioned in dealing with the *bhakti* — the cult of personal devotion — Buddhism, Shaivism, and Vaishnism achieved full-fledged forms of syncretism. The great elasticity of Hinduism in accepting divine figures extraneous to it was not exclusive to this period, either. It is sufficient to recall that Buddha himself is accepted in Vaishnism as one of the avatars of Vishnu. (Only in southern India is the Buddhavatara at times supplanted by Krishna, the hero of the *Mahabharata*.) Certainly Buddhism yielded more than did Hinduism, but this was a yielding to which the learned gave extensive theoretical justification, and which was probably accepted as a natural development by the rural population — among whom, in any case, Buddhism had never made much headway. This explains why it is useless to try to make a distinction between Hindu and Buddhist art in the work of Bengal and Magadha in the period of the Pala dynasty (eighth to twelfth centuries).

The fact remains, however, that the great cultural and pilgrimage centers in eastern India were those of Buddhism. Some of the centers, such as Sarnath, drew their nobility from the works and vicissitudes of the Enlightened One. Others were more recent. Of particular importance among these latter was the "university" of Nalanda (southeast of Patna), with its vast monastic and cult complex (Illustration 98), a center of Mahayana Buddhism probably founded in the Gupta age. Even when the political center shifted toward the west, to Kanauj, Nalanda continued to enjoy the protection the Guptas had accorded it. Hsuan-tsang, who visited Nalanda and spent considerable time there during the reign of Harshavardhana (606–647) — the king who attempted to reconstitute the imperial unity the Guptas had enjoyed — wrote of the great develop-

ment of the philosophical and theological disciplines at Nalanda. By that time, Nalanda had taken on such importance that in the thirty years following the departure of Hsuan-tsang at least eleven Chinese and Korean travelers visited the "university." Even during the Pala dynasty, Buddhism did not lose its royal protection. In fact, the new sovereigns founded additional monasteries in the region; that of Vikramasila was perhaps erected at the wish of Dharmapala (circa 770–810); if we are to believe the testimonials of the Tibetan *Taranatha* (of the sixteenth century), the learned monks of Vikramasila exerted some control over Nalanda. This, like the other religious centers founded by the Palas (Uddandapura, Somapura, Jagaddala) was to represent for the state a first-rate source of income and prestige.

The fame of the Pala universities attracted an ever greater number of students from all over India, but especially from Tibet, beginning in the time of Mahipala I (circa 988–1038). The Gupta tradition remained alive,

96. Aihole: Above: This is the front portal of the Temple of Durga, an apsidal temple with a kind of gallery running around the cella. It has been assigned to either the Gupta period or — with more likelihood — to the Chalukya period, which is the sixth century B.C. Aihole, in the Mysore region of India, contains one of the most important architectural complexes of medieval India.

97. Pattadakal: Opposite: One of the five temples at this site, this one dated to the seventh century A.D. Pattadakal is a village not far from Aihole; like the latter, it is important not only for the large number of temples on the site but because they represent both the "northern" and "southern" styles of architecture. This tower-form is an example of the former.

98.   Nalanda: Opposite: The religious center of Nalanda, situated in Magadha, was probably founded during the Gupta era, but it continued to enjoy royal protection in succeeding periods, both in the time of the Harshavardhana of Kanauj (606–647) and under the Pala dynasty (eighth-ninth centuries). In the monumental complex — identified as number three by archaeologists — are remains of no less than seven building phases, one set above the other. The stupa-tower pictured here belongs to the fifth phase; on the basis of epigraphical elements, it is dated to the sixth century A.D.

99.   Magadha: This schist relief, depicting Shiva with Uma, his *sakti*, or female counterpart, is 24 inches high; it dates to the ninth century A.D., and although of uncertain origin it comes from somewhere in Magadha. Shiva is seated on a lotus flower, with his right foot resting on Nandi, the bull, known as his "vehicle." He has four arms: the normal right hand touches the chin of Uma, the other right hand holds the trident; the upper left hand holds up the symbolic arch, while the lower left hand touches Uma's breast. Uma herself, seated on the god's knee, wraps her right arm around his shoulder while her left hand holds a mirror. Her right foot rests on a lion. (Rome: National Museum of Oriental Art)

of course, in these northeastern regions more than anywhere else, and there was virtually no break in its continuity. The artistic vitality of Bengal is evidenced, in the seventh and eighth centuries, by the rich terracotta production of Mainamati and Paharpur, and by the direct influence of the artistic centers of Bengal and Magadha, especially in the Pala era, not only on Nepal and Tibet but also on Burma and Siam (present-day Thailand). Another extremely interesting phenomenon of Pala cultural expansion involved Indonesia — Java and Sumatra — whose most significant monument, the Barabudur (circa A.D. 800), can be understood only through the religious and artistic language of northeastern India. The importation of the small bronzes from Nalanda into Indonesia also had far-reaching technical and stylistic consequences. It was precisely the intense commercial activity with southeast Asia that explains the vitality of Buddhism in the Pala reign; although with less success, it survived after the end of the dynasty, up to the Moslem conquest and beyond. To this day, Bengal is one of the few areas of the Indian subcontinent where several Buddhist monasteries can be found.

The unquestionably recognized continuity between Gupta art and Pala art has led us to consider this latter a simple prolongation or even a degeneration of the former. The fact is that Pala art not only effected far-reaching changes from the iconographic standpoint alone but also in the matter of style (Illustration 99): the image was freed from the compression between the two ideal planes — the front and the background — into which Indian art had forced it up to the Guptas (with the

100–101. Khajuraho: Two views of the temples at this site in the northern part of Madhya Pradesh. The temple of Kandariya Mahadeo is clearly seen on the left of the photograph above. Many of the temples that have made this site famous were built in the Chandella dynasty, and can be dated between A.D. 950 and 1050.

Khajuraho: Plan of the Temple of Lakshmana
1. Ardhamandapa
2. Mandapa
3. Mahamandapa
4. Antarala
5. Garbhagirha (the inner sanctuary)
6. Pradaksinapatha
The four small temples at the corners repeat the design of the inner sanctuary (No. 5); this is a recurrent device in medieval Indian architecture.

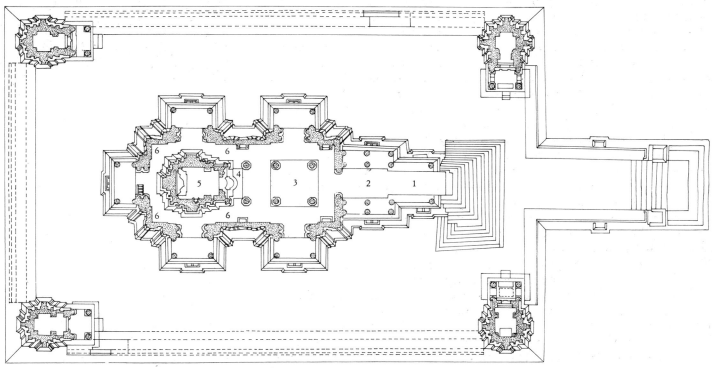

exception of the Hellenized northwest) and from the forced insertion into those levels of the rigidly geometric patterns that were attuned to the architecture of the Guptas. The stele-image typical of Pala art developed in the same way as the *sikhara* temple — sharply vertical — and the principal image took on a preeminence that was more than hierarchical.

Khajuraho and the Temples of Kalinga

Among the best-known monuments of medieval India are the temples of Khajuraho (Illustrations 100–104), in the northern portion of Madhya Pradesh. These have become especially well known to the Western world, not only because of the relative ease of reaching the locality and because of the beauty of the monuments but also because of the erotic — and to Western eyes often obscene — nature of the sculptures adorning two of the temples, that of Kandariya Mahadeo (Illustrations 103–104) and that of Visvanatha. Dedicated by the Chandella sovereigns of Jejakabhukti approximately between 950 and 1050, nearly all the temples of

102.   Khajuraho: A view of the Temple of Kandariya Mahadeo, dated to the second quarter of the eleventh century. From the decorative point of view, this is the richest of the Khajuraho temples; it is also the largest, being 100 feet high, 100 feet long, and 66 feet wide. The photograph allows us to make out the two jutting transepts, a characteristic of several of the Khajuraho temples (see the plan on page 159). Another characteristic of this temple is its high, molded foundation.

103.   Khajuraho: This is a close-up of some of the relief carvings on the exterior of the Temple of Kandariya Mahadeo. Although Al-Beruni, the eleventh-century Arab historian, merely mentioned "Kajuraha" in passing, the Arab traveler of the fourteenth century, Ibn Battuta, gave a brief but true description of "Kajarra," "where there is a large artificial lake about a mile long, with temples on its banks whose idols have been multilated by the Moslems."

AN INDIAN LOVE LAMENT FROM A
TWELFTH-CENTURY A.D. POEM

I am to die! Yet I remember, dying,
  My soul's delight — my sweet unequalled
  love,
Like a fresh champak's golden blossom lying.
  Her smile its opening leaves; and bright
  above,
Over her sleepful brow those lustrous tresses
Dark-winding down, tangled with love's
  caresses.
I die, but I remember! How it thrilled me
  This first glad seeing of her glorious face
Clear-carven like the moon; and how it filled
  me
  With tremors, drinking in the tender graces
Which, like a fine air, clothed her; and the rise
Of her twinned breast-hills, and the strange
  surprise
Of Love's new rapture! Dying I recall
  Each marvel of her beauty in its blossoms.
The large deep lotus-eyes, whence dew did fall
  Of jeweled tears; the swelling maiden
  bosom —
Heavy to bear — the long smooth arms; the
  lips
Where, like the bee, desire still clings and sips.
I die, yet well I mind, after embracing
  When hands relaxed, and gentle strife re-
  lented,
And — loosened from the gem-strings inter-
  lacing
  Their night-black threads — some wander-
  ing locks, rich-scented,
Strayed o'er her cheek and chin, how she
  would hide
Delicious flush of love, with arms close-tied
Over her happy eyes. Dear eyes! I see you
  Shining like stars out of the shade made so
Tearful for joy. Bright stars of morning be you
  Forever to this heart. Then would she go —
Her sweet head somewhat drooping — to her
  bath,
With such royal glory as the queen-swan bath.
Ah, dying — dying — I remember! Let me
  But once again behold her so — behold
Those jet brows, like black-crescent moons,
  once get me
  So close that love might soothe with comforts
  cold
The fever of her burning breast — that minute
Would have a changeless, endless Heaven in it.

            BILHANA: *Caurisuratapancsika* 1–6

Following pages:
104.   Khajuraho: A close-up of the exterior relief carvings of the Temple of Kandariya Mahadeo; the work is dated to the second quarter of the eleventh century A.D.

Pages 164–165:
105.   Bhuvaneshvar: The Temple of Lingaraj at Bhuvaneshvar (now the capital of the
State of Orissa) sits in the center of a large
quadrangular precinct (520 feet by 465 feet);
it is surrounded by a high, massive wall with
a trench, obviously useful for defensive purposes. At Bhuvaneshvar, the various temples
allow us to follow the evolution of the temple
architecture of Kalinga, as Orissa was
formerly called, from the eighth century to
the first half of the twelfth; the Temple of
Lingaraj belongs to the intermediate phase,
and is dated to the beginning of the eleventh
century.

Khajuraho — there were once 85 but only 20 survive — were built with sandstone of the soft color of leather, taken from the quarries of nearby Panna. Built more or less according to a single design, each stands on an elevated terrace in the shape of a Latin cross, with their principal axis east-to-west; their essential parts are the cella *(garbha griha)*, a pillared meeting and access hall *(mandapa)*, the entrance portico *(ardhamananda-pa)*, and a vestibule *(antarala)* separating the access hall from the cella. The more complex temples had another transept that formed, between the vestibule and access hall, a pillared hall *(mahamandapa)* that leads to the circumambulation corridor *(pradaksinapatha)*. These various parts (distinguishable in the plan on page 159) appear from the outside to be joined in a mass of masonry full of movement; through the repetition of the moldings, the sculptured friezes separated by balconies, the gradual succession of roofs over the various halls, the dynamic mass finds its crowning in the *sikhara* of the cella, a true reproduction of the sacred mountain.

Certainly among the most mature achievements of the Khajuraho complex is the temple of Kandariya Mahadeo (Illustrations 102–104), attributed to the later years of King Vidyadhara (circa 1025–1050). Erotic images are hardly exceptional in the religious art of India, and efforts to endow them with a "moral" significance — by Westerners, and in the Christian sense — derived from an attitude altogether foreign to pre-Islamic India. The meaning of those representations can certainly be explained by the philosophical elaboration of several Shaivite sects, but one should not lose sight of the fact that beneath the entire structure of Hinduism, profoundly philosophical as it is, there always lies a heavy layer of religiosity rooted in the old phallic-fertility cults.

In the particular case of Khajuraho, however, perhaps something more is involved, according to the German scholar H. Goetz, who based his observations on a reading of the drama *Prabodhacandrodaya* by Krishnamisra, written for Kirtivarman, a Chandella successor of those sovereigns who had dedicated the temples of Khajuraho. Goetz sets forth the view that the ministers of the Chandella kings Dhanga, Ganda, and Vidyadhara employed orgiastic rites of the Kaula-Kapalika sect to place these kings in a position of reigning without governing, satisfied as they were with the deification that the rites assured them. The drama of Krishnamisra, with its criticism of the Kaula-Kapalika sect, is believed to amount to the restoration, at the hands of Kirtivarman, of traditional morality. The interest of the brilliant pages of Goetz on the subject remains, even if we cannot accept his theory of diabolical machinations against the weak Chandellas, whose kingdom virtually fell apart following an ill-fated war against Mahmud of Ghazni. If nothing else, Goetz's ideas throw a clear light on the important part played by the rite for the preservation of power: the sovereign, identifying himself with the god, in the ritual mating with the sacred dancers of the temple, reached immortality in his own body and guaranteed, with the mystic repetition of the divine act of generation, the preservation of the order of all things. Goetz has even claimed to recognize, on the walls of the Temple of Kandariya Mahadeo, Dhanga, Ganda, and Vidyadhara at the moment of their identification with Shiva and his *shakti* (the feminine energy of the god); if we accept his view, these images of gods were "replaced" during the actual ceremony by those of the sovereigns in an act of ritual mating. If so, then this may have been a transitory leap beyond the limits of orthodoxy. But the sense of it is essentially what we said earlier: it was a singular way of deifying the sovereign, easily understandable in a society with a solid agricultural basis, whose elite was accustomed to the most arduous theorizing in order to absorb the ancient cults of fertility.

In the Kalinga (modern Orissa) area of eastern India, the temples of Bhuvaneshvara (Illustrations 105–109) bear further witness to the exceptional ascendancy attained by the Hindu cults, which by this time had reduced Buddhism to a subordinate position. The most ancient of these temples are the Vaital Deul, with its curved roof; the Temple of Parasuramesvara; and the Temple of Sisiresvara. These were followed by the Temple of Muktesvara (in second half of the tenth century); that of

Lingaraj (beginning of the eleventh century); and that of Rajarani (first half of the twelfth century). The Temple of Muktesvara (Illustration 109), characterized by an elegant entranceway arch, set apart from the building itself, has a porch with a pyramidal covering and the sanctuary surmounted by a *sikhara*, which in itself represents a perfect realization of the type of *sikhara* rendered famous by the largest and most complex of the Bhuvaneshvara temples, that of Lingaraja (Illustrations 105–106). Seen in the Muktesvara temple, moreover, are those vertical ribs made up of turrets, each a miniature reproduction of the *sikhara* itself. These elements — known as *urusringa* — are to be found more fully developed in the Temple of Rajarani (Illustration 107), where they have asserted an independence from the central tower against which they lean; they are

106. Bhuvaneshvar: A detail of the relief sculpture on the exterior of the Temple of Lingaraj. Such a couple, in an erotic-amorous pose, is known in Indian art as a *mithuna*.

Bhuvaneshvar: A close-up of the Temple of Rajarani. Dated to the first half of the twelfth century A.D., **this is probably one of the last built of the temples at Bhuvaneshvar. The affinity between its tower (sikhara) and those of the Khajuraho temples is evident.**

also prominent in the temples of Khajuraho — for example, that of Kandariya Mahadeo (Illustration 102).

We must conclude this unfortunately brief survey of the medieval architecture of India by looking at the Surya Deul, or Temple of the Sun, at Konarak, northeast of Puri (in ancient Kalinga). Erected during the reign of Narasimhadeva (1238–1264) of the Ganga dynasty, the temple (Illustrations 110–112) was conceived as an architectural reproduction of the chariot of the sun god Surya. This is made clear not only by the twelve large wheels carved along the walls of the platform, but also by the free-standing sculptured horses in front of the entrance, which give the impression of pulling the god's chariot. Lacking the *sikhara*, the temple has lost the ideal axis toward which the various parts of the edifice were

108.   **Bhuvaneshvar: A detail of the exterior relief sculptures of the Temple of Rajarani. The decorations consist of little "temples" or niches that contain images of gods
and *mithuna*, or amorous couples.**

designed to converge, and today it is difficult to understand its volumet-
ric relationships. We can only imagine the original appearance by referring to the better preserved temples of Bhuvaneshvara, from which the
Surya Deul must not have differed greatly. What truly distinguishes the
temple of Konarak, however, is the use of the sculpture, which by now
has overrun the entire architectural structure, in keeping with the taste
that melds images and molding in a unified effect. It is a taste that
Konarak shared with a certain type of architecture in southern India,
such as the temple of Somnathpur (1268) and the Temple of Hoysales-
vara at Halebid (Mysore); the latter perhaps represents the most genial
realization of this type of "luxuriant" architecture.

India Overwhelmed by Islam

At this point, India's tormented history once again intrudes on India's
art. Long accustomed to suffering foreign invasions from the northwest,
India did not attach much importance to the swift expeditions carried out
in the Punjab plain by Mahmud of Ghazni, an Afghan ruler of Turkish
descent who had inherited from his father, Subuktigin, a kingdom that
included the regions beyond the Indus that had been taken from the
Shahiya kings. Mahmud instigated the first significant Islamic invasion of
India (although the history of Islam on the subcontinent actually began
in the seventh and eighth centuries), but his expeditions were not so
much campaigns aimed at conquest as mere raids for plunder. In the
year 1000 he defeated the Shahiya king Jayapala; from 1010 to 1026 he
sacked the principal sanctuaries, from Mathura to Kanauj and Somnath
(Gujarat): for the Hindus, the destruction of this latter temple remained
a symbol of defeat, and to this day it is a cause for recrimination. The
death of Mahmud in 1030 brought only momentary relief for the populations of northern India; even though the attacks of the Ghaznavid
sovereign were repeated at regular intervals and had seriously im-
poverished the territories concerned, which were deprived of their har-
vests, the Indian sovereigns were unable to put up an effective common
resistance to the expeditions. Nor were they able to prepare themselves to
cope with the Moslems' attempt to conquer the area, an attempt that
inevitably would follow.
    As an offshoot of the Seljuk (Turkish-Moslem) art of Iran, Ghaznavid
art (known to us mainly from the French excavations at Lashkari Bazir,
near Qandahar, and the Italian excavations at Ghazni) represents a fairly
clear-cut break from the preceding Buddhist and Hindu works of Afghanistan. Nevertheless, it must be admitted that even the scholars know
very little of the architecture of the Shahiya period; for instance, perhaps
there is much that will yet be learned from the numerous fortifications
scattered throughout the valleys in the Swat region. When all is said and
done, our knowledge of Ghaznavid architecture is confined to too limited
a number of aspects to risk any summary.
    In any case, the Moslem conquest of India truly began with another
Afghan dynasty, that of the Ghurids, originally lords of the Ghur, the
central region of Afghanistan, which long remained outside the Islamic
area, even well into the Ghaznavid period. It was Muhammad Ghuri who,
from 1182 to 1206, the year of his death, conquered a large part of
northern India, setting up the state organization that, under the name of
the Sultanate of Delhi, was to last up to the British conquest in the
nineteenth century. One of the first architectural works of Islam in India
(leaving aside what remains of the first Arab occupation in the Sind), the
Qutb Minar of Delhi, dating from about the year 1200, was clearly a
product extraneous to the artistic tradition of India; rather, it vividly
recalls another minaret of the Ghurid epoch, the one to be found at Jam,

in Afghan territory, on the western confines of the Ghur region. But the mosque at the side of the Delhi minaret, the Quwwat-ul-Islam ("the victory of Islam"), designed to glorify Islam's conquest of the Indian territories, literally incorporated elements from the destroyed temple of the "infidels," formerly on the site. The iconoclasm of Mahmud and the Ghaznavids, which went so far as to use the idols as thresholds of mosques so that they would be continually trampled on by the faithful, here was giving way to a more "flexible" psychological attitude. The temples were destroyed (at least in the impetus of conquest), but their elements could be re-used with a certain amount of respect in the building of the temples of the triumphant religion.

It remains to be seen how much of an influence in such a development was the particular situation of the conquerors: men far from their homelands and freed from deep-rooted cultural traditions. And we use the

109.   Bhuvaneshvar: The Temple of Muktesvara, usually dated to A.D. 975. Although relatively small (45 feet long, 25 feet wide, and 35 feet high), it is one of the most elegant of the temples at Bhuvaneshvar. Particularly fine is the elaborate *torana*, which the other temples at this site do not have.

110.   Konarak: This is a close-up of one of the great chariot wheels carved along the base of the Temple of the Sun, or Surya Deul. This temple was conceived as a colossal reproduction of the chariot of Surya, the god of the sun; thus the enormous wheels, decorated with medallions on the spokes and hub. The date of this work is the middle of the thirteenth century A.D.

plural, "traditions," because of the varied make-up of the military aristocracy and the troops who made up these early Moslem invaders of India; they included many Turks of central Asia, but long transplanted into Afghanistan, plus native Afghans and even Iranians. Later, the Delhi sovereigns would continually turn to Persian art as a paramount source of inspiration; the Quwwat-ul-Islam remains a phenomenon isolated in its time. Nevertheless, the Islamic art of India was not confined to the monuments of the sultans of Delhi, and especially in the works of the peripheral cities, the presence of a clearly Indian taste may always be recognized; indeed, at times the Indian touch almost overwhelms the imported elements. In other cases, we can clearly see Indian architectural patterns adapted to the needs of the new religion.

But the reasons for venturing even this far into the Moslem period — when it is clearly not within our province to examine the monuments

THE CONSTRUCTION OF QUWWAT AL-ISLAM

This mosque was erected by Qutb al-Din Aybak. May the mercy of God be on him and on whomever prays for a blessing on the faith of the founder of this holy edifice.

In the name of God, the merciful and benevolent, he who has entered the mosque has found salvation; by the benevolence of God, it is the duty of all men who have the resources for the journey to make a pilgrimage to the House [the Kabah in Mecca]. As for whomever shall transgress this command, certainly God shall be independent of all that He has created.

This fort was conquered and this congregational mosque was built in the year 587 of the Hejira [A.D. 1191] by the Emir, great of dignity, grand and glorious, the axis of wealth and of faith, emir of emirs, the Sultan Aybak. May God bestow glory on his allies! In the construction of this mosque he employed two thousand times a thousand diliwal belonging to the idols of twenty-seven temples. May God, the great and glorious, have mercy on him and on whomever invokes a blessing on the faith of the builder of this noble edifice.

Inscription on the East gate of Quwwat al-Islam
(Delhi)

111. Konarak: The Temple of the Sun, viewed from the east side. Konarak is a small village, not far from Bhuvaneshvar, and near the coast of the Bay of Bengal. Of the damage suffered by this temple over the centuries, the most serious is the loss of the principal tower, a loss that makes it difficult to appreciate the intended proportions of the monument. A part of this tower was still standing in 1837, when James Fergusson visited the temple and made a neat and accurate drawing of it; even that modest remain was knocked down by a storm in 1848. The Konarak temple represents the final phase of temple architecture in Kalinga (Orissa), and it bears a close relationship with the Bhuvaneshvar temples, even though at least a century separates it from the last-built of the latter, the Rajarani Temple (Illus. 107 and 108).

of this era — is to establish that the Moslem invasion was quite a different phenomenon from the many preceding foreign invasions that we have witnessed — invasions that usually ended with the foreigners being absorbed by Indian culture, however much the foreigners may have modified the native traditions. This was, rather, a total overturning of an attitude toward the world, that is, toward human existence, society, emotions, and death — in a word, toward human morals. Both the contenders in this struggle were profoundly changed by the clash between Islam and Hinduism (although the orthodox of both sides have insisted on the contrary).

Indian Islamism produced architectural works of the highest order, but they have traditionally been studied as a part of Islamic art. We have not the space to upset this tradition, but we can question the sharp division between Hindu art and Islamic art. In reality, we should consider the monuments inspired by Islam and those bound up with the indigenous religions of India from one perspective so that the differences between one and the other — for they obviously exist, and they are certainly fundamental — might cease to be abstractly attributed to the different faiths that inspired them. Rather, like all the monuments of India that we have been examining, the Islamic works should be set against their social background in such a way that the religious elements would be related, like the aesthetic elements, to that particular and extremely complex socioeconomic phenomenon that was — and still is — India. That should have been the final lesson of our survey of India's monuments, a lesson applicable to all the manifold phases of India's history, religon, and art.

112.   Konarak: One of the colossal horses on the southern side of the Temple of the Sun. Each of the three stairways to the "portico" of the temple — now the tallest part preserved — had a pair of huge animals before it: two lions attacking two elephants on the east (Illus. 111); two elephants on the north; and two equestrian groups like this on the south. The horse is about 6½ feet tall, and helped to complete the image of the temple as a chariot being drawn by these horses.

APPENDICES

Ancient India and the Modern West

"It seems to me we can say that it is an infirmity of this century that in all parts of the world the sciences are in a language different from that which is spoken; it has also been the lot of all the [Indian] people to suffer from this disease."

Filippo Sassetti, Letter to Pietro Vettori *(1585)*

If India has been somewhat tardy in emerging into the modern world, there are many reasons, not the least of which are all the myths told by Indians and foreigners alike. One such described Bharatavarsa — that is, India — as the best of those parts that made up Jambudvipa, one of the continents at the center of which rises the great Mt. Meru, the axis of the world that holds up the sky and sinks its roots into the mystery of the earth. This ideal geography, always present in the cosmological speculations of India, has played, and still plays, no little role in Indians' political behavior. For along with such myths goes a complex of traditions, deeply felt by a subject population that uses them in order not to lose its individuality when confronted with the aggressive culture of invaders and colonizers. All such myths and traditions also become impediments to the development of a nation, tools for conservation but not for creation. And it is by attempting to strip away these layers of myth and tradition — both those laid down by foreigners and those built up by Indians — that we come to understand not only more about India's history but also about the monuments of India's civilization. We also may come to see how the fate of India's monumental art has been a direct reflection of India's larger fate in the eyes — and at the hands — of the Western world.

Gandhi's "Mother India" — which, even after the division that led to the establishment of Pakistan, seemed to have reconstituted the territorial and cultural unity of the Maurya, Gupta, and Mogul epochs — today reveals with more and more clarity its fundamental social strains and the apparently irreconcilable differences among the various regions. (Names such as Kashmir or Bangladesh should suffice to make the point.) True, the most deeply felt conflicts threatening to split the peoples of the subcontinent often assume the aspect of religious, racial, or linguistic differences. The acute and informed observer, however, will recognize the real causes of such conflicts: they are social causes, such as various situations of privilege for certain classes (that become improperly identified with ethnic groups), or situations of para-colonial relations between one region and another. On a political level, these contrasts take on ideological connotations, for the most part unconnected with the real roots of India's problems, which must be understood in their historical context.

In this context, the attitude toward the ancient monuments of India is important, much more so for us in the West since the study of antiquity being carried out today in India had its roots in Europe. But before we proceed to examine the official attitude of certain foreign governments toward the preservation of India's antiquities, let us listen to a few individuals' voices expressing more or less typical attitudes assumed by Europeans toward particular aspects of Indian culture. We might begin with some excerpts from the *Lettere familiari* of the Roman Pietro Della Valle, who — although he was in India back in 1623–24 — remains one of the most lively writers who has ever spoken to us about India. Della Valle clearly rejects the "monstrous fables" of the Indians, but it is not unusual for him prudently to withhold judgment and to avoid giving credence to information he has not thoroughly examined. "With other Pagan [that is, Hindu] men of learning, who are familiar only with their Indian tongue, because of a lack of a common language we could not hold discourse; therefore I reserve myself to find out with more foundation about these things and all the details of their sect in Goa . . . nor will there be lacking some Brahman scholar, perhaps become Christian, who will speak either in Portuguese or in Latin, and can furnish me with a more certain account; and if he is a Christian, he will undoubtedly give me this with more liberality and more truth than the Pagans, who I believe still do not speak willingly with us about their affairs, nor sincerely. So that trusting in better information, which I hope to have there [in Goa], I will relate here simply what I saw with my own ideas, and some other things that I became acquainted with, without a doubt as to their veracity." At other times Della Valle was struck by the suspicion that in those apparent follies there lay something that was worth investigating: "But I do not doubt that, under the veil of those fables, their ancient sages, so jealous of their learning, as barbarians have always been, have concealed from the commoners many secrets, either of natural and moral philosophy, or perhaps even of some history; and I consider it a certainty that all these monstrous figures have secret, more reasonable meanings. . . ."

It is curious that, scandalized by myths no more unpalatable to good sense than the Immaculate Conception or so many of the stories of the Christian saints, Pietro Della Valle went so far as to exalt with lyrical tones the suicide of widows, that Indian custom that reason told him was "cruel and barbarous." "If I am able to find out when it will take place [a widow's suicide on the funeral pyre], I will not fail to go and see it and to honor personally the funeral with its pitiful affection, which to me seems to require so much faith and conjugal love." Here are the contradictions typical of an Italian of the Counter-Reformation, torn between the rational and the pathetic. A few decades later (although this is to be not only a question of time but also of environment), here is the attitude — anything but ambiguous — of the Frenchman François Bernier, who wrote in a letter from Shiraz in 1668: "Now, all this great web of oddities that I have referred to . . . this furious and infernal constancy of the women who burn themselves together with the bodies of their husbands, whom often in their lifetime they probably hated . . . and finally all this fantastic heap of the *Vedas* and other books: do you not think I have rightly written on the head of this letter: 'There are no beliefs too ridiculous and eccentric for the spirit of man to embrace'?"

More than a century and a half after Pietro Della Valle, in 1790, Louis de Grandpré, an officer in the French navy, organized an expedition in order to take a Bengalese woman from her husband's funeral pyre; arriving too late, alas, he expressed his feelings so romantically: "I commiserated with that woman, in proportion to the pleasure I would have felt in freeing her and to the idea I had had of her youth and beauty." But if the romanticism of the French officer turned into an adventure, that of his colleague and contemporary, Lazzaro Papi from Lucca, Italy, did not lack for pathetic overtones when he supposed, among other causes, "a strong and desperate love in some wives that gave rise to the custom." But by this time, the sentence is beyond repeal.

It is really quite difficult for us to imagine the difficulties European travelers had in being persuaded that men could have customs, practices, and beliefs so different from those inherited from Greece and Rome. As late as 1770, a Dutch captain in the Dutch East Indies Company, Johann Splinter Stavorinus, expressed himself in the following way on the religious opinions he observed in Bengal (with less prudence, be it noted, than Della Valle had demonstrated so long before): "I have often conversed on the subject, with their brahmans, by means of an interpreter, but always found them either very ignorant of, or very obstinate in not revealing the principles and tenets of their belief. Whatever they said was so wildly absurd, and what they alleged at one time was so inconsistent with what they said at another, that I thought very little of it worthy of preservation." And, somewhat further on, the same Stavorinus described to his readers one of the most characteristic cults in India in the following manner: "Here and there were representations of a divinity, to whom they pay adoration under the appellation of 'lingam.' This is the most scandalous worship of all the numerous abominations that the superstition of man has multiplied on the face of the earth."

This gives a fair idea of how ill-disposed a typical European was to accept or even to tolerate Indian culture. And yet, less than thirty years later, the English translator of Stavorinus' memoirs added a detached, scholarly footnote to the original comment: "The 'lingam' is the image of the male organ of generation, and, in the mythology of the Hindoos, is the universal symbol of renovative nature." And even Lazzaro Papi indicated he did not want to be scandalized, although he discreetly saved the exigencies of his ethics — and those of his timorous readers — by distinguishing between the past and the present: "Moreover, it seems that the original purity of this cult was later abused and perverted by some others in less innocent times."

During the same period, a scholar like the Briton, William Robertson (1721–93), although acquainted with the recent studies on Oriental religions, trembled with indignation at those immodest cults and considered it a desecration to call their places of worship "sanctuaries." Although worthy from other points of view, Robertson's work, which had wide distribution and was translated into many languages in its day, is a monument of cultural conservatism. This "ethical" prejudice with regard to Indian customs pervaded the popular culture of Europe, largely untouched by the new methodologies elaborated by historical sciences. India, for instance, never had anyone who described her with the spirit with which James Morier presented the Persian customs to Europe in his work of the early nineteenth century, *The Adventures of Hajji Baba of Ispahan*. And yet the last decades of the eighteenth century were years of intense research, destined to cast light in a completely different way, at least for cultured persons, on the relationship between European and Oriental traditions. For Indo-European linguistic unity was, as we shall see, a concept acquired during this period, and in 1784 there appeared the article by Sir William Jones (1746–94) with its extremely resonant title: "On the Gods of Greece, Italy and India."

Comparative research on ancient religions would later be most successful, but for the moment we need only observe how different is the attitude of the person who sees only "superstition" in foreign customs, from that of the person who looks first and foremost for a historical link between distant and separate facts. Thus European culture came to accept ancient India on an equal footing, so long as a distinction was made between past and present: one should not even think of comparing modern Indians with modern Europeans — that is, with Christians! Here is what J. Carnac, a member of the Asiatick Society, wrote to the president Sir John Shore in 1795, introducing him to an article by J. Goldingham on the Elephant cave (on an island in the harbor of Bombay): "This gentleman argues ably in favour of its having been an Hindu temple; yet I cannot assent to his opinion. The immense excavations cut out of the solid rock at the Elephanta, and other caves of the like nature on the island of Salsette, appear to me operations of too great labour to have been executed by the hands of so feeble and effeminate a race as the aborigines of India have generally been held to be, and still continue." Carnac certainly had no doubts about the rigor of his logic, and whoever has traveled to the Orient knows quite well how widespread — two centuries later — such analogies and unshaken convictions still are among so many Western residents. (These are the same persons, by the way, who provide "first-hand" information to the mass media, and thus exercise such an influence on outsiders' views of India.)

By now it should be understood that Westerners' lack of comprehension of Indian culture was not limited to the religion and customs but also extended to the figurative arts. It would certainly be interesting — but also, I fear, monotonous — to give a series of quotations to shed light on this phenomenon. However, it should be noted that the aesthetic condemnation of Indian art was formulated only in relatively recent times — in any case, after the rebirth of Classicism in Europe. (Recall that Winckelmann's *Geschichte der Kunst des Altertums,* the work that first articulated the Western classic aesthetic, was published in 1764.) Up to this time, the scorn for the subjects represented — often obscene in the eyes of Christians ("truly devout representations for such a Temple," Della Valle had sarcastically written) — was usually accompanied by a certain admiration for the majesty of the works or for the perfection of the details, but seldom by an aesthetic judgment, negative or positive.

But when Western aesthetic values began to be imposed, we encounter such lines as these, written by Ernst Haeckel, a prominent German naturalist who hardly lacked acumen in his observation of things and who went to India and Ceylon in 1881: "Be it understood that it is not a question of true beauty when speaking of Indian sculpture, so grotesque and overloaded with ornaments. The repulsive and abnormal union of the parts of the human body with those of animals, the gods with three heads (Trimurti), the grotesque and grimacing faces, the bodies with several breasts, eight arms, eight legs, etc., fill me with disgust, and I belong to that small number of heretics who agree with our Goethe concerning the absurd caricatures of the temples of Elephanta." These words were suggested to their author by a visit to the temples of the Elephanta cave (and imagine what he might have said had he visited the temples of southern India) and Haeckel confused many things seen in India with others that are not Indian. The tone is that of one who rejects what is unfamiliar in a blind frenzy, with the preconceived conviction that only his world expresses the just, the beautiful, and the honest.

Significantly, when Haeckel passed on to Karli, he was pleased to meet with greater simplicity and composure in these Buddhist sculptures compared to those in the Hindu temples. But is Buddhist art really Indian? "After A.D. 300," wrote Vincent Smith earlier in this century — an English authority on India we shall speak of again shortly — "Indian sculpture properly so called hardly deserves to be reckoned as art." Note those phrases: "after A.D. 300" and "Indian sculpture properly so called." We might well ask what is Indian sculpture not "properly so called" after A.D. 300 — the Indo-Portuguese sculpture of Goa? Most probably Smith, with those two delimiting phrases, wanted to make a clear distinction between what is Indian and "recent," and what is "ancient" and of foreign inspiration. In any case, now read what Theodore Duret said about a visit he made to the Lahore Museum in 1872 together with Enrico Cernuschi. (The latter became famous for his activities as a patriot in Italy, and for his collection of Chinese and Japanese art, which he donated to Paris — the present-day Cernuschi Museum — which had received him when he was in exile.) Duret wrote that everything led him to think that the Indian Buddhists, masters throughout the rest of Asia, had themselves received the gift of sculptural art from others. But from whom? "The collections in the Lahore Museum reply: they got it from the Greeks." And thus we are all satisfied. Yes, India has produced beautiful things, but when? Before A.D. 300. And before A.D. 300 who was in India? The Buddhists, naturally, much less "Indian" than the Hindus, and certainly much more inclined to take suggestions from foreigners, particularly (and who could doubt it?) the Greeks. I may be excused, I trust, for having presented this line of reasoning by drawing upon different passages from different authors. But if it is a concept that no one has ever expressed in its entirety, it is certainly the basis for many of the essays and judgments on Indian art up to fairly recent times.

The Lahore Museum! Few museums have played such an important role in the formation of a solid base of knowledge of a country's past (and with a concomitant effect on the evaluation of its present) as this collection. As far back as 1892, it received 600 visitors a day, something of a record for museums of that time. Perhaps some will recall the white-bearded Curator whom Kim introduces to a Tibetan pilgrim in Rudyard Kipling's book, and the spontaneous mutual understanding between the old Buddhist and the learned Englishman, united by diverse but converging interests in an art that, in a Lahore swarming with Hindus and Moslems, found its habitation in a building in which the ideals of a foreign administration were expressed architecturally. But before arriving at the Lahore Museum and the other major museums of India, the study of Indian antiquity had to travel a long road. We cannot afford to take the same journey but will limit ourselves to some essential considerations.

It is difficult to say when scholars approached Indian antiquity with the spirit of true practitioners of archaeology. There were some early precursors, among whom it is worth recalling our old companion, Pietro Della Valle. Not content with describing a temple and the images venerated in it and the rites performed there, he would also give a rather detailed plan of the edifice. "And so that one can understand this history, I will describe here below the plan of the Temple with its cloister and porticos as well as I can, by sight without having any exact measurement of it." Or there was the Italian from Calabria, G. F. Gemelli Careri, who around 1695 visited the island of Salsette, where present-day Bombay lies, and penetrated it in order to reach the "famous Pagodas of Canerin" — that is, the caves of Kanheri. He left a lively account of this visit in his memoirs (published in Naples in 1700) in which appear such curiosities as his description of the two stupas carved out of the rock. "One might judge that [the two domes] served as sepulchres for ancient nobility; but there is no sign from which one can assert this with certainty, there being no opening through which they might have put the bodies, or the ashes, inside; rather, one discerns that inside they are not empty but are worked only on the exterior in the shape of domes."

Archaeology in the modern sense was, in the beginning, an import to India. It began as an antiquarian pursuit, thanks to the interest shown by a group of enthusiasts who, in 1784, established the "Asiatick Society" at Calcutta. The founder was Sir William Jones, the man who had first revealed in a systematic form the affinities between Sanskrit and Persian as well as the relationships among Greek, Latin, and the Celtic and Germanic languages; this gave rise to a series of studies that might be said to characterize the entire nineteenth century's intellectual activity. (It can hardly be overlooked, by the way, that all this activity, to the extent that it affected India, was part and parcel of the British Empire, which from the mid-eighteenth century had become virtually synonymous with India.) Among the aspects of Indian civilization that the Asiatick Society meant to investigate, "Antiquities and Arts" were explicitly mentioned; but the program outlined by Jones was anything but restrictive. "If now it be asked, what are the intended objects of our inquiries within these spacious limits, we answer *man* and *nature;* whatever is performed by the one, or produced by the other." Nonetheless, it is understandable that the major interest would center on languages and literature. And it was through the medium of inscriptions that (thanks to H. T. Colebrooke and H. H. Wilson) Indian antiquarianism took on the character that we might define as "scholarly research." We might even nominate 1841, the year of the publication of Wilson's work on the Afghan antiquities, *Ariana Antiqua,* as the beginning of true archaeological research in this part of the world.

The half century after the foundation of the Asiatick Society represented a period of intense activity devoted to the collecting of material, reliefs of monuments, and especially the inscriptions that were printed in the pages of *Asiatick Researches,* the society's journal. But this was isolated work at best; the British government and the India Company — the commercial operation that had swallowed up India for the Empire — except for a generalized interest, did not demonstrate any desire to support a serious program of exploration and conservation. However, in 1800, the Marquis of Wellesley commissioned Francis Buchanan to conduct a survey of the Mysore territory; this task, basically topographical and statistical in nature, did not neglect the archaeological approach, and it represents the first instance of interest on the part of the British government in India's antiquities.

Yet we cannot speak of a cultural policy that actually concerns itself with the monuments of a country's past until such time as effective preservation laws are passed. In the first thirty years of the nineteenth century, to be sure, Lord Minto (Governor-General of Fort William from 1807–13) worried about the preservation of the Taj Mahal; while the Count of Moira (between 1813–22) ordered restoration work to be carried out at Sikandara. But in the same period numerous monuments were demolished under official orders, and during the governorship of Lord Bentinck (1828–35) there was actually a proposal to demolish the Taj Mahal in order to remove the marble slabs of the work and then to cultivate the earth on which it stood! So, too, although the caves of Ellura had been described in detail by Sir Charles Warre Malet in 1794, as late as 1824 Captain John B. Seely accused his own "powerful, scientific and generous nation" of being "barbarians, even worse than the Mussulmans" if it did not see to the conservation of the monuments of Ellura; "for we add canting professions and heartless lamentation to our regret. Affecting to venerate antiquities, and the monuments of a passed age and mighty people, it is our duty to endeavour to maintain, as far as we can, their original beauty and design; for while we esteem and admire these venerable and singular works, it becomes us imperatively to preserve them." It was during this same period, not so coincidentally, that Lord Elgin took the marbles of the Parthenon to England (1819); meanwhile, in India, Colin Mackenzie was stripping the stupa of Amaravati, whose reliefs, after many mishaps, likewise ended up in the British Museum.

Both Elgin and Mackenzie represent the romantic-enthusiastic attitude toward the works of antiquity, an attitude hardly sensitive to the value of the same works as documents of a people's history. But others were doing valuable, if less publicized, work. James Prinsep, secretary of the Asiatick Society from 1833 to 1840, was responsible for deciphering the *brahmi* and *kharosthi* scripts — an exceptional achievement in itself; beyond that, Prinsep helped to create a school of researchers who approached the problems of India's past systematically and who thus laid the groundwork for the succeeding and, as we shall see, better organized archaeological work. Among the scholars influenced by Prinsep were James Fergusson, whose work on Indian architecture (1855) is still a basic reference book (and which has been reprinted as late as 1967), and Colonel Meadows Taylor, one of the first to realize the importance of stratigraphy in archaeological excavations.

No less important than the work of the scholars was the activity of certain artists who furnished the European public with precious documentary material at a time when photographs and other forms of mass media were unknown. Drawings executed on the spot in India reached the English public for the first time with the publication of *Select Views of India* (1785–88) by William Hodges. And when the drawings of Thomas and William Daniell were engraved in steel and reproduced in various publications, we can say that the European public had finally received true, if selected, information on the countryside and monuments of India. Particularly worthy of mention is the series of the *Oriental Annual, or Scenes in India* (1834–39), which represented a qualitative leap toward objectivity compared to the highly imaginative illustrations furnished by other publications of the time.

And yet, some decades after the truly monumental work of the Daniells, the official survey programs requested by London remained a dead letter in practice, sharing the same fate as the program proposed since 1848 by Alexander Cunningham, the future director-general of the archaeological service in India. After the bloody phase of the Indian revolt of 1857–58, the governor of India seemed to realize the urgent need to establish some sort of organic cultural policy. The Asiatic Society of Bengal, which in 1860 received an annual sum of 50 Pounds sterling from the government for its zoological collections and an equal amount for its publications on Oriental studies, had been under pressure for some time to hand over its collections to the government. This was achieved only when the government declared itself ready to carry out a project of an Imperial Museum, "for the collection and exhibition of specimens of natural history in all its branches, and of other subjects of interest, physical, economical, and historical." Thus the Indian Museum of Calcutta was born, and thus, too, did the English begin to relinquish their claims on India's own heritage.

In the short period from 1861 to 1866 the first Archaeological Survey of India — which must be identified with the goals of Alexander Cunningham — was born, functioned intensely, and suddenly ceased to exist. There then followed a few years of confusion until, in 1871, Cunningham returned to his post as director-general of the reformed Archaeological Survey. Dissolved once again in 1889 at the suggestion of its director-general James Burgess, Cunningham's successor, the survey was established again, this time definitely, in 1902. In the meantime, however, despite all the interruptions and uncertainties, such a mass of work had been undertaken as to fill one with astonishment and admiration, especially if we consider the small number of collaborators Cunningham could count on. The results of this fertile period are collected in the volumes of the *Reports of the Archaeological Survey of India*, the *New Imperial Series*, and the *Epigraphia Indica* published during those years.

By this time, too, a new idea was surfacing. The concept that ancient monuments could be utilized for the imperial mission began to make headway in the minds of the British administrators and politicians. The exploitation of antiquities for political ends is a phenomenon that should not surprise an aware modern individual. It was no accident, either, that the appointment of John H. Marshall to head the reorganized Archaeological Survey in 1902 almost coincided with the publication of Vincent Smith's *The Early History of India* in 1904. Although we cannot accuse Smith of having voluntarily provided an interpretation of Indian history for political purposes, certainly the ideas he expressed — not only in his *Early History* but in its successor, *The Oxford History of India* — fit perfectly within the official propaganda framework. Smith's interpretation of India's past corresponded with the widespread sentiment that the Pax Britannica, by guaranteeing the unity of the Indian nation and the centralization of its administration, was almost a blessing for India's future. Sir Aurel Stein, a leading archaeologist — who in the same period coordinated his scientific work with various "political expeditions" in the northwest and in central Asia on behalf of the Indian government — was not insensitive to this thesis. Vincent Smith regarded the Gupta empire as the apex of Indian civilization and tended basically to recognize in the British administration of his time the efficiency of the "happiest" moments in India's ancient history, with the addition of that "benevolence" that he almost always refused to see in the ancient sovereigns.

In short, the myth of the "great empire" (of which the British version was the living example) as the greatest good was taking hold; in this sense, Smith was in perfect agreement with another, certainly no less important if far more popular writer on India — Rudyard Kipling. This shared "climate" of opinion also explains why the need was felt to preserve those monuments that represented in the most tangible way the connection between ancient Indian culture and the British Raj: that resulted in the Ancient Monuments Preservation Act, which became law in India in 1904. Ironically, though, by the time this law was put into effect, Britain would find it easier to preserve India's monuments than its own empire; indeed, the decades that saw the twilight of Britain's political role in India witnessed one of Britain's greatest gifts to India: the aid it gave in discovering India's ancient past. Sir John Marshall was not only responsible for the organization of excavations (including those at Taxila) but also for the introduction of new criteria and techniques, such as scientific restoration and the use of chemical analyses. Sir Mortimer Wheeler, who headed the Department of Archaeology from 1944 to 1948, deserves the credit for reorganizing the organization and for the introduction of the most rigorous stratigraphic techniques.

Today, Indian archaeology has become essentially oriented around the prehistoric and protohistoric periods, as a reaction to the previous tendency to concentrate on the "great moments" of India's history. Among the tasks to be accomplished, however, remains a proper revision of the historical period based on archaeology and on a more correct foundation of historical-religious studies. The end of the last century and the first half of this one have witnessed a flourishing of studies on Buddhism and the other religions of India. But most of these aim more at determining the supposed "absolute" contents of the various faiths than at understanding the position of these religions in the social context in which they developed. Even today, it is not unusual to read "scholarly" works on Buddhism and Hinduism that seem to be written by Buddhists and Hindus preoccupied with propagating their faith or confuting the heresies of their adversaries.

India is still waiting for the destruction of the myths created about her past by a not entirely disinterested group of Indians as well as by foreign scholars who occasionally transfer their concern for the esoteric to their researches. The subtle and genial logic of the Mahayana Buddhist sages, the mysticism of the Shaivite texts, the cosmic visions of the *Upanishads*, the philosophical-religious productions of the cultured élite — even these have not yet resolved Indian religiosity. Adding one's own lucubrations to those of such past traditions means renouncing the function of the true historian-archaeologist; it is one more contribution to the idea that "the sciences are in a language different from that which is spoken." The contribution of archaeology to India should be fundamental in putting an end to this "infirmity," which belongs to our age no less than to the one in which Filippo Sassetti wrote about India. In this lies perhaps the Western world's last chance to understand the true India.

Chronological Chart of Indian History

DATES	MAIN EVENTS
B.C.	
pre-2500	Early phases of Indus Valley Civilization
2250	Peak phase of Indus Valley Civilization: Harappa Culture: centered in Harappa, Mohenjo-daro, and other sites
1750	Decline of Indus Valley centers; possibly due to climatic conditions, possibly to first incursions of Aryans from region north of India
1500	Vedic Period begins with emergence of Aryan culture in northern India
800	Aryan culture widespread in northern and central India; iron coming into use
600	Magadha (eastern region) becoming major political force in India
563–483	Lifetime of Siddhartha Gautama the Buddha
c. 520	Darius I, Achaemenid Emperor of Persia, conquers northwestern India
365	Nanda Dynasty expands power of Magadha
327–325	Alexander the Great passes through India
321	Chandragupta Maurya inaugurates family dynasty with its imperial ambitions
268–232	Asoka, greatest of the Mauryan dynasty: tries to shape Indian religious and social life to own political aims
c. 200	Bactrian Greeks becoming influence in northern India
185	Mauryan Dynasty ends as Shunga Dynasty dominates Magadha
c. 100	Sátavahana-Andhra Dynasty on the rise
72	Shunga Dynasty ends
50	Rome extends trade to southern India
A.D.	
c. 78	Kanishka, a Kushan, becomes king; Kushans to be power in northwestern India for several centuries
130–150	Rudradaman, a Shaka (Scythian) king in western India
c. 200	Satavahana dynasty disappears as effective power
c. 320	Chandra Gupta I takes throne and inaugurates Gupta Dynasty, which lasts to about 600
c. 500	Huns control northern India
500–900	Succession of dynasties and warring kingdoms divide India: major powers were the Pallavas, Chalukyas, and Palas
c. 900–1200	Cholas emerge as leading power in south; spread influence elsewhere in India and southeast Asia
997–1030	Raids by Moslem forces from Afghanistan in northwestern India
1192	Mohammed Ghuri defeats Indians with Turkish-Afghan force
1200–1526	Moslem Turks and Afghans establish Delhi Sultanate; exercise political and cultural influence in India
c. 1340–1565	Vijayanagar Dynasty dominates southern India
1526	Babur defeats Sultan of Delhi and thereby brings Mogul power into India

Recommended Reading

There are numerous books that readers can turn to for more detailed knowledge of the various aspects of ancient India that this volume has been able only to touch upon. What is offered here is a selective list of those works that are most accessible — in terms of recent editions, price, and level of approach.

General History and Culture
Allchin, Bridget and Raymond: *The Birth of Indian Civilization* (Penguin, 1969)
Auboyer, J.: *Daily Life in Ancient India* (Macmillan, 1965)
Basham, A. L.: *The Wonder That Was India* (Taplinger, 1968; Grove, 1959)
Gokhale, B. G.: *Ancient India — History and Culture* (Asia, 1960)
Kosambi, D. D.: *Myth and Reality: Studies in the Formation of Indian Culture* (Humanities, 1962); *Ancient India* (World, 1969)
Rapson, E. J. *et al.* (ed.): *The Cambridge History of India* (Cambridge Univ., 1955–70)
Thapar, Romila: *A History of India* (Penguin, 1966)

Specialized Historical and Archaeological Studies
Allan, J.: *Catalogue of the Coins of Ancient India* (British Museum, 1936)
Banerjee, Guaranga: *Hellenism in Ancient India* (Calcutta, 1919)
Marshall, John: *A Guide to Taxila* (Cambridge Univ., 1960)
Narain, A. K.: *The Indo-Greeks* (Oxford Univ., 1957)
Puri, Baij: *Cities of Ancient India* (Verry, 1966)
Ray, S. C.: *Early History and Culture of Kashmir* (Verry, 1971)
Taddei, Maurizio: *India* (Geneva, 1970)
Tarn, W. W.: *The Greeks in Bactria and India* (Cambridge Univ., 1938)
Wagle, Narendra: *Society at the Time of Buddha* (Humanities, 1969)
Wheeler, Mortimer: *Indus Civilization* (Cambridge Univ., 1968)

Religious Life
Berry, T.: *Religions of India* (Bruce, 1971)
Conze, Edward: *Buddhism: Its Essence and Development* (Harper-Row, 1959), *Buddhist Texts Through the Ages* (Harper-Row, 1954)
Davids, T. Rhys: *History and Literature of Buddhism* (Verry, 1962)
DeBary, William (ed.): *The Buddhist Tradition in India, China, and Japan* (Modern Library, 1969)
Eliot, Charles: *Hinduism and Buddhism* (Barnes & Noble, 1962)
Embree, Ainslee (ed.): *The Hindu Tradition* (Modern Library, 1966)
Ross, Nancy: *Three Ways of Asian Wisdom* (Simon & Schuster, 1968)
Warder, A. K.: *Indian Buddhism* (Verry, 1971)
Weber, Max: *The Religion of India* (Free Press, 1958)
Zaehner, Robert: *Hinduism* (Oxford Univ., 1966)

Art and Architecture
Bachhofer, Ludwig: *Early Indian Sculpture* (Hacker, 1971)
Barnet, L. D.: *Antiquities of India* (Verry, 1964)
Barrett, D. and Gray, B.: *Painting of India* (Geneva, 1963)
Bhattacharyya, B.: *Indian Buddhist Iconography* (Verry, 1968)
Brown, Percy: *Buddhist and Hindu Periods: Indian Architecture* (Int. Pub., 1965)
Bussagli, Mario and Sivaramamurti, Calembus: *Five Thousand Years of Art of India* (Abrams, 1971)
Coomaraswamy, A. K.: *History of Indian and Indonesian Art* (Smith, 1965); *Introduction to Indian Art* (Int. Pub., 1971)
Glubock, Shirley: *The Art of India* (Macmillan, 1969)
Goetz, Hermann: *India: Five Thousand Years of Indian Art* (McGraw-Hill, 1959)
Hallade, Madeleine: *Gandharan Art of North India and the Graeco-Buddhist Tradition* (Abrams, 1968)
Havell, E. B.: *The Art Heritage of India* (Int. Pub., 1970)
Kar, Chintamoni: *Classical Indian Sculpture* (Transatlantic, 1950)
Lippe, Aschwin: *Art of India: Stone Sculpture* (Asia House, 1962)
Marshall, John: *The Buddhist Art of Gandhara* (Cambridge Univ., 1960)
Mawry, Curt: *Folk Origins of Indian Art* (Columbia Univ., 1969)
Mehta, Rustam: *Masterpieces of Indian Sculpture* (Int. Pub., 1971)
Munsterberg, Hugo: *Art of India and Southeast Asia* (Abrams, 1970)
Rosenfield, J. M.: *The Dynastic Arts of the Kushans* (Univ. of Calif., 1967)
Rowland, Benjamin: *The Art and Architecture of India: Buddhist, Hindu, Jain* (Penguin, 1967)
Sarkar, H.: *Studies in Early Buddhist Architecture of India* (Verry, 1966)
Volwahsen, Andreas: *Living Architecture: India* (Grosset, 1969)
Zimmer, Heinrich: *The Art of Indian Asia* (Princeton Univ., 1968), *Myths and Symbols in Indian Art and Civilization* (Princeton Univ. & Harper-Row, 1963)

Recommended Viewing

Nothing makes the world of ancient India seem so real as a visit to the actual sites; failing that, the next best thing is a visit to a museum with a collection of Indian art and artifacts. Some of the finest are these:

GREAT BRITAIN:
Brighton: Art Gallery and Museum
Cambridge: Museum of Archaeology and Ethnology
Durham: Gulbenkian Museum of Oriental Art and Archaeology
Edinburgh: Royal Scottish Museum
Leeds: City Museum
London: Victoria and Albert Museum
Manchester: University Museum
Oxford: Ashmolean Museum

U.S.A.
California: Los Angeles: County Museum of Art;
        San Francisco: Center of Asian Art and Culture
Illinois: Chicago Art Institute
Massachusetts: Boston: The Museum of Fine Arts
Missouri: Kansas City: Nelson-Atkins Museum
New York: New York City: The Metropolitan Museum of Art
Ohio: Cleveland Museum of Art
Pennsylvania: Philadelphia Museum of Art
Washington: Seattle Art Museum

There are still other collections of Indian works in North America, some highly specialized, some more general, but all open — within certain restrictions — to the general public. The list that follows, in conjunction with those singled out above, should allow people everywhere throughout North America to start an acquaintance with this great civilization.

Colorado: Denver Art Museum
Connecticut: New Haven: Yale University Art Gallery
Maryland: Baltimore: The Walters Art Gallery
Massachusetts: Cambridge: Harvard University, Fogg Art Museum
Michigan: Detroit: Institute of Arts
Missouri: St. Louis: City Art Museum
New Jersey: Newark Museum;
        Princeton: Princeton University Art Museum
New York: New York City: Brooklyn Museum;
        Asia House Gallery (occasional exhibitions)
Oregon: Portland Art Museum
Pennsylvania: Philadelphia: University Museum, University of Pennsylvania
Virginia: Richmond Art Museum
Washington, D.C.: The Freer Gallery;
        Smithsonian Institution
CANADA:
Montreal: Museum of Fine Arts;
Toronto: Royal Ontario Museum

Credits

The reworking of plans and drawings, done by Giuliano and Giovanni Battista Minelli, was based on the following works, with the kind permission of their respective publishers:

V. S. Agrawala: *Indian Art* (Varanasi, Prithivi Prakashan, B 1/122, Dumraon Kothi, 1965). *Ancient India* (Archaeological Survey of India, New Delhi). H. G. Franz: *Buddhistische Kunst Indiens* and *Hinduistische und Islamische Kunst Indiens* (Leipzig, E. A. Seemann). R. C. Kak: *Ancient Monuments of Kashmir* (New Delhi, Sagar Publications, 18 Indian Oil Bhavan, New Janpath Market, 1971). G. A. Pugachenkova: *Skul'ptura Khalchayana* (Moscow, Iskusstvo Publishing, 1971). Benjamin Rowland: *The Art and Architecture of India* (London, Penguin Books, 1953).

The drawings of the Tepe Sardar stupa were done by Nicola Labianca. We want to thank Dr. Domenico Faccenna, Director of the Rome National Museum of Oriental Art and of the Italian Archaeological Mission in Pakistan, for the plan and the photograph of the sacred area of Butkara I as well as for objects from his museum reproduced in this volume; Dr. Paolo Consiglio for his participation in the photographic work; and the Novotsi Agency for illustrations 34 and 35. Photographs numbered 28, 36, 37, 38, 78, and 79 are by Mrs. Francesca Bonardi; photograph 39 is by Professor Umberto Scerrato; and photographs 26, 27, 32, 33, 42, 73, 76, and 77 are by the author.

Quotations from the following works, to whose authors and publishers we extend our thanks, are used within the text: J. Auboyer: *Introduction à l'étude de l'art de l'Inde* (Rome, Istituto Italiano per il Medio ed Estremo Oriente, 1965). M. Hallade: *Inde: Un millénaire d'art bouddhique* (Fribourg, Office du Livre, 1968). Benjamin Rowland: *The Art and Architecture of India* (London, Penguin Books, 1953). G. Tucci: *Asia Religiosa* (Rome, Partenia, 1946). W. Y. Willetts: *An Illustrated Annotated Annual Bibliography of Mahabalipuram* (Kuala Lampur, Dept. of Indian Studies, Univ. of Malaya, 1966).

The passages cited in the appendix-essay, "Ancient India and the Modern West," are to be found in the following works:

Bernier, François: *Voyages de François Bernier Docteur en Médecine de la Faculté de Montpellier, Contenant la Description des Etats du Grand Mogol, de l'Hindoustan, du Royaume de Kachemire, etc.* (2 vols., Amsterdam, 1709–10)

Carnac, Jacques: *Supplemental Volumes to the Works of Sir William Jones, Containing the whole of the Asiatick Researches hitherto published, excepting those papers already inserted in his Works,* Vol. II (London, 1801)

Della Valle, Pietro: *Viaggi di Pietro Della Valle il Pellegrino, Descritti da lui medesimo in Lettere familiari. . . . , Parte terza* (Venezia, 1667)

Duret, Theodore: *Voyage en Asie* (Paris, 1874)

Gemelli Careri: *Storia dei viaggiatori italiani nelle Indie Orientali,* by A. de Gubernatis (Livorno, 1875)

Grandpré, Louis de: *Voyage dans l'Inde et au Bengale, fait dans les années 1789 et 1790* (Paris, 1801)

Haeckel, Ernst: *Letters from a Traveler in India* (1884)

Jones, William: *The Works of Sir William Jones,* Vol. I (London, 1799)

Papi, Lazzaro: *Lettere sull'Indie Orientali* (Filadelfia-Pisa, 1802)

Robertson, William: *An Historical Disquisition Concerning the Knowledge which the Ancients Had of India* (London, 1791)

Sassetti, Filippo: *Storia dei viaggiatori. . . . , op. cit.*

Seeley, John B.: *The Wonders of Elora* (London, 1824)

Smith, Vincent: *The Early History of India* (Oxford, 1904)

Stavorinus, Johann Splinter: *Voyages to the East-Indies,* trans. by S. H. Wilcocke (3 vols., London, 1798)

INDEX

190

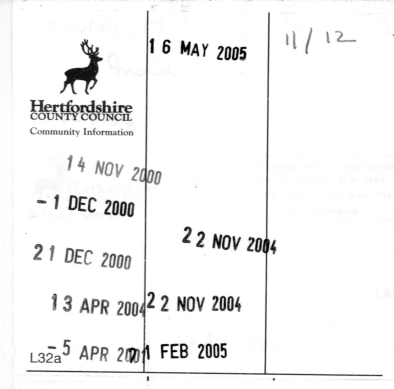